After being reborn in a la[...] London in June 1989, Kirk [...] music world for thirty-five years as a promoter, performer, (almost) popstar and clubbing travel pioneer.

His thoughts have appeared in Mixmag, DJ Magazine, Time Out, Ministry and (ironically) The Sun. In 1999 he set up Radical Escapes: the world's first holiday company catering exclusively for clubbers, and has taken over 10,000 people on holiday to Ibiza alone.

His debut book 'rave new world: Confessions of a raving reporter (Nine Eight) won an ARIA award for Audiobook of the Year in 2024 and has been the UK's most popular dance music title since publication (June '22). His ground-breaking one-man spoken word show has appeared at Glastonbury Festival, Edinburgh Fringe and in UK theatres.

After working with all the biggest names in dance music, Kirk now lives in Devon with his wife, two sons, a cat that is mute, and his tinnitus, which sadly isn't.

rave new world PRESENTS

# planes, trains & amphetamines

## CLUBBING HOLIDAY CONFESSIONS

# Kirk Field

First published by Velocity Press 2025

velocitypress.uk
ravenewworld.co.uk

Printed and bound in Great Britain by Clays Ltd, Elcograf S.p.A.

Cover design: Paul Palmer-Edwards
Typesetting: Paul Palmer-Edwards
Editor: Paris Ferguson

PAPERBACK ISBN: 9781913231958
EBOOK ISBN: 9781913231965

GPSR
Publisher: Velocity Press, London, United Kingdom
EU Authorised Representative: Easy Access System Europe -
Mustamäe tee 50, 10621 Tallinn, Estonia, gpsr.requests@easproject.com

# CONTENTS

# INTRODUCTION

Music tourism is one of the fastest growing trends in leisure travel. According to a study by the World Travel Market, the global music tourism market is expected to reach over £9 billion by 2028. From Taylor Swift's Eras tour boosting the UK economy by a billion pounds, to the 3.3 million people who visit Ibiza each summer, music holidays are big business.

It could be argued that dance music devotees kick-started the trend; from Ibiza and Miami to Ayia Napa, Croatia and Malta, clubbing and tourism are entwined like a DNA strand.

London's unlicensed mid '80s warehouse party scene was directly influenced by the post-disco movement in New York. Laker Airways £99 return flights from London allowed the capital's DJs to experience Brooklyn block parties. It was whilst on a lads' holiday in Ibiza a group of them would discover the new dance culture. The rest is history.

The rise of the low-cost carriers in the '90s allowed a generation to return to the source. For the rave generation, going to Ibiza wasn't merely a summer holiday, it was a rite of passage.

The desire to *dance somewhere different* grew. While Ibiza cradled house, techno and trance, Ayia Napa reverberated to UK garage, Goa gave birth to psytrance and Holland's gabber and hardcore culture provided the foundation for the countries' rich dance music festivals – now tourist destinations in their own right.

Empowered by the spirit of adventure and emboldened by the internet, the world was suddenly our oyster – even if the travel industry was a clam.

The major tour operators, still selling bar crawls and wet-T-shirt culture to a new breed of holidaymakers were either unaware or unwilling to accept a cultural revolution had taken place. Club 18–30's infamous slogans included 'Beaver Espana' and 'Girls, can we interest you in a package holiday?' above a photo of a hunk in tight trunks. Not forgetting the irresponsible, 'You get two weeks for being drunk and disorderly.'

Alcohol??? That was sooo '80s, the kids had moved on.

Club 18–30's motto may have been, 'Your granny wouldn't like it', but neither did anyone else who cared about the soundtrack to their week in the sun.

As a result, when the new century took off, package holidays were in decline. For the first time, the internet empowered the independent traveller to avoid the package holiday experience altogether. Durations were no longer limited to seven or fourteen days. It was now possible for guests who were more 'scene' than 'herd' to fly out just for the weekend.

I recognised that package holidays were being shunned by the very people who were searching to replicate the same shared experience the dancefloor offers. But while it's true independent travel works well for couples or a small group of friends, it can't offer the shared group experience and economies-of-scale financial benefits that a package holiday can.

But to understand clubbing travel, you have to understand the dancefloor. It's where individuality melts into something far bigger. It's where 'I' becomes 'us'. Like many, I lost myself and found a family in the rave scene. Individuality melts into something far bigger.

*'When a number of bodies of the same or of different magnitudes are pressed together by others, they are said to be mutually united, and taken together they are said to compose one body or individual'*
– Baruch Spinoza

I knew this group dynamic was the key to delivering a package holiday with a difference. This is why cosmopolitan twentysomethings – archetypical independent travellers – will surrender that cool little boutique hotel they've found and flying out on a Tuesday morning 'cos it's cheaper than a Friday night, and stay somewhere maybe not quite so niche, because it means they get to be a part of *The Shared Experience*.

A decade earlier, despite having no journalistic training, I started writing about the raves I attended, because no one else was doing it from the raver's perspective. In late 1999, inspired by a nightmarish 2wentys holiday in Ibiza, I decided to do the same with holidays, putting together party-orientated packages with an approach and soundtrack which reflected the new culture I was a part of.

This is the story of what happened when I pioneered a new kind of tourism for guests who weren't interested in spending the night in a four-star luxury bed (or, come to think about it, any bed!) – for whom a healthy tan raised suspicion rather than envy, suggesting the owner had spent more time on the lounger than the lash and who cared as much about the soundtrack as the suncream.

It was a golden era; Ibiza was at its bacchanalian best, Holland took festival production to another level with mega daytime raves and the snow-covered hills alps came alive to the sound of British DJ culture.

I've told it as it was because I want to paint a vivid picture of a wild new century filled with come-alive-at-sunset hedonists, all blissfully unaware of the terror attacks, climate emergency and global pandemic waiting beneath the horizon. The book doesn't glorify (or gory-fy) for the sake of it. I just reflect on what happened. Holidays are sometimes gritty and graphic as well as glossy and glamorous.

In the last twenty-five years, I've promoted holidays and overseas festivals which have been attended by over 100,000 people, taken over 15,000 people to Ibiza and flown over a million miles (for one of our smileys!). Although some names have been changed to respect the confidentiality of my guests, everything you're about to read happened.

Expect misadventures in the sun, snow and on the high seas, along with my forays into 'psychic travel'. Hold tight, it gets turbulent...

*'Travel makes a wise man better, and a fool worse.'*
–Thomas Fuller

# 1

# THE TEN COMMANDMENTS
## OF CLUBBING HOLIDAYS

'The coppers in green are cunts. Don't mess with them 'cos they'll beat the fuck out of you... or even worse.'

The self-important 2wentys's rep stood sweating at the front of the hotel transfer bus, addressing his captive audience of new arrivals.

Ever since we'd boarded the coach an hour ago, he'd trundled out a tiring tirade of know-all Ibiza insider info to one hundred exhausted ears. Where to drink, where not to drink, where to club, where not to club, to not miss the bar crawl and reps' cabaret. All of which could be booked at the welcome meeting tomorrow morning at ten, prompting someone to vocalise everyone's feelings, 'Ten o'clock in the fucking morning? We're on 'oliday! Yer 'aving a bleedin' laugh, fatty.'

A group of lads at the front erupted in laughter. For a brief moment, everyone saw through the branded tour operator T-shirt and beyond the sweat-soaked forehead and caught a glimpse of Gary Smithwick from West Bromwich, who, due to his likeness to Lou Costello, the short, rotund one in Abbott and Costello, was known as Lil Louie. Though he would tell any guests that he was named after the DJ Li'l Louis Vega. But Gary wasn't so much a Master at Work as a masturbator at work, pleasuring himself with endless ejaculations from a tiny microphone that his pink, fat fingers wrapped themselves around like cheap Richmond sausages.

Gary wiped the sweat from his brow. His status hung in the balance, and he knew it. Lose us now and it would be a long and fruitless week. He needed to act. He searched for salvation, and it was duly delivered. As the bus crawled forward in heavy traffic, they drew alongside a green-and-white VW van with the words GUARDIA CIVIL. Next to it a group of broad-shouldered men in uniforms surrounded a skinny scooter rider in a white Space singlet but no helmet. One policeman drew a baton and thwacked the lad at the back of the legs, causing him to collapse in a heap.

Gary seized the moment. 'The coppers in green are the Guardia Civil, the Civil Guard. They aren't from 'round here. They're from the mainland, see, so they don't know anyone and can't be bribed or persuaded to turn a blind eye like the local coppers can. None of 'em speak a word of English – least that's what they'll tell ya, so they communicate with their batons. If you give 'em any shit, they'll take you in. And that's when the fun really starts...'

By now the entire coach were swivelling their heads back and forth from the military-style police contingent outside to Gary and back again like a Centre Court crowd following a long baseline rally.

'Don't give them any lip 'cos they'll beat the fuck out of you, or even worse.'

'What could be worse than being beaten the fuck out of?' one lad in an Arsenal shirt asked under his breath, prompting more sniggers.

Upon hearing this, Gary walked a few paces down the central aisle until he was adjacent to the lad who had provided his cue. At full stretch, the normally curly microphone lead ran to the dashboard resembling a tightrope, taut and strained. Like a dog straining at his leash, the fat, sweaty rep knew this was the limit of his influence and the last chance to assert his authority otherwise it would be a long week.

'Allow me to explain.'

The coach fell silent.

'They're all nasty fuckers, but there's one particular nasty fucker called Carlos, who's bald as a coot with a big handlebar moustache. Carlos just loves to shove his baton where the sun don't shine, and I don't mean Scunthorpe.'

Upon hearing this, a girl sat opposite me who'd been feeling unwell for some time wretched, vomit spewing out from between her fingers as they cupped her mouth.

'They tell the hospital that the poor buggers "resisted" arrest.'

He paused to make a 'quote, unquote' gesture with both hands, momentarily relaxing his sausage-like grip on the mic which darted out of his hand like a crossbow bolt, hitting the windscreen of the coach with a CRACK, narrowly missing the driver who shook his head resignedly. Although his English wasn't good, he sensed that Gary was a tit. The only Spanish words he'd heard from his mouth were 'Vamos, señor!' whenever he closed the bus doors. He'd also noticed how at the end of each week, departing guests wouldn't give him the same warmth or respect they showed to other reps.

'Sorry about that, I'm lethal with a mic, me. You have been warned! Now then, where was I? Oh yes, a Geordie lad last week was admitted to Can Misses hospital with a ruptured rectum after a date night with Carlos.'

Gary crouched in the aisle and addressed the lad in the nearest seat who asked the question. 'Now, that's worse than being beaten, isn't it?'

The lad, like his mates, stared ahead, the blood drained from their faces as they wondered if they'd perhaps landed in Feltham Young Offenders Institute by mistake.

Gary jumped up again, his sense of authority restored. 'Next hotel, The Brisa, make sure you take all your personal belongings from the coach. If you leave yer passport on the bus, don't expect to get it back... not for free at least. Welcome to the jungle!'

This was my first taste of a package holiday in Ibiza. I'd booked a last-minute 2wentys holiday for £159 per person including flights, transfers and accommodation in August 1997 as it was the cheapest way I could spend a week on the island promoting my white label, a reworking of the Subliminal Cuts piano house classic 'Le Voie Le Soleil' with a soaring vocal hook added and invited my mate Marten, who was going through some choppy waters, a much-needed break to join me.

My track didn't go far, but as so often in my life (and yours, too, if you stop and think about it), it opened the door to another path. It was while on this god-awful bus which had taken over an hour to reach my hotel from the airport just ten miles away that I first caught a glimpse of what appeared to be a gap in the package holiday market – a visible void in vacationing.

We eventually emerged pasty-faced and dehydrated from the bus like those mobile cattle crates you sometimes see on motorways and we stumbled into our hotel, where we had to wait for another half an hour to check in because Gary was too interested in chatting up two girls from Rhyll rather than helping the poor receptionist by asking everyone to get their passports ready and asking some to wait in the adjacent bar area.

## First Night Madness

The first night on holiday is always the wildest. When that suitcase is opened, all the problems, stresses, frustrations and tensions from back home burst out like a bunch of demented butterflies.

With pockets bulging and adventure beckoning, there is little consideration of tomorrow. *THIS* is what you've been waiting for all those months. No matter how tired you are from the red-eye flight, or how little you've eaten, with no regard for hydration or pacing yourself, you hit the town like a drone strike hits a Jihadi jeep. Bang!

Although it's light when you get to bed, the sun's not quite visible – which is just as well as it would dazzle you with its brightness, highlighting last night's souvenirs scored on your skin; the cigarette burn from the girl dancing too close in Play 2, the singed eyebrow from the Flamin' Sambuca you spilled in Koppas and the bruised toe from that security wanker who deliberately stamped on your foot when you *finally* left that downstairs dive bar where the girls walked around with their tits out; 'West End Warrior's' battle scars you wear with pride for the rest of the week. You fall onto the bed still wearing the shorts stained with garlic mayo from the kebab you dropped into your lap as you sat at the fountains and fell asleep. At least you hope it's garlic mayo. There was a grope in a doorway with some Scottish bird, but after the amount you'd drunk, an erection was out of the question, let alone ejaculation… you hope.

Just as you drift off you can hear a distant hammering. You think it's someone doing DIY, but then you hear your name being called. You rise and stagger to the door, dragging your aching body like a stylised somnambulist. After struggling to unlock it you realise it wasn't locked in the first place and pull it open.

'Welcome meeting in ten minutes downstairs, this is your only chance to book the bar crawl and cabaret.' Gary's face looks wider than ever; a pink, fleshy satellite dish from which two piggy eyes surveyed the wreckage. Without replying, you slam the door shut and through the door hear, 'Be there or be square!' as his trainers squeaked down the corridor.

Back in your bed you could hear Gary knock on other doors, an unwelcome Prison Officer announcing slopping-out time. His rapping solicited one of two responses: complete silence or, 'Fuck off!'.

At least, this was my experience.

By programming a welcome meeting before midday after the first night out, it showed that either the tour operators didn't understand their guests or treated them with disdain. I pulled out the folded 2wentys booking confirmation from my trouser pocket. On the reverse, I'd scrawled THE TEN COMMANDMENTS OF CLUBBING HOLIDAYS I'd started on the bus the previous day which already stated the first two points:

1. NO MULTI-DROP HOTEL TRANSFERS TAKING MORE THAN ONE HOUR

2. NO MENTION OF BUGGERY WITH BATONS

I now added the third:

3. NO WELCOME MEETINGS BEFORE 1 P.M.

Throughout the week, the Jack the Lad reps would waltz past us in the lobby, inflated by their sense of self-importance. Each rendezvous was seen as an opportunity to upsell an excursion: bar crawl, drinking games, a glass-bottomed boat tour or the inevitable ride on an inflatable plastic banana which was being towed by a speedboat. Second only to the undoubted highlight of the week, the Wet T-shirt Contest. Girls were cajoled into entering and any hesitancy to do so was met with derision. Prompting more notes:

4. DON'T TREAT GUESTS AS SEX OBJECTS; AND

5. TREAT ALL GUESTS THE SAME REGARDLESS OF HOW ATTRACTIVE THEY MAY BE.

Although we were in Ibiza at the height of the '90s clubbing boom, they acted like we were in Benidorm or Torremolinos in 1983. The only club I can recall them recommending was UFO which was on a Monday at Es Paradis. This had a half-decent line-up and took place in a unique setting, but in the late '90s, Monday in Ibiza was Manumission – 'the world's biggest club night in the world's biggest club', attracting around 10,000 people each week and featuring a random, interactive performance element – it embodied Ibiza. Their infamous sex show led to British tour operators eschewing the night. Well, that's what they said. In reality, the amount of commission a rep could make on a Manumission ticket was less than half they could make on a ticket for UFO, so while one night was talked down ('they slaughtered a goat on stage last week', 'someone caught VD from a toilet seat'), the other was talked up and promoted the hell out of – simply because it paid them more commission. I pulled out a pen and wrote:

6. ALWAYS OFFER THE BEST PARTIES

7. DON'T BE INFLUENCED BY COMMISSION.

I was dismayed at how much contempt they showed to their guests – who they clearly saw as nothing more than pockets full of money and panties full of pussy. When their fun was interrupted by someone requesting some help in changing the room or how to report a theft, they would employ evasion tactics with the expertise of a politician. If the guest persisted and wanted to complain, they would agree to a nine o'clock meeting the following morning, knowing that nine times out of ten the guest wouldn't want to sacrifice a night of their holiday for a meeting about a balcony facing a dusty car park rather than a glistening ocean. The reps would always turn up, spend fifteen minutes routinely going through next week's rooming list with the hotel management, before leaving with a knowing glint in their eye. After their no-show, the guest and their complaint were not seen again until departure day when they would sheepishly board the coach to the airport, their name ticked off the list by the triumphant rep and a 'See ya next year, lads!'

Like Nazi stormtroopers or coppers at a demo, they were only following orders – and just like Nazi stormtroopers or coppers at a demo, this was no excuse for their actions.

The reps' training began when they were taken to the airport shortly after arriving in Ibiza for the summer season.

Resort manager Jamie was a fast-talking scouser who came from a family of car thieves, shoplifters and drug dealers. 'I'm the black sheep of the family, the only one to make an honest living,' he'd tell people, before adding, 'well, honest-ish.' He'd risen through the ranks using guile, ambition and some incriminating Polaroids of a private party with the previous resort manager and, as a result, now 'ran' San An. If this was a military movie, Scouse Jamie was the crewcut sporting, lean, mean regimental Sgt Major whose job was to knock the motley crew he was presented with into shape, transforming them into a smarmy army of pocket-picking, sun-tanned salesmen who personified the company whose logo was emblazoned across their chest; fun, frivolous, flirty – and five years behind the curve in terms of what was cool, hip and happening.

I could imagine the rep's first day of the summer season was spent meeting with the first 2wentys' guests of the summer at the airport. Standing on the viewing terrace with a complimentary drink in front of a dozen new uniformed reps, Jamie had just finished outlining the golden rules of engagement with the guests:

'…and finally, NEVER, EVER ask them if everything is okay, or if they're enjoying their holiday. That's just asking for trouble. Keep it to a nod or a smile, unless you're selling something, or just keep walking by. This goes for the cute ones too. If you have to shag 'em, do it later in the week, or they'll be on your case for the rest of their stay. And always wear a johnnie or better still, get Harry on the boat, as we say out 'ere. They can't get pregnant that way.'[1]

A plane appeared in the blue sky over Jamie's right shoulder which grew larger. He checked his fake Rolex.

'Fuckin' great, bang on time. The pilot must need a shite. Here's the first week's arrivals. Let's watch them disembark.'

Ten minutes later, a Boeing 737 with '2wentys' written along the fuselage came to a stop around one hundred metres away from the viewing terrace. A stairway was attached to

---

1 Cockney rhyming slang for ejaculation, spunk (Harry Monk) on the (Boat Race) face and title of former Club 18-30 rep Colin Butt's book and TV series *Is Harry On The Boat?*

the front door and the passengers began to leave the aircraft.

Jamie gestured for the new reps to crowd round and passed a pair of binoculars from a box to Gary Smithwick from West Bromwich. 'What do you see, son? Describe it for everyone,' Jamie insisted.

Gary closed one eye, then the other. He'd never used binoculars before and couldn't see anything. With one eye open he glanced to the side of the lens pressed up against his face and stated definitively, 'People are leaving the aircraft.'

'No shit, Shylock. What kind of people?'

'Guests.'

'Whose guests?'

'2wentys' guests.'

'They're *your* bloody guests, Gary. Now, take the lens caps off and it might help.' This prompted laughter all around, only serving to increase Gary's stress.

Jamie removed the lens cap and handed the eyeglasses back to him.

'Now yer cooking with gas! What are your guests carrying?'

Gary could now make out blurred shapes which sharpened as he twisted the centre dial. 'Erm, rucksacks. Some have got those small suitcases, one or two have what look like stereos?'

Jamie, growing impatient, said, 'Yes... yes... but what's in their pockets?' He made a circular motion with his right hand, the gesticulation of impatience.

Gary turned the dial on the binoculars to get a closeup of their pockets without success.

'I... can't see... they keep moving.'

Jamie shook his head in comic despair. 'Great, they're alive then. Have a guess, Gary.'

'Wallets, keys, passports?'

'Now we're getting there. What else is in their wallets, Gary?'

Gary, still frantically twisting the focus in an attempt to see into their wallets, unconvincingly stuttered, 'Erm, credit cards, driving licence, organ donor card, maybe...'

'Organ fucking donor card. Anything else?' Jamie was now in full patronising mode.

Gary felt the veins in his temple pulsing. 'A photo of their mum?'

Jamie snapped, grabbed the binoculars from Gary and presented them instead to the rep standing next to him.

'Paul, please help Gary. What do people carry in their wallets?'

But before Paul could answer, Gary had his eureka moment and blurted out, 'Got it! Cash!'

Scouse Jamie grasped Gary's shoulders with both hands and stared into his eyes, his forehead only inches away from the other's with an intense stare and proudly proclaimed, 'You may make a rep yet, Gary.' Then, with a cheesy Chris Tarrant accent, he calmly asked, 'For one million pounds, Gary, whose cash is in their wallet?'

Gary paused and, lacking conviction, eventually muttered, 'Theirs?'

Jamie threw his head back in exaggerated anguish, eyes tightly closed, as if willing Gary on.

'Is that your final answer? Final answer, Gary?' his voice began to rise in intensity.

'Yes.'

Jamie released him in disgust, almost pushing him away like a lover rejecting the advances of a cheating partner.

'Let's ask the audience. Anyone, whose cash is in their wallets?'

After ten seconds which saw Jamie pace up and down exasperated at the increasing silence, he paused, turned to face his audience and, holding his hands out like Christ the Redeemer in Rio, bellowed, 'Yours! They've got *your* wages in their wallets – and it's your job to take it from them.'

He then moved amongst the intake of reps, addressing each one with a sentence or two before moving on to the next; his knowledge works his way through them like a virus; unseen and undeniable.

'Ask any bar owner in San An who are the best guests, and they'll all tell you it's the Brits. Sure, the ei-tie's look flash, but four of 'em will share two cups of cappuccino, making it last an hour as they sit on the best pavement table, dripping in their posey designer threads. The Spanish ain't got any money and the Germans don't leave Playa D'en Bossa where they only drink in German bars anyway. But a Brit saves up all year for his 'beeffa blowout. He'll arrive with a bulging wallet and treats his cash like Monopoly money, 'cos it's not real if it ain't got Her Maj on, right?'

He continued, 'If he's got any notes left by the time he gets home, he considers it a wasted opportunity. Holiday money quite literally burns a hole in their pockets. So, what they arrive with, they spend. They call it spending money for a reason! This is why your job is easier than selling double friggin' glazing. Your guests actually *want* to spend their money! It's just a case of whether you get it or the lap dancers on their last night do. Or, if they don't make it out on the last night 'cos they haven't drank any water since they arrived, and are on a drip in Galeno, he'll leave it with the fuckin' Pacha shop at the airport.'

His tour complete, he returned to the front, adding, 'The

existence of which is proof – if any was needed, Gary – of my truth.' Taking back the binoculars, he stepped back and opened his arms like an opera singer, exalting those gathered in a climactic call and response:

'Where are your wages?'

'In their wallets,' came a mumbled, staggered response.

'I SAID, WHERE ARE YOUR WAGES?'

'IN THEIR WALLETS!'

'Where?'

'IN THEIR WALLETS, IN THEIR WALLETS, IN THEIR WALLETS!' Their eyes burned with fire as they clapped their hands and chanted. They were now engaged and energised and filled with the spirit of all-inclusive bars, standing erect like a nipple in a wet T-shirt, while possessing the vision of a glass-bottomed boat in a sandy, turquoise bay.

Jamie nodded in acknowledgment. *Now* they were ready for work. He walked through them like a Messiah who'd just shown them the light, calling them to follow him to the arrivals lounge to meet their 'prey, oops, sorry, I mean guests'.

'C'mon, it's payday!'

For the first time in his life, Gary Smithwick felt like a hunter rather than its prey.

However, he failed to relieve me of any money. I booked no excursions, rode no jeeps, crawled no bars, ogled no nipples and straddled no inflatable bananas. By Friday, Gary had given up and instead of hassling me over my Full English in the hotel cafe/bar, he shook his head solemnly and uttered, 'Very disappointing, Mr Field, very disappointing,' like a teacher who could see the obvious potential in a pupil ebb away in a series of detentions and dubious friendship groups.

The week ended with me being knocked awake once again

by a uniformed frown with a clipboard.

'Bus to the airport is outside. *Everyone's* waiting for you,' the blonde in a 2wentys shirt spat in a West Yorkshire accent.

After repeatedly trying to sell me excursions and failing, they had no interest in me other than getting me off the island as soon as they could.

Through squinting eyes I muttered, 'The plane leaves at half-past nine. What time is it?'

'6.15 a.m., as stated downstairs on the noticeboard. You have to be there two hours before the plane leaves. And it'll take the best part of an hour to pick everyone up from all their hotels, especially if they are naked...' Her disgusted gaze lowered to the towel I'd thrown hastily around myself to open the door. In my haste to answer it, I'd made the schoolboy error of grabbing a hand towel rather than a larger one. The lack of material meant I was unable to fold the two sides together, so I held them together with my left hand... except there was a small gap, between which my post-pill penis peeked out, like a bashful button mushroom between two white curtains.

'Not very impressed, Mr Field. We'll wait for ten minutes and ten minutes only.'

I'd had enough. I knew Ibiza had a small airport which was swift to navigate, and this was more about vacating rooms allowing them to be cleaned and absolving themselves of responsibility: as once a guest goes through security, they are no longer the responsibility of the resort staff.

I didn't know this at the time however, but I did know that I didn't need to leave my bed three and a half hours before my flight left – especially as I'd only got into it twenty minutes beforehand.

'I'll make my own way to the airport.'

'I must advise against that. If you choose to make your own way there, you must understand we are not responsible, should you miss your fli—'

I slammed the door. Was I her guest or her prisoner? I found a pen.

8. NO REP UNIFORMS. STAFF WILL WEAR BRANDED T-SHIRTS ONLY.

I managed another hour snoozing, ate breakfast downstairs and asked the receptionist to call a cab. We still managed to arrive at the airport at the same time as the 2wentys bus. My cheery wave at the blonde rep was met with an icy stare and a frown... which was directed at my groin area, followed by a shake of the head.

After checking in, I sought out the head rep who was stood with the blonde rep and graciously thanked him for showing me how not to do a package holiday.

'You're welcome, pal. See you next year!' His response showed he wasn't listening, and only reinforced my belief that if ever I decided to work in travel I could do better. A lot better.

At the departure gate I made a note:

9. DON'T ASSUME THERE IS NO COMPETITION OR TAKE YOUR GUESTS FOR GRANTED

On the plane home, I added another:

10. NEVER COMMENT ON THE SIZE OR STATE OF A GUEST'S GENITALS, NO MATTER HOW LARGE, SMALL OR SHRIVELLED THEY MAY BE.

And just like that, I had my ten commandments. No climbing mountains or heavy slabs to carry.

## Afterglow

Although my white label was played in Privilege by Jon Pleased Wimmin and received support from some big names, I couldn't afford to press up the 500 copies needed to get a nationwide reaction or a position in the *Mixmag* Buzz Chart. Go to www.ravenewworld.co.uk or check out the audiobook edition if you want to hear it.

---

**Top Tune: Belo Horizonte – The Heartists (Original Mix) {VC Recordings}**

---

## BEHIND THE BROCHURE

A few years ago, I organised an Ibiza package for a club brand who attracted a large group of ravers from the north of England; a surprising number of whom hadn't previously left the UK. This is always a worry. Culturally naive and unused to international travel, they are more likely to become incapacitated by drink (as they aren't used to the generous Spanish measures and the 'local' brands of spirits used in some bars), be involved in a road accident (as they don't look left instead of right when crossing the road) or lose their passport (as they've never had to take care of one before).

One such case involved a first timer called Jade, who I'd noticed was a little worse for wear when checking in, as many guests are, having started their holiday the night before at the airport. She called me in a panic. I advised her to check everywhere again and then report it lost/stolen and apply to the British Consulate in Ibiza Town for an ETD (emergency travel document) to enable her to return home. This would cost her £100 for the paperwork and £100 in taxis, money she just didn't have. We urged her to borrow some from a friend or relative, or face being stranded in Ibiza – advice she ignored. She was adamant it would turn up, and if it didn't, mistakenly believed the airline wouldn't just leave her in Ibiza, as she had 'photo ID': she'd show them her Facebook page.

On the morning of her departure, Jade messaged me. She'd remembered she put it in the safety deposit box in her room when she first checked in, as we advise our guests to do, but couldn't remember the code. I told her to ask the hotel receptionist who would be able to help.

Ten minutes elapsed before she called again, blubbering that someone must've taken it as the safety deposit box was empty. Jade travelled to the airport and, as expected, was refused boarding and was making a nuisance of herself at the check-in desk.

It was at this point the hotel called me to say they'd found her passport in her room. It was in the microwave.

# 2

# ARMIN VAN ROADSIDE

*'This whole world is wild at heart and weird on top.'*
 – David Lynch

It's no secret that Ibiza is a crazy place. Devotees believe it possesses a unique energy which can act like a vortex; an unseen hand stirring up emotion and sending you spinning to places you never thought you'd go.

Add into the mix a long tradition of hedonism, the easy availability of drugs, a scorching-hot sun and that's a pretty potent cocktail to drop into...

August. San Antonio felt like a city besieged by bass; a Balearic Beirut with a beatbox booming from every flag-draped balcony. It was high season, and everyone was high.

Everyone except myself and Marten, who had recently moved to Australia and was unsure it was working out as he'd wanted. I figured a few days in Ibiza would sort him out. I offered to show him the island's nightlife, as he'd been a bit of a face in the New Romantic scene and a resident DJ at Leeds Warehouse in the early '80s.

He accepted my offer of Ibizan therapy, but on one condition...

'As long as I don't have to dance.'

I was baffled. That was what I was most looking forward to doing, losing myself in the crowds at Privilege, Amnesia and Pacha.

He explained he hadn't ventured onto a dancefloor for over fifteen years – when a group of boozed-up rugby types mercilessly ridiculed him for the way he danced, surrounding him before pushing and kicking him like he was a piñata, leaving him traumatised on the dancefloor in a club in Sheffield.

This was a challenge I was eager to accept. Dancing at the orbital raves was my salvation and is the purest form of expression; our body (and soul) freed from the brain, connecting with universal vibrations and others. I *had* to get him dancing again.

If I succeeded, he'd feel better about himself and break this hoodoo.

He expressed an interest in taking some E to help dissolve his inhibitions, which I thought could be beneficial if certain criteria was met, namely that the pill was clean and came from a trusted source, and that I kept an eye on him as you should do with a novice.

Finding pills in Ibiza isn't hard. Every worker can sort you out as many made a living from dealing to tourists. If they get into debt they're told to do a run to the mainland and bring in a shipment. If they are unlucky, and it's late in the month and the number of seizures haven't hit the target, the customs will be tipped off and they'll be sacrificed (no matter how pretty they are…).

Every September in San An, there'll be a cull of the 'foot soldiers'; it's all part of the deal the drug 'Generals' do with the police. They get some arrests to make it look like they're on top of things, the Generals get to deflect the heat, and by the time this happens, everyone has made their money (and by everyone, I mean both the Generals and the police).

But I needed a more discreet and credible source than a random worker who've been known to swap or adulterate clean pills, safe in the knowledge the buyer will be off the island in a matter of days.

So, we headed for a game of pool in a well-known bar along the beachfront when the manager (who we'll call Stan) recognised me from a previous trip when I'd interviewed Judge Jules there. After a brief chat, I asked if he could help me get Marten back on the dancefloor. He replied that he could, but the items in question were at his house a few kilometres away in the hills out towards San Jose. He asked if I had a scooter, which usually I did, but as this was a flying visit, I hadn't brought my licence, so offered to follow him in a cab. He was unsure, thinking it may be a trap. He knew I was a journalist and probably suspected I'd been turned by a tabloid.

'Tell you what, I finish in half an hour, have another beer and jump on the back of my moped and we'll whizz up there together and I'll drop you back.'

He was somewhat overweight, and the two of us on that 49cc hairdryer was a tall order. Not surprisingly, as soon as we got out of San An and turned off onto a dirt track, it died.

After abandoning the steaming moped, we walked the last mile or so in the searing heat along the rural lane, and after thirty parched minutes reached his village: a one-street terrace of small white houses.

After gulping down two glasses of water, he rolled a huge cone-shaped spliff. I didn't smoke and just wanted to pay him for a couple of pills and then start the long walk back, but it felt rude to rush him and, clearly out of shape, the poor guy looked shattered.

He offered me the spliff, which I declined, meaning he smoked the whole thing himself, with me on passive stoner duty, unable to avoid inhaling the big blue cloud of smoke which hung like a spectre in the room, at one point momentarily morphing into Caspar the Friendly Ghost.

After a slurry of slurred chit-chat Stan was melting into the sofa, a perspiring amorphous blob through the blue haze. I reminded him I really had to leave as I had a long walk ahead, and Marten would be wondering where I had got to.

Placing the spliff in his mouth, he reached down and, from beneath the cushion, extracted the stash of pills – a plastic bag of white tablets the size of a balloon. As he clumsily leaned forward, the lit end of the reefer caught the plastic bag – which instantly dissolved, spraying tablets everywhere: a spectacular eruption of ecstasy pills bounced and rolled in all directions on the terracotta-tiled floor, disappearing under every item of furniture. It was like a Class A Skittles advert. Some fell into Stan's lap, leaving him with a pile in his crotch. Countless more vanished down the backs and side of the sofa. The whole room was peppered with pills.

Instinctively, I got on my hands and knees and started picking up the small white tablets, placing them in my left hand.

'Fuck me, mate! How many pills were in that bag?' I enquired through the head-fuck haze.

'500, but there are always a few more 'cos it's not good to be under in this game,' he replied, winking.

As I carefully picked them up I began counting, placing them into my sweaty palm as I scrambled round on all fours, counting out loud as I recovered each pill. 'Thirty-five... thirty-six... thirty-seven...'

Someone was at the front door. Stan groggily rose, shedding even more pills, some of which fell into my hair, whilst holding the remnants of his stash, a limp piece of smouldering plastic in his left hand. Spliff in hand, oozing like a smoking gun, he opened the door. I looked up from my handful of pills to find a uniformed policeman on the doorstep, grinning at me. Behind him was a police car. I froze. I'd been set up. Why would he do this? The policeman pointed to me and said something in Spanish; Stan replied and, instinctively, I stood up, ready to be arrested. Then the policeman said, 'Hasta luego, amigo,' and Stan closed the door.

'What the fuck is going on, Stan?' I demanded.

'Easy, fella, it's only Pedro, my neighbour.'

'But the smoke... the pills... we were caught bang to rights.'

He smiled and beckoned me to follow him into the kitchen, where he opened the shutters.

'Take a look at his garden.'

Nervously, I peered out to see five-feet-high marihuana plants filling his garden.

He winked and gestured to his spliff. 'Where do you think this comes from?'

I was incredulous. 'Don't his neighbours say anything?'

He smiled. 'Take another look.'

Beyond next door's back garden, there were more plantations. Closer inspection revealed they were all at it – every single house on the street was growing weed!

Dumbstruck but relieved, I went back to my counting. We recovered 497 of the buggers. I felt paranoid that Steve would think I'd pocketed them, but he was relaxed and trusted me.

He wouldn't take any payment as he appreciated they were for therapeutic use and that I had to walk back.

But I didn't walk back, I was one hundred metres down the road when Pedro stopped and gave me a lift in his police car! Although nervous, I couldn't really refuse, so I jumped in and swallowed hard. The ten-minute journey lasted an age. The silence was crushing. The bar couldn't arrive soon enough. Marten was waiting outside, hands in pockets, peering up the street. Already a little nervous at being left on his own in Ibiza when I went off to score, you can imagine his expression upon seeing me sat in a police car!

I opened the door. 'The game's up, mate, you best jump in the back, they want a statement from you...' Marten stared wide-eyed and trembling. '...only joking, meet Pedro!'

We had a brilliant night in Manumission. After initially swaying on the dancefloor with his hands in his pockets, my friend gradually loosened up. They say 'dance like no one's watching'; in Manumission it was easy. People either had their eyes closed as they communed with the kick drum or stared agog at the old lady on stage who was peeling potatoes whilst sitting on a toilet.

On noticing her, Marten beckoned me closer, 'Fuck, this stuff is strong, I'm glad you only let me take a half, I'm hallucinating big time.'

I would've told him not to worry, and that it was only a part of the show – if I'd been sure it *was* only a part of the show – so I smiled reassuringly and handed him a bottle of water.

Marten danced all night, and we even made it to The Ship for a few pints of Guinness after leaving Privilege at 5 a.m. We'd jumped in a waiting cab and drove down the winding lane which joins the main road at a roundabout, ringed by a metal fence. At the bus stop nearby a group of revellers noisily waited for the Discobus. One of them was waving what looked like a prosthetic arm like a flagpole. Marten and I exchanged glances but said nothing, both of us thinking it was another hallucination. I wondered on the way back to San Antonio how he came to be in possession of the plastic limb. Was it his mate's who'd given it to him for safe keeping? Maybe he'd found it in the club, meaning a one-armed clubber would be waking up tomorrow and going through that 'Where's my phone?' routine, checking pockets and under the bed for his missing limb.

We got back to our apartment a little delayed by a police incident which partially blocked the road just outside San Antonio. A battered Fiat was the prey, probably clubbers driving under the influence. Marten went to his room,

'A top night, Mixmaster Dosemaster, what time does our flight leave?'

'9.15 tonight, get some sleep,' I replied, before adding, 'great to see you dancing again, mate.' He gave me the thumbs up and disappeared, looking forward to a long sleep.

Just as I drifted off, there was another loud knock on the door. This was repeated a few seconds later.

'Mr Field, Mr Field, open the door,' a female voice sounded, demanding entry.

I pulled some shorts on and opened the door.

A red-faced 2wentys rep stood there fuming, clipboard in hand. 'The bus to the airport is waiting for you and your friend. If you don't come now, we'll leave without you.'

Oh shit, the flight home wasn't departing at 9.15 p.m., it was 9.15 a.m. – schoolboy error!

I put the kettle on and took a mug into Marten's room. As I opened the creaking wooden door, he stirred.

'I've got good news and bad news, which do you want first?'

'The bad news,' he said in a gravelly voice.

'The plane leaves at 9.15 this morning, not tonight.'

His eyes shot open and he sat bolt upright like Nosferatu, rising from his coffin. 'What's the good news?'

'I've made you a nice cup of tea.'

It remained untouched. Ten minutes later, we'd packed and were in a cab speeding to the airport, hallucinating and sweating like two death row prisoners on DMT.

We just made the plane, giving our fellow passengers two hours and twenty-five minutes to regret that neither of us had the time to take a shower for over twenty-four hours.

The tale of this night doesn't end there, however. I returned to Ibiza the following summer. There were roadworks on the main road as roundabouts and a tunnel at San Rafael was being constructed in readiness for the road expansion.

As we crawled along, I struck up a conversation with the cab driver who'd picked me up from the airport. While he welcomed the plans for a dual carriageway, he expressed a concern that faster journey times would lead to more accidents, and as we came to a halt at the roundabout near Privilege, he pointed out the metal fence which was installed to keep clubbers from straying into the road and told me about an incident which took place the previous summer...

5 a.m. a battered blue Fiat screeches out of the car park behind Privilege. Its occupants, four inebriated Italians, sway in unison with each bend, the two girls in the back laughing as they're squashed together as the car swerves around the

roundabout at speed. The front passenger, a male in his late twenties, extends his tattooed arm through the open window, outstretching his fingers to feel the balmy night air. Bliss – but then his upper arm meets the thin metal bar of the fence which frames the roundabout, effectively slicing through his soft flesh like a cheese wire. His limb detaches from his body, leaving only a few inches of flesh flapping from his shoulder. Upon seeing this, he immediately passes out from the pain and shock. From the back seat the girls, swapping tongues in a druggy girly kiss, shriek at being sprayed with what they thought were droplets of water from their mischievous front-seat passenger. Except it isn't water; it's blood which is sprayed rhythmically from his severed shoulder. Blissfully unaware, with her eyes closed, the blonde on the driver's side wipes her friend's face with a free hand whilst continuing to probe her mouth with her tongue. The plink plonk of minimal house is turned up even louder, drowning out the Policia Local car which pursues them, siren blaring and blue lights flashing.

After four kilometres, just outside San Antonio, the police car draws level and points to the roadside. The party car pulls over, and with music still blaring, the passengers nervously wait for the officers, who first walk slowly around the car to fully take in the scene. The girls cease their snog and two pairs of eyes, framed by blood-splattered faces, follow the torch beams which slowly encircle the vehicle like slow-motion spotlights.

After returning to the driver's window, the torch shines at the CD player. The policeman shrugs, questioning why they haven't turned it down or off.

The driver, totally away with the fairies, misunderstands and replies, 'Sirillo!'

The officer reaches in, silences Sirillo and removes the

ignition key.

'Español?' the officer asks.

'Italiano,' comes the reply.

'English?' A compromised tongue is offered.

'Si.'

Shining his torch on the front passenger, still unconscious, the policeman asks the driver, 'Your friend – what happened?'

The driver notices his friend sleeping and says, 'Mario, svegliati leggero!'

Svel-yatti lejero. *Wake up, lightweight!*

The police officer gestures for the driver to get out of the car and walk around to the passenger side to see the carnage framed in the open passenger window.

'Santa Maria! Oh Jesu! Mario, Mario!' He makes the sign of the cross and puts his head in his hands, screaming, 'No, no, noooooo!'

The girls in the backseat look at one another, and upon realising they are covered in blood, also start to scream.

This wakes the passenger, who takes one look at his severed arm (pause) and passes out again.

The cab arrived at my hotel. My head was spinning. I recalled the group waving a prosthetic arm as we drove past last summer. But could an arm really be ripped clean off? I asked him how he knew all this detail. I suspected he was exaggerating, or that it was an urban myth.

'My brother was the policeman. I have a photo from the evidencia file,' he replied, dipping in and out of Spanish, as he handed me a receipt.

'Really? Can I see it?'

'Of course. I send on WhatsApp now, what is your number?'

My phone pinged. I paid him and got out of the cab.

The grisly image revealed a severed arm lying at the kerb-side. The forearm bore a tattoo bearing the word *Libertad* – Italian for freedom. And it had found it.

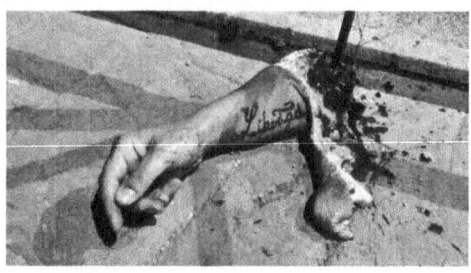

*Yes, it really happened (photo from cab driver).*

## Aftercare

Both the amphetamine amputee and his arm were airlifted to Palma, Mallorca to be reunited. Sadly, the operation wasn't successful. The driver was charged with possession of cocaine, ecstasy, drink driving, failing to report an accident and driving a car which had no tax or insurance. He received a custodial sentence but got off lightly compared to his mate in the passenger seat, who, in addition to losing his right arm, had to find €178,000 for the helicopter ride and treatment as he didn't have health or travel insurance. The old lady on stage in Manumission peeling potatoes whilst sitting on a toilet was indeed all part of the show... I think...

> **Top Tune: Magic Carpet Ride – Mighty Dub Katz
> {Southern Fried}**

## BEHIND THE BROCHURE

Never go on holiday without travel insurance; it can save you a fortune if things go wrong. But like all financial schemes can be taken advantage of by the unscrupulous, for whom a slip on the steps is blamed on the tiling rather than the Tequila shots, a hired moped crash is the fault of the loose wing mirror, not the NOS balloon their pillion passenger shared with them as they rode along. When they run out of cash, they'll swap their phone for a wrap and report it stolen the next day. The reputation of Brits for making dodgy claims is no secret.

As a result, it's easier to win the Nobel Peace Prize than to obtain a crime reference for a stolen camera or phone from the Guardia Civil in San Antonio, Ibiza.

Some hoteliers now insist guests who've specifically requested a balcony sign a disclaimer exonerating the hotel of any responsibility in the event of an accident.

Magaluf, 2019: a young British tourist blamed spilled water around the hotel pool for slipping over, breaking his shoulder bone and numerous ribs.

His €37,000 claim for medical bills caught the attention of the insurance company at the same time a video circulated on social media, showing an identical young man drunkenly trying to leap from the same hotel onto the top of a nearby tree. He missed both the tree and the payment, and ended up covering the €37,000 bill himself.

In 2021, José Antonio Ferragut, Councillor for Tourism in Sant Antonio, was asked by *Diario de Ibiza* what his ideal visitor would be. His reply was, 'Ones who don't use the emergency services and know how to use a balcony.'

# 3

# IN BED WITH A FRAUDSTER

In 1999, my wife Catherine suggested that rather than pay money each week to a landlord, we should look into buying a property. She was a successful session musician playing violin for major acts while appearing on numerous television music shows in a female string quartet. Coupled with a few days teaching at a school in Enfield, she was financially comfortable. I was also busy; regularly earning from my weekly column in TNT Magazine, penning freelance features for Time Out and Ministry magazine, handling press for London's busiest weekly club night, Freedom at Bagley's, while supplementing my income as a dubious MC, fronting club PAs for various producers who had no desire to drive to Wigan and Wakefield on a Saturday night to promote their record.

Unlike Catherine, who was legit, my earnings were rather more, let's say, 'casual'. I was usually paid in cash and the amount varied from month to month depending on the chart position of the tracks I was promoting, and the amount of extra events happening at Bagley's, or the success of that year's Kiss FM listener ski trip I'd conceived and managed in Mayrhofen, Austria.

So, I figured it was impossible for me to get a mortgage.

I wasn't alone. Many self-employed 'gig' economy workers were in the same boat.

But in 1998, how people earned their money was changing, so they introduced self-certification mortgages. Suddenly, I was in the ballpark. I could get a mortgage simply by stating how much I was earning. But my financial advisor told me that although I wasn't doing anything illegal, my multi-revenue streams looked too messy, and advised me to register myself as a business.

But doing what?

'Do what you're best at,' was Catherine's sage advice. As a 'jack of all trades', I excelled in doing lots of things to a passable standard, but what did she think I was best at?

'Showing your friends places you love,' she replied. 'You're happiest when you take people to Ibiza or Mayrhofen – and you do it really well because you care about the place and your guests.'

Over the next few days, I thought about her words. If I could find a way to make money from my passion, I'd be in business... literally!

I knew clubbing and travel were likely to be volatile and wanted to protect myself from creditors. I was advised to create a Limited Company, of which I would be Managing Director.

Radical Escapes Ltd was registered with Companies House in the dying days of the last century. It was set up by Chris Lunn & Co who was introduced to me as 'accountant to the stars'. Mr Lunn represented Sadie Frost and many of the Primrose Hill party set, along with another few thousand media types who worked in theatre, film, music and television. He was unlike any accountant I'd met, previously or since – he was interesting. We spent more time discussing a shared love of mountains than tax affairs. He told me not to try contacting him in June, as he'd be trekking through the Himalayas. I thought it was cool to have such a free-spirited accountant. In retrospect, it was a red flag. The more boring your accountant is, the better. You want an administrator, not an artist.

Upon receiving confirmation of incorporation, I thought it odd that the share certificate showed one share belonging to one Christopher Lunn. When I questioned him, he told me it was a goodwill bond. 'A tiny gold watch, if you like, all my clients agree to it.' Although this sounded unusual, I went along with it. If it was good enough for the stars, it was good enough for me. Who was I to argue?

My wife wasn't so sure, suspiciously inspecting the claret-and-yellow-striped paper clip that held the covering letter together. With an eyebrow raised she mused, 'Bespoke paper clips? Who has paper clips in company colours?'

Nonchalantly, I ignored it.

He'd advised me to register for VAT, and was shocked to hear when I told him that shortly after filing my third quarterly return, Radical Escapes was selected for a visit by the VAT inspector.

'This is most unusual, I've never known an inspection so soon. I can only advise that you have some quality coffee on the boil and cooperate fully, you have nothing to hide.' There was a pause before he added, 'But be careful. If they get their teeth into something, they won't let go.'

The sums involved were miniscule. I'd claimed back £658 of VAT in the three quarterly returns, a drop in the ocean compared to the amounts other companies were claiming. This was a new world to me. As Sole Officer with Significant Control of a Public Limited Company, I'd be responsible for any financial irregularities and face legal action resulting from any investigation. I went through the figures again. All seemed in order, but what if I'd made a mistake and been filling in the forms incorrectly?

The dreaded day arrived. At precisely 9 a.m., a small man in a grey suit carrying a black leather briefcase opened my gate and walked the six steps to my front door in Seaford Road, Enfield.

'Mr Field, Radical Escapes? I'm Charles Tonkin from Her Majesty's Customs and Excise responsible for investigating VAT fraud, may I come in?'

By the time he'd crossed the threshold I was already shitting myself. I was unused to such formality and felt I was out of my depth.

When I set up Radical Escapes, I had to select the areas the company would work in. I chose 'tourism, events and music'. A few weeks before the VAT inspection, the border force at Harwich had searched every one of my 652 guests prior to boarding my club cruise to Hamburg. I raised a complaint

'Mr Field, you organise events – effectively "raves" as far as we can ascertain – which involve crossing borders. Your events are of interest to the authorities, and therefore warrant increased surveillance,' they told me.

From then on I was paranoid, I suspected they were tapping my phone. I was aware HMRC are a proper firm, and that crime bosses are usually taken down for tax evasion rather than by a bullet. With nothing to pin on me, had Harwich Customs alerted HMRC to pursue me and close my business, using any small financial discrepancy they could find?

'Can I offer you some of the finest Colombian, Mr Tonkin? It's got a real kick.'

What did I just say? But Mr Tonkin was still in the hallway studying the walls and ceiling, and never heard me as I was facing away from him and had entered the lounge.

'I'm sorry?'

I poked my head back around the doorframe. 'Coffee, from Columbia. It was on offer, you see; I usually buy Italian.' Now I was overcompensating. I needn't have worried; Inspector Tonkin was miles away looking at the spiderwebs in the cornice of my hallway and craning his neck to the fuse board above the front door. I darted back inside to bring him the coffee, which was radiating a caramelised, nutty aroma from the kitchen. When I returned, he was in the lounge still peering at the bare ceiling. 'Okay, I give up. Where do you keep them, then?' he asked, accepting the coffee.

'My accounts? They're here on the table.'

'I was referring to the chains.'

'Chains?'

'Chains and padlocks, shackles and handcuffs. You *are* an escapologist, aren't you, Mr Field?'

It transpired that the reason for the early VAT inspection was that (the soon-to-retire) Mr Tonkin was an escapologist nut, and chose me for investigation because of my company's name. I tried to temper his disappointment by giving him an old book I had about Harry Houdini. I think it worked; after a few hours of grilling and following an external audit I was contacted to be told everything was in order, and Radical Escapes were subsequently left alone.

The first few years were lean; sporadic earnings from listener trips and Ibiza holidays which I struggled to get paid for. As a result, I couldn't justify the high fees Christopher Lunn & Co were charging, and he stopped representing me a few years later.

In 2010, I was on the tube and picked up a well-thumbed copy of the Evening Standard and came across a headline which screamed:

*Accountant to the Stars Faces £117 million Fraud Inquiry*

The full-page feature told of the arrest of a 'showbiz accountant' who, it alleged, had swindled the UK Government out of an estimated £117 million pounds through sharp practices. Although the character in question (a former bankruptee) had many famous clients including BBC newsreaders Joanna Gosling and Fiona Armstrong's company Paradox Productions, it also emerged he wasn't actually registered with any accountancy body at all! After the jury failed to reach a verdict in 2014, he was acquitted but was convicted at the retrial in December the following year. His words echoed in my head, 'Once they get their teeth into something...'

In early January 2016, following a lengthy investigation and voluntary cooperation by many of Lunn's unsuspecting clients which totalled £20 million, Denis Christopher Carter Lunn was found guilty of four counts of Cheating the Public Revenue of in excess of £6 million and was sentenced to five years in prison. I understand his clients from 2005 onwards were investigated for tax discrepancies and many found themselves having to pay bills of up to £160,000. If Radical Escapes had really taken off in those early years, I may have been one of them. However, because he holds a share, I'm technically still in partnership with a convicted fraudster. I suppose I could get the share removed, but it would mean changing this chapter title!

I chose the name of the company, Radical Escapes, to reflect both the extreme nature of my holidays and to acknowledge a holiday is a release from reality. A very famous club in Ibiza's original name was The Workshop of Forgetfulness, but it looked messy on T-shirts, so Amnesia was chosen instead. The name had advantages and disadvantages...

In the early noughties, Radical Escapes was approached by Tierry Donard, a French film director to manage the UK launch of his movie, *Perfect Moment*. This was the latest in the *Nuit de la Glisse* series of feature-length films shot on 35mm which captured stunning exponents of extreme sports; surfing, free-running, extreme ski and snowboarding, kite surfing, freefall parachuting and wingsuit flying. It was a class product, and we both felt Radical Escapes was a good fit brand-wise. I wanted to deliver something out of the ordinary, and my idea was that after the red carpet premiere in Leicester Square, everyone would be taken in blacked-out buses to London Zoo, where, amongst the reptiles, they would be entertained by the UK's premier breakdancing crews who I knew.

People are always looking for unique venues, and when I heard it was possible to hire The Reptile House at London Zoo, I figured it would be ideal for the after-party. All my emails were ignored and my telephone calls unreturned. Weeks went by, and while I'd tied up Warner Brothers Leicester Square, printed and sent out the invites (including complimentary transport to a secret after-party venue), I still hadn't managed to speak to anyone at the zoo. Eventually, I was told the venue wasn't available on the date I'd requested. So, I confirmed my Plan B, The Limelight on Shaftesbury Avenue. Although it was only a minute's walk away from Leicester Square, I'd promised complimentary transport and had to deliver it. So,

I booked a dozen rickshaws who ferried the guests the few hundred metres to the club!

No one was aware that I'd planned to hold it in the zoo, and it was a great party. Break crews excelling themselves, a montage playing on a big screen and music from Chris Phillips from Kiss FM, Radio One producer Paul Thomas and the fab Bex Tbx. Tierry and his sponsor Philips were very happy, so all in all, job done.

A couple of months later, I was invited to an album press launch at the Reptile House in London Zoo through my TNT Magazine column. At some point I was introduced to a member of staff and expressed my disappointment at the lack of cooperation when I tried to book the venue.

'Really, that's a shame. What's the name of your company?' the girl asked.

'Radical Escapes,' I replied.

Her reaction was immediate. 'Please excuse me, I'll be back in a moment.' She brushed past me and disappeared into the crowd, returning a few minutes later with two burly security men who asked me to go outside into the courtyard with them.

I was incredulous, first they ignored a potential client, then they wanted to throw me out?

'What on earth have I done?'

'It's more what you'd like to do,' sneered one security guard. 'You animal lib lot don't realise you'd cause more distress and death if you got your way and freed the animals.'

'What are you talking about?' I asked, bewildered.

'We've been made aware there's a plot to access the site using our private events, from which undercover animal liberation campaigners will hide until the public have left, then facilitate the escape of the animals,' he said, a tight grip on my bicep.

Suddenly it all made sense. My email address was radicalescapes@btinternet.com. They suspected my movie launch party was a cover for a mass escape attempt.

I was allowed into an office where I showed them my event pages and the link to the trailer of the film on an office computer. They apologised profusely, and were so embarrassed they offered me a discounted hire to be taken in the following twelve months. I was also given a London Zoo mug!

> **Top Tune: Play at Your Own Risk – Planet Patrol {Tommy Boy}**

## Afterglow

Some years later, my attempts to volunteer as an Official Prison Visitor (OPV) were similarly rebuffed. OPVs visit prisoners who rarely, if ever, have visits from friends or family members. Every application I sent was ignored. I told my wife, who asked me which email account I was sending them from. 'Radical Escapes,' I replied. 'Wait, you don't think they...' Sure enough, when I resent the email from my personal account I received a swift response. It was a rejection (which is just as well, as Gary Glitter was moved to the prison I applied for and would've been amongst those eligible to receive visits, which I would've found very challenging).

I've still got the claret-and-yellow-striped paper clip, which a woman's intuition was right about.

## BEHIND THE BROCHURE

Guaranteed sun and getting a tan has always been the main driver of holidaying in the med, the reason why Brits choose San Antonio over Saarf-end and Magaluf over Margate.

The seventies' million-selling holiday anthem, Viva España, summed up how it used to be:

> *When they first arrive, the girls are pink and pasty /*
> *but oh so tasty as soon as they go brown*

It used to be possible to tell how long my guests had been on holiday simply by looking at their skin; pale (recently arrived), red-raw (2–3 days), peeling (4–5 days), red-raw *and* peeling (6–7 days).

Then spray tanning took off, creating Cretan complexions without the carcinoma. These days getting a fake tan is an important part of the oh-so important pre-getaway ritual which can also include lip filler appointments, a course of slimming jabs and posting an obligatory airport pint photo.

But sunless tanning can provide a false sense of security. I was once called to a room by a couple of female guests who looked like someone had been using a blowtorch on their shoulders. It was genuinely horrific. I remembered them from the welcome meeting, and gently chided Ruby Mae and Courtney for laying in the midday sun for hours on their first day, explaining how much stronger the sun was in Ibiza than Preston.

'But we paid full whack for a Bridal spray tan course to build a base, haven't we, Courtney, luv?'

Courtney, luv (not to be confused with Courtney Love),

who was also laying front down on her single bed, removed her teeth from the pillow she was biting to manage the pain and grimaced, 'Too fucking right, babes, we're getting a full refund from the buggers.'

# 4

# HOLIDAY HISTORY

Although I've made my living for over twenty years selling them, the 2wentys holiday I described earlier was my first and only experience as a guest on a package holiday. As a family we never went on them. Indeed, Her Majesty's Passport Office were blissfully unaware of my existence until my school trip to France when I was twelve. Summer holidays were instead spent persevering a ten-hour drive to a modest B&B in the west country or searching for a caravan site in the gathering gloom in the Yorkshire Dales which didn't belong to the Caravan Club. If only the AA roadmap had differentiated between (members-only) Caravan Club sites and farmer's fields with a standpipe and toilets which doubled as a singles' bar for daddy long legs and clumsy moths, it would've saved us hours of dragging our Sprite around country lanes. All too often our back seat hopes of a cosy Horlicks sat around a Formica table watching a tiny black-and-white portable telly dissolved in a passenger seat cry of 'Oh hell! It's another bloody Caravan Club site. Keep going, Brian.'

Given the price of fuel after the oil crisis in 1973, I couldn't help wondering if it would be more economical to join the bloody Caravan Club.

Their sites assumed the status of a mythical forbidden land; the towbar equivalent of the Holy of Holies or King's Chamber in the Great Pyramid, off limits to all but the chosen elite.

What could make them so special? As we disconsolately drove away, the thick perimeter hedge concealed its hidden treasures. Having never seen inside one, my over-active ten-year-old mind imagined a lush Shangri La with heated swimming pools, hot tubs and goalposts with nets. In researching this book, I finally found out. In order to qualify as a CL (certified location), a Caravan Club-designated site needed to possess the following riches: an emptying point for chemical closets, a safe drinking water supply, a bin for dry rubbish and, the jewel in the caravanning crown, public liability insurance cover.

So along with Father Christmas, the tooth fairy, Lance Armstrong and the electoral system, the Caravan Club resides in the 'not what I thought it was' drawer.

When we did find a non-CC site, we'd spend the week sheltering from the inevitable Yorkshire rain, which would assault the tinny roof like an angry snare roll as we played Scrabble whilst enjoying a flask of my mum's delicious potato hash. Eagerly passing around a bag of Mother's Pride (white, of course) to dip into the Tupperware bowls we ate it from. Mum used to sell it, see. Not the bread, the Tupperware. The kitchen cupboard was a tribute to pale pastel-coloured plastic. Occasionally, she'd throw Tupperware evenings; you know like today people throw Anne Summers parties. Except it was the flexibility of the dishes rather than the dildos which excited 1970s housewives. Back then it was the container they were concerned was airtight, rather than themselves.

Other kids went to exotic destinations like Mallorca and Benidorm, returning with gravy-stained faces and their names on bullfighting posters. While my mum and dad clearly knew it was the '70s, as we ate Angel Delight, Arctic Roll and watched *It's a Knockout!*, they refused to join in with everyone else in the great working-class exodus to the Costa Del Sol. Looking back, I got all the worst things about that decade; Coronation Chicken vol au vonts whilst watching *The Black and White Minstrel Show* (in between the power cuts), but didn't get to experience the ultimate '70s holiday cliché: taking off for two weeks in Torremolinos.

To be honest, I wasn't too fussed with missing out on foreign food and flamenco, it was the journey there and back I wanted to experience. I longed to fly, see. I'd gaze at vapour trails scarring clear blue skies and spend hours listening to air traffic control handing passing flights to the next sector on a short band radio. As a kid, the nearest I ever got to the departure lounge on any summer holiday was a family daytrip to Heathrow airport in 1972. It was there I first caught a glimpse of a jumbo jet from the viewing gallery. It was like looking at the future. If Concorde had turned up, I'd probably have spontaneously combusted.

Flying defined the era – 'the supersonic seventies' they called it on the Cadbury's adverts. It was the start of space travel. A few years earlier I'd stood on the drive with my dad and he'd pointed up at the moon incredulously, saying, 'You can't see them, but there's a couple of blokes walking around up there.'

It felt like the dawning of a new age. By the year 2000 I figured I'd probably be living on the moon, never mind visiting the bugger, wearing a one-piece jumpsuit and eating Sunday roast in a pill. Air travel was its aspirational, glamorous and sexy little sister. According to the adverts they even gave you free 'in-flight' *Cinzano Bianco*. I didn't know what *Cinzano Bianco* was, but figured if Joan Collins drank it, it must taste good.

We were the only ones at the airport that day without a suitcase or a pair of binoculars. So near and yet so far. Looking back, that day was like an aviation lap dance; I could look but I couldn't get involved. I left frustrated and wished we'd gone to Whipsnade Zoo instead to see the monkeys masturbating like Chris from up the street had on his holidays. I needn't have worried, they were still at it when we visited a few days later.

I realised that the only way I was going to get airborne was to do it myself. But on £1.65 a week pocket money and no passport, there was only one way to do it other than hijacking a plane (which, along with quicksand and celebrity paedophile rings, was all the rage back then) was to join the Air Training Corps.

I worked hard in air cadets and must've shown some leadership qualities because within eighteen months I was the senior cadet in my squadron. Each summer, Flight Sergeant Field was selected for week-long attachment to an RAF station. But rather than being sent somewhere exotic such as British Honduras or Cyprus, we'd be dispatched to the highlands of Scotland or, if we got really lucky, Germany.

I was over the (by now heavily footprinted) moon to be sent to an edgy, frontline, cold war air base.

This meant flying in an actual plane! I've still got the sick bag and embossed seatbelt sign I prised from the seat in front as souvenirs.

Space cadets (as the RAF lads referred to us) would spend each day of the week attached to a different section of the airfield, to gain work experience and show us that there were many other jobs available after you failed your pilot selection course at Biggin Hill.

One day in Air Traffic Control (blue-carpeted calm and forever quietly sipping tea), a day with the Military Police dog handlers, where we'd be dressed in sacking and provide the prey for the dogs to chase. I wondered if you could rely on them to tackle a target if they were dressed in a shell suit and Nike Jordan's rather than padded sacking, but didn't raise it. On one occasion we were shown the NCO's mess. This is where non-commissioned officers, Corporals and Sergeants relax after a long day shouting at their privates. Each squadron has a mascot, a motto and a crest. But this particular squadron also had something else. As we were shown along the corridor outside the bar, we paused in front of a rather grand gold frame mounted on the wall. In the centre of the frame was a light brown, slightly curved cylindrical object.

My host stepped back to admire it. 'Our pride and joy. What do you think of it?' he asked. His moustache twitched as he stood noticeably to attention, beckoning me to do the same with a deft tap of his cane against my leg.

'Very nice. Is it the squadron frankfurter?'

After appreciating the geographical reference with a nod of admiration, he shook his head and beckoned me to approach it, so my nose was almost touching the glass. Closer inspection revealed it was crumbling.

'Hmmm. Is it a religious relic?'

He thought for a moment, twirling his moustache so it formed a point. 'It is to us, sonny, and to any proud Englishman.'

He briskly threw his right arm out to the side, before bending it at the elbow, bringing his hand to his right eyebrow and instructed, 'Salute the Royal poo, laddie.'

I joined him in saluting the shit. This would explain why I needed to be stood to attention.

He explained how the Queen's Flight would transport the monarch on long-haul flights. On one occasion, a plan was hatched to capture the royal flush. They loaded on an extra loo just for Her Maj and monitored who went for an in-flight number two, removing and replacing the chemical toilet unit after Lizzy had abdicated the throne. The prize was then dried and coated with a plastic bonding agent. Imagine a joke dog poo and you'll get the picture. I was then sworn to secrecy holding a photo of the Queen and given a cup of coffee and custard cream.

Years later, I regaled this tale to a mate who provided personal security to celebrities. Like most of these guys, he was ex-military. His area of work was the Royal Family. 'Sweeping' wherever the Queen would spend the night outside Royal residences, checking for bombs and bugs and ensuring no nutters were hiding under the bed. In addition to ensuring the safety of the monarch, his duties also included ensuring the Queen's privacy and dignity weren't compromised. Inside his black rucksack, alongside the electronic gizmos and night vision goggles, was a small potato. After establishing which ensuite loo the monarch would be using, he'd hand the potato to a colleague who was in radio contact and instruct him to drop it into the bowl from toilet-seat height whilst he stood silently in adjacent rooms listening out for the 'PLOP'. Only when he was satisfied the regal dump couldn't be heard was the room allowed to be occupied by anyone other than her Her Royal Highness.

During my week on the base, I spent a day with the engineers whose task it was to replace the engines in the Buccaneers and Phantoms and manage the armaments. It was late afternoon, and I was sitting nonchalantly on a tarpaulined trailer chatting to a mechanic who was laying on his back on the ground beneath a jet engine. It was the height of the cold war and talk of Armageddon was everywhere, so I couldn't resist asking the question that had been on my lips ever since getting the posting.

'Are there any nuclear weapons on this base?'

Without stopping whatever it was he was doing, he agitatedly replied, 'That, we are not allowed to divulge, but if you keep kicking your fucking legs against that missile you're sat on, you'll find out soon enough, sonny.'

As a student and government artist, Someone who claims unemployment benefit and is said to be 'drawing the dole' I continued to be unstained by the package holiday experience. I'd watch Judith Chalmers on *Wish You Were Here* like a spotty youth watches porn, not even daring to imagine it was me experiencing the endless buffet, and 'tasty local cuisine'. The alternative, Club 18–30 similarly held no mystique, coming across like a sunburnt equivalent of a provincial nightclub, the entry to which demanded proper shoes, a shirt with buttons all the way to your belly button and an unquestioning attitude to the resident DJ's preference for chart disco over punk, ska and goth records.

It was obvious Club 18–30 catered for the mainstream, not weird anorexics like me. Post-holiday stories of blowjobs in hotel whirlpools, gang fights with groups of Geordies and all-you-can-drink-and-spew bar crawls from my mainstream mates only served to reinforce my aversion to the package holiday throughout the '80s.

This probably explains why in the early '90s I was so eager to accept whatever overseas assignment *Mixmag* offered me. It was a chance to fly somewhere for free.

So, when I boarded that 2wentys bus in 1997, I was naive to the ways of the package holiday world, and utterly horrified at what I found. They say the way to boil a frog is to put it in cold water and slowly heat it, so it doesn't notice the subtle change in temperature and boils to death. My first youth package holiday experience was a violently bubbling cauldron which this frog immediately saw for what it was and hopped away. I hope this explains why that week had such an effect on me, and spurred me into action in forming Radical Escapes.

## Aftersun

Looking back, I'd be very surprised if what I experienced as an air cadet – shooting live ammunition, combat training with bayonets, flying in a dual-control two-seater training planes and flying solo in a glider at the age of sixteen *without a parachute* – would be allowed in the current health and safety obsessed society. Defence cuts have bitten deep, the ATC is funded by the RAF, who understandably prioritise the nation's defence over teenage kicks. Half of glider squadrons were disbanded in 2016, and the Department for Education recently ended its grant for cadet forces. This seems short-sighted. With Kier Starmer seemingly intent in provoking WW3, who does he think is going to sign up to fight the Russkis, other than Space Cadets and Pongos (an air cadet reference for Army Cadets born of the saying, 'where the Army goes, the pong goes...')?

> **Top Tune: Wood Allen – Airport '89 (12" Club Mix)**
> **{BCM}**

## BEHIND THE BROCHURE

In the early noughties, a premium vodka brand offered an activation which sounded imaginative, innovative *and insane;* taking 700 UK clubbers for a night out in Ibiza.

The contestants – couples (mates or romantically linked partners) – would assemble in branded bars in Glasgow, Manchester and London in possession of their passport. Every couple was given a glowstick, 350 of which would turn red when broken. These were deemed the winners, who would be whisked off to the airport, where they'd board a privately chartered Boeing 747 bound for Ibiza – to party all night for free in Space (this is a worthy prize in itself), before being whisked back to the airport at dawn to catch the Red Eye back to blighty.

To avoid the possibility of flight delays, the aircrafts were privately chartered at a cost of £300,000 each, The Cuban Brothers were booked as in-flight entertainment and Space were paid in advance for theming, admission and drinks.

Additionally, the risk assessment involved them booking 200 hotel rooms in the event of illness, food poisoning or fatigue.

All in all, the jape cost in excess of a million pounds.

The day before the trip, Ibiza taxi drivers went on strike, blockading the airport. No one could get in or out of the terminal.

The BBC Evening News led with tearful interviews of distressed families with small children struggling with the cramped conditions in the searing high summer heat.

The brand and agency wisely decided not to proceed, but as it was only hours before the event was about to start, they couldn't cancel the aircraft and so had to pay in full, despite them never taking off, meaning Cuban Mike Keat's joystick remained untouched.

# 5

# AN ENGLISHMAN
# IN NEW YORK

Before I relive my misadventures, I'd like to take you to New York in the summer of 1988 for what was, now I look back on it, my very first clubbing holiday...

The silhouette of a slight figure, strolling with a cane beneath a fedora along 4th Avenue Manhattan, was as incongruous as it was familiar. I'd spent the previous five days crossing the Atlantic Ocean on the QE2 reading a book called *The Wit and Wisdom of Quentin Crisp*, which I found erudite and entertaining. A quotable, relatable 1980s Oscar Wilde, he was a pre-internet influencer, a gay rights campaigner when being gay was a crime, an author, performer, philosopher, outsider, dandy and icon, whose words resonated with my mid-twenties' 'outsider' persona.

I justified my persevering as a struggling, unsigned singer in a band rather than getting a 'proper job' with his idiom, 'It's no good running a pig farm badly for thirty years while saying, "Really, I was meant to be a ballet dancer." By then, pigs will be your style.' I never even knew he lived in New York.

He drew closer, his facial features now recognisable; a powder-faced kindly aunt in a turquoise silk cravat. As he drew level, he stopped and delved into a pocket of his scarlet velvet jacket and produced a key. He inserted it into the door he was standing beside. I had to move swiftly. I stepped forward.

'Mr Crisp, it's a pleasure to meet you. Can I just say that what you said about the pig farmer and ballet dancer was absolutely correct.'

I held out my hand. He drew his head back slightly to get a better view of me, looked me up and down, graciously accepted my hand and declared, 'My dear, everything I've ever said has been absolutely correct.'

He removed his small, warm hand, pale and translucent and framed in a lavish lace sleeve, and returned it to the key protruding from the door lock. He turned both the key and his head. 'Make the most of your time here,' he said, before nodding his farewell and disappearing indoors.

What a coincidence! Sixteen million people lived in New York in 1988 and I bumped into the one who I'd spent the previous five days studying!

This chance meeting gave me the confidence to explore what was a dangerous city at the time. The Big Apple was a rotten apple – in the grip of both the crack and AIDS epidemics. A homicide was recorded every five hours, but Quentin had told me to make the most of my time here – and as everything he said was 'absolutely correct', I felt it was only right to do as he told me.

I found myself in New York that summer's day as a last-minute replacement for my manager's elderly mother – who, a few days prior to departure, had temporarily blinded herself whilst peroxiding her hair. This meant she was unable to travel and accept her son's golden wedding anniversary present to her and his stepfather: a transatlantic crossing on the QE2, three nights in The Big Apple, before a flight home on Concorde.

Concorde! The delta-winged, droopy-nosed, supersonic jet defined the era: the 'supersonic, space-age '70s'. For someone who dreamed about flying, Concorde was the ultimate rush – literally: you could fly faster than a rifle bullet on the edge of space. From its windows, you could even see the curvature of the Earth... WHILST EATING CAVIAR!

It was the five days and nights getting out there which was the problem. Although the QE2's maiden voyage was one of 1969's technological landmarks along with the moon landing and Concorde, it was a pretty distant third. Adverts may have boasted 'The only thing QE2 has in common with other ships is that she floats' as the strapline, but in my mind she was just like the rest of them; a forever-moving, vomit-inducing, life-threatening tub of torment.

Me and the sea just didn't get on. The first time I crossed the channel was on a school trip to France. The next time I set foot on a ship was the previous spring when I toiled to Zeebrugge on the Herald of Free Enterprise. With no money to book a cabin, my girlfriend and me spent a sleepless night in unforgiving chairs at the stern of the ship. The following week it sank, killing 193 people when someone forgot to close the bow doors, which were located directly below where we'd been sitting the week before...

I vowed to avoid the sea from then on, and hadn't been on a ship since. My resolve to remain on land was only reinforced when I accepted an offer from a psychic-minded friend to undergo past life regression. I hoped to discover my 'previous life' involved me being Alexander the Great, Voltaire or George Mallory, but instead had to settle for a humble sailor who drowned in a sea battle in 1870. But so passionate was my love of flying that the chance to crunch caviar on Concorde and check out New York's clubs was too good to miss.

On my bucket list was the 'Vatican of Disco': The Saint, The Limelight, The Tunnel and a place called The Vault.

We set sail from Southampton one bright June morning. The only thing my manager (who we'll call Guy) asked was I keep his stepfather company in the onboard bars and casinos, and enter the passenger talent competition – both of which I executed to satisfaction. The first task was more challenging than the latter. William was a seasoned barfly and had an impressive capacity for alcohol and late-night bonhomie with rich American widows. The talent show (imagine The X Factor on the Titanic, and you'll get the picture) took place in The Grand Lounge after the harp recital (never was the saying 'from the serene to the ridiculous' more apt). Competition wasn't what you'd describe as stiff, more static. Four rich American widows, all of whom statuesquely laboured through a Gilbert and Sullivan operetta. By way of contrast, my animated Elvis medley with the house band was an epileptic fit in the key of E and fake leather trousers. Whether I won the silver platter for my singing, gyrating, or just because I was the only entrant demonstrably still breathing was unclear, but at least it gave me mum something to stand on top of the telly.

I must've been the only passenger under the age of fifty on that crossing. My youth, coupled with the absence of Ralph Lauren logos on my clothes and cheap trainers, led to me often being apprehended by senior staff while walking around the carpeted corridors. 'Use the service corridors!'

they'd snarl. They didn't believe I had the social status to be sharing a boat with the likes of Omar Shariff, John Mills and Jimmy Saville. They weren't wrong. Each night I'd drink in the crew bar where drinks were a fraction of the price of anywhere else on the ship.

I'd spend the days jogging around the deck and reading, whilst I was kept entertained by Quentin Crisp's wit and wisdom, Guy was fascinated by a new book called *The Art of the Deal* by the comically named Donald Trump. I told Guy I didn't know how anyone could take him seriously with a name like that.

I should mention that I was frontman and singer for a band in London at the time. This would explain my pillar-box red hair which was immaculately coiffured into a quiff. I'd wear a matching scarlet military jacket with more gold braid than is healthy for a man; a rouge ensemble which would turn heads, stop traffic and elicit shouts of WANKER! from every building site I passed.

Although I'd dyed it black for my transatlantic adventure, upon arriving in Manhattan, my red Hussar blouson and immaculate quiff, coupled with an air of frontman self-importance came in useful as we left William to charm the oldies in the hotel casino and went clubbing.

This enabled me to walk to the front of the queue at The Limelight, a former church whose congregation now included pop icons, supermodels and movie stars. Normally, upon arriving at a venue, Guy would beckon the door manager over and explain the self-important scarlet spectre before their eyes with two words: 'Kirk Field.' In provincial England this would be met with, 'Who? Never heard of him,' and an invitation to join the back of the queue. But this was downtown

Manhattan, where stars were born every week. As long as I looked and acted the part of a star, I figured I'd be fine. And so it was; they waved me through and even asked me if I was with Mr Dillon's party. Unfortunately, Guy shook his head.

Once inside the VIP area, we could see Matt Dillon holding court in the VVIP area for which we didn't have the right pass.

After a few hours, we asked a cab to take us to The Tunnel, a nightclub in a former railway terminal complete with tracks, cages suspended from the ceiling and music I'd never heard before. EVERYONE was dancing, most with their eyes closed; shirtless gay guys, their bodies glistening with sweat, danced next to Puerto Rican girls moving their hips like I'd only ever seen in films.

I was shocked to find them using the same toilets. It was the first unisex public toilet I'd ever seen with partitions rather than cubicles, which throbbed to every kick drum beat and shuddered as one with the bass. Like an awestruck child I explored the catwalks and gantries, braving the regular drips of sweat from the dirty brickwork. This was unlike any nightclub I'd been in before; industrial and anonymous. And seductive as hell.

I stood behind the DJ, who appeared to be captivated by the seamless, pulsing rhythm as everyone else was in there. I asked a handsome young security fella who was guarding the entrance to the tunnel behind the decks what he was called.

'Junior Vasquez,' came the gravelly reply.

'And what's this music called?'

He looked at me and smiled knowingly. 'This is house music… I guess it hasn't reached England yet, huh?' I shook my head, which drew a smile. 'It will…'

He told me he was an actor, but loved working as a bouncer

as he could listen to house music, and would even come in on his nights off to dance.

Years later I was watching *The Fast and the Furious* and couldn't place where I'd seen the actor playing Dom before. I suffer from proso-pag-nosia – face blindness – so it was his voice which I recognised.

It was Vin Diesel.

## Act Like You Belong

At 1 a.m. I hailed a bright yellow cab outside our hotel.

'Where to?'

'The Vault, 10th Avenue, between Little West 12th and 13th streets, please.'

The driver weighed me up through the rearview mirror. My nostrils told me he'd had garlic mayo with his supper followed by a cigarette. He hadn't showered since yesterday.

'A couple of fags?'

'Sorry, we don't smoke.'

'I said, are yous a couple of fags? 'Cos if you ain't, I can't see why you'd want to go to Devil's Playground.'

I remember reading in Time Out how New Yorkers don't beat around the bush, or waste time with unnecessary small talk. They get straight to the point, and they are not afraid to tell it like it is.

Or like they think it is...

'Listen, mate, I'm not a fag. My friend here may qualify, and I haven't got a problem with that. The Vault is a mixed club where anything goes.'

He shrugged. 'Anything except me, I don't go there. I'll take ya to the meat market. It's a two-minute walk to the AIDS factory.'

Cars screech around the block checking out the working girls touting for business. I say girls, but closer inspection revealed most of them were pre-surgery transgender women. The meat market was in night mode; instead of carcasses on hooks, the flesh came in leather. It was Grindr in bricks and mortar, and abounded with sex clubs which included The Hellfire Club, Manhole and The Mineshaft which attracted swingers and thrill-seeking celebrities who felt safe. I'd been told about The Vault by a drinking buddy Dave Ball from Soft Cell. The British bands would be taken there by US record company girls when they played New York. He told me he'd seen Freddy Mercury and Al Pacino in there. It was a place I just had to witness if I was to make the most of the city as Quentin Crisp had instructed.

We were walking across the square feeling vulnerable. A rat scuttled across our path, hunched and laboured, carrying a used condom in its jaws. Christ, even the vermin's twisted. I had four cans of Sapporo lager tucked across my chest concealed by my black leather biker jacket as The Vault had no liquor licence (which was ironic, as there was no shortage of lickers). The Japanese beer body armour made me look like a top-heavy He-Man.

We walked down what looked like a litter-strewn Sesame Street. Up ahead a group of black teenagers sat around a stoop[2].

They spotted us approaching and stood up, blocking the sidewalk. Shit. My heart beat increasingly faster against the aluminium beer cans.

We drew level. There were seven or eight of them.

---

2    A stoop is a New York term for a flight of steps at the front of a house

'Keep walking,' I quietly said to Guy

'Fuckin' hell, Kirk,' he replied, exasperated.

The strong smell of Ganga and acrid chemicals filled my nostrils. A Rasta type sat on the steps, dreadlocks cascading like rusty waterfalls over his clearly silicon breasts as he smoked a small pipe. Breasts? His bulging eyes were enhanced by mascara. A pair of ebony thighs sprouted from a pink Lycra microskirt before disappearing into a pair of black PVC thigh-high boots which fixed him to the stained steps.

A tall man in a faded Bob Marley T-shirt stepped out in front of me.

I shifted to the side. He followed me. I shifted back. He did likewise.

'Base?' His breath enveloped my head, an acrid cloud of burnt plastic with hints of ammonia.

Do I speak and let him know I'm English? I thought. One of the unwritten rules of travelling is that ghetto tourists are fair game. But before I could decide Guy politely declined their kind offer of crack cocaine in his gentle Irish lilt and ushered me onwards, and away from the gaggle. Resisting the urge to look back to see if we were being chased, I kept looking straight ahead, whilst walking as fast as I could.

Up ahead on the corner I saw a lit doorway, a Hell's Angel type stands sentinel. We'd confirmed we were not lost and knew the name of the establishment. He invited us in, took $100 off us and explained the rules: 'No fucking. Spanking, whipping, jerking and sucking are fine. Check your weapons at the door and no means no.'

Footnote: In order to remain open through the mid-'80s AIDS epidemic the backroom and glory holes were removed in New York sex clubs.

As we waited for the small steel cage elevator another sign read: 'Act like you belong'. But it was the small sign next to it which caught my eye:

*Official HQ of the Fist Fucking Society of America*

I was intrigued; a fellowship for fisting! Who knew?

How did you join? I imagined entry was probably a slow process requiring a certain positioning and patience, but once you were in the lodge of lubricators, things were more relaxed and there was perhaps a surprising capacity for upward mobility. Their motions were naturally decided by a show of hands. Such was their enthusiasm, I reckon every hand in the room shot straight up, allowing them to punch through their agenda like the well-oiled body they were.

The Hell's Angel doorman walked past. Across his shoulders, a name was embroidered onto the leather waistcoat which hung from his gym-toned torso: LUCIFER. NYC. It was perfect. If it had said RUPERT it wouldn't have felt like we were about to take an elevator ride into Hades.

There were four floors and a basement – each, as I was to discover on my travels – catering for its own target market: a multi-story menagerie of messy mischief which was wrong on so many levels.

The wrought iron elevator lift shaft was effectively the spine of The Vault; a suspended cage which ascended and descended depending on the depth of your desire and depravity.

We rode it one floor up. The door rattled as we opened it and stepped out. Preferring to retain our trousers, we declined the services of the clothes check and found a bar. Sure enough, the only beverages available were iced tea or water. Hardcore pornography flickered on a cheap TV set high in a corner. There was no volume, but you could follow the plot easily enough.

We found an empty table. A few couples sat around in silence looking bored. A single man dressed in sharply creased beige trousers and expensive-looking shiny loafers perched on a bar stool. In contrast to everyone else we'd seen he was somewhat incongruous with his neat knitwear and healthy complexion, and looked familiar.

We cracked open our cans of Sapporo which hissed like a couple of angry asps. The first can didn't touch the sides. It was a hot June night, and I was parched. I needed to pee and asked the girl behind the bar, who was at the very least topless, for directions. Without speaking, she pointed to the lift, then moved her finger down and held up two fingers.

I took the lift down two floors and emerged into a dark corridor. Ahead, a sign hung lopsidedly: THE DUNGEON. To my left there was a brightly lit room which I figured was the toilet. The porcelain urinals on the left indicated I was correct. As I walked towards them, in my peripheral vision I caught a glimpse of someone to my right, who was sitting down in what appeared to be a large ceramic bowl.

Just as I positioned myself at the urinal and unzipped my PVC trousers a pleading voice echoed around the otherwise empty room, 'Pee on me?'

I looked to my left, through a gap in the large bowl and saw a chubby grown man in his fifties dressed in a nappy sat cross-legged on the floor.

'Pleeeease pee on me.'

I ignored him and tried my best to pee, not on him, as he'd requested, but in the urinal, but I couldn't.

He repeated this phrase as I stood there with nothing coming out. Each second lasted a minute. It was a dilemma the likes of which I'd never encountered before or since.

I always try to do 'the right thing' – but what was the right thing in this situation?

He was here by his own free will, and with no great effort could I make him happy. No one would ever know. What would otherwise be a wasted pee could instead make someone's night. One man's piss is another one's pleasure, you might say. What was causing my reluctance? The act itself, his gender – or the fact he was dressed as a baby?

Eventually, my bladder overruled my reticence. The sound of my piss hitting the aluminium urinal drawing a 'Noooooo!' from the big baby in the big bathtub as he realised he'd lost out.

I couldn't wait for it to end. Eventually I tucked myself in, zipped up my fly and walked out, without washing my hands as I wanted to avoid the big baby, figuring he wouldn't pick me up on it.

I hurriedly departed to a shout of, 'Meanie!'

I decided not to mention anything to Guy, who was distracted by the scene which had developed in my absence. The familiar-looking guy at the bar had both hands on a mane of bronze hair in his lap; at the same time his head faced the ceiling as he received fellatio. Upon completion, she removed her head and wiped her mouth. It was the crack whore in the plastic miniskirt and thigh boots. He looked down benignly and thanked her. This was the first time I'd seen his face. It couldn't be, could it? I whispered his name to Guy, who squinted before silently mouthing, 'Oh, my God, yes, it's him!' He was a world-famous golfer whose secret will remain exactly that.

Guy told me he now needed to pee and asked for directions. I went through the bar girl's sign language routine, and he left.

Ten minutes later he hadn't returned, so, emboldened by two cans of Sapporo and a miniature bottle of JD in my trouser pocket that I'd taken from the hotel minibar, I set off in search of him. I needed another pee in any case. I couldn't face the guilt of depriving the baby again, so I found another toilet and walked in to find a girl kneeling in the same kind of bowl.

She had ample breasts with pierced nipples, short-cropped hair with big brown eyes heavily surrounded with kohl and wore a rubber minidress decorated with a spider web pattern. This was an all-together different prospect. Our eyes met. She held an A4 laminated sign that read:

*For $5 you can pis on me*

This threw me. The pee power dynamic had shifted. Giving a golden shower to someone who wanted one was one thing, but paying for it was a whole different ball game. It suggested that rather than possessing a penchant for piss, money was her motivation. Maybe she hated golden showers, but needed the cash to help her get through college or buy food for her infant. Once again my head span, confused which was the morally correct course of action.

She could probably hear my mind whirring as I stood there staring at her.

'Well, whaddya say?'

I had to say something, but the four words which came out were, in retrospect, embarrassing.

'The baby doesn't charge.'

'He's gotta lotta growing up to do,' she sneered. 'Now, you

wanna pee on me or what? 'Cos if you ain't, make way for someone who will.'

I was unaware that there was someone else standing behind me. It was the golfer. As I shuffled off to the urinal, I paused, turned around and, pointing at her sign, said, 'You're missing an S. Should be P-I-S-S,' smiled and put my thumb up as if to say, 'don't mention it, you're welcome.'

The sportsman whipped out a $5 note followed by his '9 iron' and proceeded to play 'the yellow water hazard' with the control and aim you'd expect an open-standard sportsman to possess. I'm not going to lie, I couldn't resist watching. The arc of urine sprayed over her neck and breasts, causing them to gleam beneath the unforgiving fluorescent lights. She caught me looking and threw her head back, adeptly positioning herself so the golden jet disappeared into her open mouth, occasionally swallowing. The golfer was clearly relishing his hole in one – as was the girl. She may have been missing an S, but she was careful not to miss the pee, I thought, as I left the room.

Back in the bar I sat opposite Guy, ruminating that there are times and places to point out spelling errors, and that a sex club is probably not one of them.

We were both absent-mindedly gazing in silence at the TV in the corner at a trio of surprisingly agile rubber nuns. There was no eye contact. Was I a loser for not paying her $5? I wanted a second opinion, but my head was still spinning, so I sat silently watching the rubber nuns – which although an arresting image, didn't dislodge the one I'd seen upstairs. What's the saying? Once you've seen something you can't unsee it?

We walked down the corridor past a pinball machine which

was being played by a slim blonde in a black pillbox hat. Her light hair was tied back, her face semi-hidden by the black lace veil. In between plays, she sucked seductively on a cigarette holder. Her pert breasts were naked and jiggled as she pushed the flippers at the end of long shiny black rubber gloves. She was sexy as hell. Mainly because she completely ignored everyone else in there. I must've passed her half a dozen times during the next few hours. She intrigued me as she was in a world of her own, totally relaxed and at home in the environment. Although topless, she held more mystery and allure than everyone else in there put together. I thought about talking to her, but she never took a break from the pinball machine and exuded an air of untouchability.

I found myself in the couples' lair, which was formerly known as the BANG MY WIFE room but had rebranded after the 'no fucking' rule came in post-AIDS. Reassuringly, there was still lots of fun to be had. A Captain Mainwaring type was being whipped by a dominatrix on a sofa, while a guy with a beard masturbated as his Readers Wife-type partner, a forty-something peroxide blonde peeled a pineapple, carefully gouging out the centre. When she'd finished, a brief nonverbal exchange occurred which informed the moment had arrived for him to ejaculate into the pineapple, which she then drank from before offering it around, asking, 'Pina Colada, anyone?'

'Are there show's every night?' I asked the bar girl later, referencing the Pineapple Two.

'Oh, Frank and Fran, they're just guests, they come every Thursday.' She did however confirm there was a dizzying calendar of perversions laid on for regulars, which included slave auctions ('always a roadblock'), toe sucking summits, the Hot Wax Olympics, Fist Fucking Society meetings, uniform nights (emergency services half price) and the club's own 'Leather Claus' handing out gifts at Christmas.

Another room contained a large wooden X and what looked like a two-seater electric chair paired with a gynaecologist's contraption with stirrups. This was occupied by a shirtless, spiky peroxide-haired male wearing leather trousers. He appeared to be waiting for someone. As I entered, he looked up expectantly, before looking away and cursing under his breath. First the baby, now the Billy Idol wannabe; I was causing disappointment wherever I went – except The 'Ladies Who Love Ladies' room, which I hovered outside like an errant schoolboy waiting to enter the Headmaster's Office to receive a caning.

Guy appeared. 'Let's check out The Dungeon and then leave.'

I agreed. It was 3.30 a.m., had been a long day and I wasn't interested in The Cell Block (whose noisy occupants had scared me off venturing into), and was wary of the basement, which was known for being the grittiest. This was where Al Pacino researched the gay S&M scene for the film *Cruisin'* some years earlier.

The lightbulbs, like most in there, were bare and glowed red, the black ceiling soaking up what little light they gave. Shadowy figures huddled in corners emitting groans. More TVs hung on the walls playing endless porn which showed ever-erect flesh in action. Even the stale air was well-hung; a cocktail of sweat, poppers and spunk. It stuck in my throat – the air, I mean. It was hard to identify security. Everyone except me and Guy looked like bodybuilders. In retrospect, they were probably the ones with trousers on – but in The Vault even that wasn't a given. The room was dominated by a large cage into which stepped a muscular man wearing only boots. A naked figure on all fours was led on a leash across the floor, which, on having to make way for him, I became aware was sticky. This isn't unusual for carpeted venues. It was at that moment I'd had enough. It was only when I reached the door did I notice there was no carpet – it was concrete.

As we emerged it was getting light outside. The pale sky of a June morning and calm, clean, dawn air brought me back to reality. Refrigeration trucks rumbled. Men in white coats unloaded carcasses on metallic frames, clattering and shouting to one another.

I turned around for one last look at The Vault and saw a spotlit mannequin dressed in black leather and a gimp mask, hanging outside of the building above a cloth sign which read AFTERNOON DELIGHT. What a place!

The following week, back home over a pint at the Drum & Monkey pub just off Abbey Road, I was telling my mate Dave about my night at The Vault. He persuaded himself the guy in the gyno chair wasn't a lookalike but Billy Idol himself, who lived a five-minute walk away at the time and was in the midst of his drug-fuelled debauchery. The identity of the girl playing pinball in the pillbox hat may have been revealed a few years later when Madonna released her 'Sex' book, some of which was shot in The Vault, as was the video for her song, 'Erotica'. There's a photo of Lucifer in there also, with whom she appears to be enjoying a good tongue wagging...

A few days before, as we sat at JFK waiting to take off, there was a technical problem which took an hour to resolve. This was my chance to ask Guy.

'Did you see the baby?'

'The baby?' Guy continued to stare straight ahead before

realising. 'Oh Christ, yes. You could've warned me.' He shook his head, half laughing.

'Yes, sorry about that. Did you…?'

'Did I what?' He glanced at me before looking away again.

'Did you… do what he asked?'

There was a long pause. He finished his drink and put his Walkman headphones on. 'That's between me and the baby.'

We never spoke about it again.

## Aftersun

The Vault was co-owned by Anthony Rotundo (considered to be 'the real Tony Soprano') and it witnessed many secretive celebrity visits after Madonna's profile-raising promotion. In 1996, the club had to close to make way for a road-widening programme. A top lawyer was hired who noted that as the building was rented, no compensation could be claimed other than for permanent fixtures. So, work hastily commenced installing numerous sinks and toilets salvaged from municipal dumps, and everything in there was welded or bolted to the floor. The City of New York paid out an astonishing $1.8 million dollars of taxpayers' money for replacement equipment which included '*[One] custom-made torture chair, double-sided with seven leather restrainers each side and with cross bars, spectator platform facing hitching post, a hanging rack, a leather sling, and a gynaecologist's examination chair, steel frame.*'

Quentin Crisp inspired Sting's 1992 hit 'Englishman in New York'. Struggling actor Marv (Mark) went on to star in over twenty blockbusters under the stage name Vin Diesel. His love of dance music remains, he collaborated on a track with Steve Aoki and appeared onstage with Dimitry Vegas at Tomorrowland in 2024.

I never did get to ride Concorde, a technical issue meant we flew back in a 747. Twelve years later one exploded in Paris and the aircraft was phased out, so I'll never get the chance again.

> Top Tune: Englishman in New York – Sting (Ben Liebrand DMC Remix) {A&M}

## BEHIND THE BROCHURE

Odd things happen in hotel rooms. During a student ski holiday in Mayrhofen, Austria, the temperature in the resort was a bone-numbing minus 15 degrees Celsius, so we took the decision to check the students' heating and water was working by visiting each accommodation block by car. One room was particularly reluctant to grant me access. It belonged to some medical students from a university in the North West who'd turned their apartment into a rehydration suite, setting up an intravenous fluid drip with which they tackled their hangovers… which probably explains why they were the only students never late for morning ski lessons!

# 6

# FROM PIRATE RADIO TO THE SHIPPING FORECAST

*'Fail we may, sail we must.'*
— Andrew Weatherall

At a corporate race day at Chelmsford which was sponsored by Essex FM, with whom I was running ski holidays for their listeners (more on this later), I was introduced to the guy who was responsible for marketing at DFDS Seaways, and who it fell to fill cabins on the companies' glamorous-sounding forty-eight-hour 'mini cruise breaks' on the (very unglamorous) Harwich–Hamburg freight route. No one had ever pulled off an international clubbing trip as there were obvious logistical, safety and security implications of putting a rave on the waves, not least the presence of HM Customs and Excise officers with their rubber gloves, dogs and moral opposition to all untaxed drugs.

But with my proactive ally's support, if I could find an older, dressy crowd whose bar spend was considerable, and whose music was accessible to the general public with whom they would be sharing the boat, I figured I may just be able to pull it off.

In the late nineties, Future Perfect at Hanover Grand in London attracted a glam and gorgeous crowd which in turn attracted the likes of Leonardo Di Caprio, Val Kilmer and the supermodel set. I knew the promoter, Toni Tambourine, from the early '90s rave days (where he'd invariably be banging a tambourine on a dance podium, hence his name). On hearing the concept, he presented it to Hanover Grandee Twysden Moore, who loved it. In early November 1999, the world's first ever international club event 'The Perfect Cruise' set sail with a line-up which included K-Klass, Rhythm Masters and David Dunne from Atlantic 252 radio, along with Future Perfect resident Craig Jensen. 7 Magazine, who I wrote for at the time, hosted a second area which was headlined by the Balearic beatniks A Man Called Adam. Clare Fray and Tara McDonald hosted, podium danced and vomited, executing all three with naughty nautical glamour.

Although everyone loved the concept, and the pre-event press was very positive, ticket sales were negative, and I was looking at a considerable loss. A few days before the event I received a call from Andy Cato who had seen a feature in the press and asked if Groove Armada could play. 'It's a perfect fit! With our name, we should be playing this event,' he urged. He was right, of course, but much as I loved their sublime track, 'By the River', I explained that I had no budget left, and reluctantly told him I couldn't accommodate them this time. Andy was still really keen for Groove Armada to play, and offered to do it just for travel and accommodation expenses which was amazing as they were huge at the time. But this would've been another £500, and as the event was less than a week away, it was too late to announce them and bring in any more punters (there was no internet or social media back then, remember). I was looking at an £8,000 loss, and when you're already losing a lot of money it's hard to throw more away, so I politely declined his kind offer. But it showed me that this concept caught people's imaginations and had legs (as it turned out, it was sea legs we needed).

I was nervous in any case, as my maritime experiences up to that point suggested I didn't belong on the briny.

## Veering slowly, losing identity...

It was early November, and anyone reading this who's spent any time detained at the pleasure of the North Sea will already be grinning.

This is the time of the year when the ocean toils like a boiling, angry cauldron of green angst. Huge swells lift any vessel unfortunate to be at its mercy ten metres or more, before letting them drop, just to watch them fall and crash like malicious kids running riot in a ceramic shop, gleefully dropping Wedgewood plates onto a concrete floor, unconcerned by their fate. I'd heard the stories, but figured it couldn't have been as bad as they told me... could it?

In the days leading up to The Perfect Cruise I found myself tuning in to The Shipping Forecast on Radio 4. This timeless tribute to our island status is a throwback to a slower, more sedate era. A time when Britain ruled the waves. The dreamy orchestral 'Sailing By' introduction, the timeless and authoritative narration reinforced by the orderly clockwise procession of the quirkily named maritime areas comforts even those not at sea, reinforcing tradition and spreading calm in the midst of the various tempests which rage all around our sceptred isle. Or in this case, off the southern coast of Iceland.

By the time I'd finished working on these events, I was a regular listener to the forecast and able to distinguish my Dogger from my Rockall and my Viking from my German Bight.

The morning of the event I set my alarm for 5.15 a.m. in order to catch the 5.20 a.m. bulletin. What I heard made my blood run cold:

*'German Bight, Humber, Thames: South Westerly, gale 8 to storm 10, severe gale 9 to violent storm 10, squally showers, then rain. (Visibility) moderate becoming poor.'*

This wasn't a weather forecast; it was the end of the world. I tossed and turned in my bed, practising for the voyage ahead and waited for the clock to tick to 8.30, when I knew someone would be in the office at Harwich.

'Have you heard the forecast? Is the ship still sailing?'

A DFDS employee tried to allay my fears. 'The Danish Met office are saying it's not as bad as the UK Met Office believe. We're a Danish company, remember. We'll make a decision at midday, so prepare to sail, but be aware there could be an order to batten down the hatches.'

'Batten down the hatches? What the hell does that mean?'

'It will mean no one will be allowed outside on the deck and everything *must* be secured.'

Footnote: This term originated in the navy, where it signified preparing for a storm by fastening down canvas over doorways and hatches (openings) with strips of wood called battens.

This hardly filled me with confidence. I had two trucks full of sound and lighting kit en route to Harwich from Cornwall, and the production plan involved building a couple of three-storey-high PA stacks and erecting a couple of lighting trusses over the decks (these were the days of vinyl, remember).

I met my assistant Kei for breakfast in a greasy spoon cafe on Holloway Road, and ordered the 'belly buster' as a condemned man facing the execution chamber would doubtlessly do. 'Dead man eating!' he quipped, but I wasn't laughing.

This was my company's first event and I had lots of press onboard. If it was cancelled at the last minute or the DJs couldn't play because of the storm, I doubt I'd recover from the reputational damage. In other words, I'd be sunk.

Looking back, in terms of operationally challenging venues in which to put on a rave, there can't be many more difficult than a North Sea ferry in a Force 9 storm. At midday I received a call that the sailing would proceed, but would arrive in Hamburg an hour later than scheduled due to expected sea conditions.

The crossing took eighteen hours, departing three hours late after the boat train from Liverpool Street carrying all my guests and most of the DJs took twice as long as usual to make the hour and a half journey due to 'the wrong kind of leaves on the line'.

This baffled me. Apart from tea leaves and tree leaves, what kind of other leaves are there?

As the tide was rising, the boat couldn't wait indefinitely, and almost left without everyone due to the surprise leaves. So, just to set sail felt like a major achievement in itself.

Leaving Harwich, the route veered north and followed the Belgian and Dutch coasts, before hanging a sharp right into the mouth of the calm waters of the River Elbe, prior to finally arriving in Hamburg, once dubbed as the 'naughtiest city in the world' by George Harrison.

When I boarded, Kevin Allen from the suitably named Fearless Audio was lashing the PA stacks to a central pillar in the Columbus Lounge under the doubting faces of the Danish crew, who clearly thought the whole idea was insane but had no other option than to facilitate this idiocy. Which had been sanctioned by the UK marketing and sales arm as a new group market.

As Event Director I was asked to address my guests across the ship's Tannoy system behind the reception desk. Whether it was the nerves or it just happened automatically whenever I got a mic in my hands, I lapsed into MC speak.

'*Yo! Listen up, crew. This is a shout out to all da Perfect Cruisers! You know who you are. How you feelin'? I can't hear you, I said, HOWWW YOUUU FEELIN'?*'

The middle-age Danish ladies on reception froze. The Ship's Purser, whose office was located behind, looked up from his papers, mouth open. I paused and reconsidered my delivery.

'Erm, anyone here for The Perfect Cruise, please assemble in the Columbus Lounge in fifteen minutes to receive your wristbands and a complimentary welcome drink, thank you.'

The Purser nodded in agreement, clearly relieved the ship hadn't been hijacked by a pirate radio DJ from Hackney.

One of the Danish ladies on reception drew my attention to the weather forecast which had been pinned to the reception desk.

'I hope you don't suffer from seasickness,' she said, 'it will be a rough couple of crossings.'

Amidst all the planning, preparations and promotion, I'd been so wrapped up in the concept that I'd failed to consider one important factor – something you would think would be a primary consideration when deciding to work on the ocean. I'd completely forgotten I suffered from acute motion sickness.

From being a small boy being driven around the Lake District on a Sunday afternoons by my parents, to decorating Vivien Butterfield's dress on the waltzers and spraying sick over the queue below from *The Wild Mouse* roller coaster in Morecambe funfair, to multi-vomits on the Holyhead to Dún Laoghaire ferry; at the slightest sign of movement, my face would turn green and my fellow travellers would run for cover.

Just when I thought my life couldn't get any worse, it just did – and what's that she said about BOTH crossings? I'd also failed to register that the sea could be rough ON THE WAY BACK ALSO. Myself, the dance press and my poor naive guests had signed up for forty hours of torturous turmoil with nowhere to escape or respite other than a few hours in an Irish pub on Europe's largest red-light district, the Reeperbahn.

In that split second, I told myself that I wasn't going to allow myself to be seasick. I needed to hold the event together. These people were there because of me, and I had a responsibility to them. This was my bright idea, and I couldn't be seen to be suffering. The kind lady behind reception gave me a pill[3]. 'This will help, along with iced water with lime,' she said, winking at me. 'Keep your eyes on the horizon, don't fight the motion, but go with it, and you'll be fine.'

I did as she said, and ever since that day I haven't suffered seasickness since – allowing me to manage over a hundred parties on boats on the North Sea and around Ibiza without

---

3. I later discovered the pill was a placebo as they aren't allowed to offer anything to passengers which may cause an abnormal reaction, or extreme allergic reaction. It did cause drowsiness however – not ideal for a clubbing cruise!

any problems. For the record, this is my only 'mind over matter' victory, despite adopting a similar approach to my other phobias (dentists, heights and snakes), they remain lurking in my mind's recesses but at least I no longer toil on the sea.

Sure enough, as we headed eastwards towards the Belgian coast the swell continued to grow and the North Easterly wind hit the ship sideways on, causing her to roll, which resulted in everyone on the dancefloor moving *en masse* a few steps to the right and then to the left as the ship tilted back and forth. After a few hours we headed northeast, directly facing into the prevailing – and strengthening – wind. As it was effectively a head wind, it allowed people to dance like they've never danced before. Riding the waves of weightlessness which, for a few seconds, gently lifted them off the floor, creating an illusion of a levitating group of ravers. Essentially creating a room which rose and fell like those moving floors in fun houses at the fairground. Everyone moved backwards for five seconds, before shuffling to a halt, experiencing the 'lift', before the entire dancefloor shuffled forward in one choreographed movement like a murmuration. Hilarious to watch, but a nightmare in which to play vinyl. We had to repeatedly bring in more quilts to bed the decks on, and add an ever-growing number of two-pence pieces to the stylus with Blu Tack to weigh it down as the ship violently rose and fell.

Standing at the bar was even harder, if you didn't hold on, you'd find yourself staggering back five paces, levitating for a few seconds before being thrown towards the bar again. People became adept at holding onto their drinks throughout this 'dance', accommodating for the ascending and descending with an outstretched arm like alcoholic automon.

If you lost your balance, there was little chance of getting up again. In mid-storm at midnight, I found Toni Tambourine engaged in a swimming race across the carpet to the bar with his mate Brian who he introduced to me.

'This is Brian, he's a singer in a band.'

I shook his hand, and my discomfort must've been evident.

'Except for the weather, is everything going okay?' he asked.

I mumbled something back about this being the most nerve-wracking show I'd ever done and that no one could understand what I was going through. He said he sympathised as he'd recently gone through a similar ordeal.

'Really, was it on a cruise ship?' I asked

'No, Madison Square Garden, duetting with Bowie.'

It was Brian Molko from Placebo. Sheepishly, I swayed off.

We arrived in Hamburg looking and feeling like we'd been in a spin dryer for nineteen hours, with people utilising the short four-hour 'shore leave' to walk the length of the Reeperbahn, which I'd been bigging up as a destination worthy of booking the trip for.

When the shuttle buses deposited us, the only red lights were on the traffic lights. The strip clubs, peep shows, restaurants, cafes and even the bars were shut. The signs said they opened at five. It was one.

The only thing visibly open along the whole street was a grubby KFC. Eventually someone found a sex shop which was open; an establishment called PRIVAT VIDEO KABINS.

We walked in and David Dunne who was covering the trip for Atlantic 252 and 7 Magazine struck up a conversation with the owner, a seedy leather-jacketed gangster type who was smoking what looked like a thin cigar.

David's interest was piqued by a contraption on a wall of one cubicle below the TV monitor. Moulded hands complete with nail varnish on foam arms framed a pair of fake rubber breasts.

'Excuse me, what is this?'

The unshaven gangster took a drag of his cigar and paused like he was recalling an English phrase. He exhaled and spoke at the same time, the acrid smoke forming a succession of word clouds.

'Tittenwichs.'

'Tittenwichs?' David repeated.

The proprietor of all things porn grabbed the breasts and thrust his hips against them, then looked around as he cupped the latex mammaries in his coarse, smoke-stained fingers.

'Tittenwichs, ja?'

'Ahh, it's a tit wank machine!' David couldn't contain his mirth.

Even The Star Club, where The Beatles learned how to be a live band whilst speeding their tits off was underwhelming, having been turned into a bland '70s shopping mall. Some guests had suffered enough and abandoned ship by taking a cab to the airport and jumping on the first flight back to blighty. Like a post-nuclear war landscape, those who remained were jealous of those who were no longer there.

I was relieved that the return leg wasn't quite so bad. The storm was relenting, and most people took the opportunity to sleep for the four hours we slid serenely through wind farms, poppy fields and chemical production plants of the river Elbe. Except Simon Morrison who was covering the trip for DJ Magazine, and who was already ensconced in the bar celebrating the completion of the first part of his Teutonic Food and Place Trilogy – having eaten a hamburger in Hamburg. He spotted me walking by and raised his glass.

'Just a frankfurter in Frankfurt and Wiener schnitzel in Vienna to go! Anchors away!'

Simon's write up, like all of the press we received, was super positive. All in all, financial aspect aside, this was a concept which had real potential. But I needed to get some better dates and avoid the North Atlantic winter storms. I'd demonstrated to the ferry company that I was responsible and could handle the delicate on-board politics, broke their bartake with the hundred and twenty people who attended and the resulting favourable press proved that it was a concept which would appeal to clubbers seeking something new.

> **Top Tune: Placebo – Without You I'm Nothing**
> **(Brothers In Rhythm Club Mix) {Virgin}**

## BEHIND THE BROCHURE

'Souvenir hunting' is a scourge. I've lost count of the times hoteliers call me complaining that one of their room number signs is missing.

'Is it room 303?' I ask, knowing the answer.

'Yes! How did you know?'

I'll then explain to the poor hotelier the significance to dance music devotees of the sacred number, explaining the importance of the Roland TB-303 bass synthesizer in the genre.

Students are particularly fond of souvenir hunting. When I took student groups to alpine mountain huts I'd usually receive an inventory of missing items the next morning: antlers mounted on a shield, dried edelweiss in a vase, numerous cowbells and a stuffed marmot, all of which we'd recover as their holdalls were searched before we let them board the buses back to Blighty.

The most memorable pilfering took place on a trance cruise to Amsterdam in 2015. As we were pulling into Newcastle on Sunday morning an announcement was made over the Tannoy:

'Can the passengers who've removed a wheelchair from the corridor on Deck 6 please return it immediately, as the lady who owns it would like to leave the boat. Thank you.'

# 7

## RUNNING WITH THE ~~BULLS~~ *Pills*

While Future Perfect were great to work with, they indicated they weren't interested in repeating the event. I needed to find the right promoter to grow this concept with. I tried another one of my clients, Kiss FM, for whom I put together a Valentine Cruise featuring breakfast show stars Streetboy and Dave, Matt 'Jam' Lamont, Andy Morris and Jay C & Squirrel, who were big at the time. The gender imbalance was a worry; seventy-five per cent blokes with most of the girls spoken for. So, it turned into a lad's weekend. A roofer from Romford lost £1,700 in the casino before we'd even left the port. I remember thinking the wall-mounted breasts in the PRIVAT VIDEO KABINS were in for a busy few hours.

The return crossing once again took place in a storm and turned a speed garage night into a line dancing hoedown, sending girls wobbling along blue-carpeted corridors to their cabins to swap their glitzy heels for trainers.

I asked everyone to fill in reaction sheets. One girl nailed it; 'The concept's great, but all the men are mingin'.'

However, the Kiss cruise reinforced my reputation with the ferry company as a professional and responsible safe pair of hands. This is always important to corporate entities, who have their shareholders and brand reputation to worry about.

I still had exclusivity on this, but word was getting out. My man in marketing was being called up by some big London promoters who'd heard about the first few cruises. I knew they wouldn't want to work with Radical Escapes, and that they'd definitely rub the Danish crew up the wrong way with their attitude and fuck it up for everyone. I couldn't let that happen. I'd worked hard for very little return.

Having survived dates in November and February, I appealed to the ferry company for one in the summer. My persistence paid off when they said I could have an initial 500 beds in late June at £23 each, but on the condition I would commit to them upfront. This meant if I didn't fill them I'd still have to pay in full for them. This was a big risk – £50,000, but if I could find a crowd who were easy-going, looking for adventure, wanted to travel and who were fiercely loyal to their promoters, I knew I was on to a winner. The concept was unique and by the late nineties, London was the clubbing capital of the world, people went out seven nights a week and dance music ruled the charts. I just had to plug into the right crew.

Through my freelance writing I knew all the major promoters personally, and started attending their nights to suss out how their crowds behaved, how they dressed and what they spent over the bar: all of which would tell me whether they'd be suitable.

David and Allen, promoters of the legendary Torture Garden had heard about the cruises and were keen to explore floating their fetishes. A prospect which shivered me timbers, somewhat, conjuring up visions of cat o' nine tail floggings in the Columbus Lounge, keel-hauling sessions beneath the

Casino and rubber sailor girls prowling the decks. As for what would take place in the onboard sauna, the mind boggled.

I reluctantly shared my doubts. 'I don't think it will go down very well with the fifty-odd lorry drivers who share the boat, not to mention the general public. I remember that last time there was a group of Belgian nuns onboard.'

'Oh, you'd be surprised what those lorry drivers get up to in lay-bys and service station car parks,' replied David.

'Not to mention the nuns...' added Allen, with an eyebrow raised.

'Or the general public for that matter,' David concluded. 'We get all types at our parties, from forklift truck drivers and supermarket check-out girls to managing directors, celebrities and £150-an-hour lawyers.'

They were right, of course, but a TG crowd did what they did feeling they were surrounded by like-minded people who had a stake in maintaining secrecy. A cross-channel ferry was public, not pubic, transport. So, we shook hands and parted, both parties realising that it wasn't to be.

My search continued apace. On Monday morning, the ferry company gave me a week's deadline to send them the signed contract or they'd unblock the beds, and the golden opportunity of a June/July cruise would be lost, along with my exclusivity deal.

Weekly weekend clubs like Freedom at Bagley's, who I handled press for, weren't interested because it didn't make sense losing their crowd. Other promoters were keen, but honest enough to tell me that their crowd didn't drink anything other than tap water, or that their crew didn't own passports as they were so young and had never been overseas. Another major London promoter initially told me he was interested but told me his aspirational, posey crowd would only book 'VIP' Commodore Cabins, and not be seen dead slumming it in the standard ones. As we only had twelve commodores, this wasn't feasible.

There was always an obstacle. I needed a crew who weren't overtly sexual, spent well but weren't too obsessed with status, who were experienced enough to handle an afternoon in Hamburg after an all-night party and not lose their passports or sanity.

Every day that week the ferry company called me asking me to return the signed contract and pay the first twenty-five per cent deposit on the cabins. This amounted to £12,500, which I planned to borrow from my bank as a short-term loan. The bank agreed, but despite being a Limited Company (meaning I had limited liabilities), they demanded my house as a guarantee. This meant if it all went tits up, I would lose my house. I never told my wife Catherine this – just like you, she's hearing about it for the first time!

I was on the verge of giving up. The then-free weekly magazine for Aussies living in London, TNT Magazine dropped on my mat. It was sent every week as I wrote their clubbing section and, amidst the Aussie Rules results, an interview with the bald bloke from Midnight Oil and endless job adverts, I had a eureka moment.

'OF COURSE... AUSSIES!' I shouted out, startling Catherine as we sat at the kitchen table. She looked at me, quizzically.

'The crowd I'm looking for is right beneath my nose! My Aussie, Kiwi and South African readers trust me, just love travelling and their club scene isn't dependent on costly big-name DJs.'

Distributed free at tube stations, TNT had a print run of 60,000, though in reality was read by over 100,000–150,000 pairs of eyes due to it being left on the tube and picked up and passed around the (over)crowded accommodation in which antipodeans lived.

In the noughties, West London's Shepherds Bush and its neighbouring boroughs Acton, Hammersmith, Fulham and Putney were Aussie enclaves; 30,000 of them on a rite-of-passage working holiday, using London as a base to hop around Europe while grafting and partying.

The Aussie in London demographic changed radically in the '90s. Prior to the rave explosion early in the decade, antipodeans arriving in the UK were content spending their time downing pints of Fosters in The Walkabout or getting muntered on snakebite to strippers while moshing to Jimmy Barnes in Sunday swill-fest 'The Church'. The highlight of their trip was the bucket list tour of Europe; a few months in a smelly van stopping off at Pamplona, Gallipoli, La Tomatina and Oktoberfest.

The post-rave arrivals were aware London was the epicentre of the clubbing explosion and were eager, young enough and demographically organised to not only experience but create their own scene. Sure, they still wanted to run with the bulls in 'Pamps' and throw tomatoes in Spain, but they were also open to exploring new frontiers and witnessing the new hedonism emerging from the planet's clubbing capital.

I realised that these Aussies, Kiwis and South Africans were as interested in running with the pills as they were running with the bulls – all they needed was a boat big enough to accommodate them.

Upon arriving in London, they were often bewildered as

to where to begin their clubbing education. The choice was vast. By the mid '90s, the clubbing explosion was into its seventh year, and had split into a dizzying array of sub genres; funky house, glam house, hard house, handbag house, hard bag house, garage, speed garage, techno, trance, tech-trance, drum and bass and big beat. And that was just on a Tuesday.

Dress codes were also creeping in, as small boutique venues and promoters vied for the coolest crowd. After a few years of baggy tops 'n' trousers, glow sticks and bum bags, glam was very much in. It was all a world away from the come-as-you-are ethos of the early years of rave culture, attractive for those who had already experienced the first visceral throbs, but not for the wave of Aussies and Kiwi virgin clubbers who sought an easily accessible soundtrack which they could enjoy in the few clothes they'd arrived with in their rucksacks.

So, as they weren't catered for, they did what immigrants have done since the beginning of time: they created their own scene.

Realising that after attending The Church and other Sunday daytime clubs, no one wanted to go home. Eammon Kilgraff and Wayne Hart hired a dingy basement of a West End pub and threw an unofficial after-party which was still cracking on at nine the next morning. The same 150 turned up each week generating a family atmosphere. There was no dress code, attitude or well-known superstar DJs. AND IT WAS FREE.

The refurbishment of the pub meant they had to find another venue (a former London Underground branch tunnel behind the Astoria called 'The Tube') which involved paying a hire fee. So, they had to start charging for admission and were concerned no one would pay to attend what was a previously free party. But they had the three elements every promoter needs to grow: trust, loyalty and their own sound.

I'd been a part of the rave scene throughout the '90s and witnessed some hedonism, which cooled as the first generation of ravers got older and more sensible. These Southern scenesters may have joined the party late, but boy, were they making up for it.

They even turned going home into an extension of the party. There was no shortage of Aussie-rented, large semi-detached houses with gardens which were happy to host a party. One house party specialist like Macey Munro was all it took to turn a quiet suburban Sunday afternoon in Acton into a full-on, neighbour-annoying, bass-pumping, arms-in-the-air, hard house-heaving rave.

A decade after the tabloids had introduced the world to acid house, club culture was big business with DJs asking for five-figure sums. Club nights were now considered brands with registered logos; corporate entities who exploited multiple revenue streams which included their own record label, mix CD series, a merchandise range and overseas residencies in Ibiza.

The down-underground scene by comparison was a decade behind, and still possessed an honourable not-for-profit passion to party driven by a DIY punk spirit of making your own music and not playing by the rules.

In 1997, Time Out asked me to write a feature about the scene after I told my editor Dave Swindells that the busiest nights in the capital featured DJs he'd never heard of. The feature alerted even bigger venues and British clubbers who weren't interested in glam house and garage nights. It was official: the Aussies and Kiwis were leading the charge (and they were certainly charged...).

This was a self-contained scene. A tight-knit clubbing community which stuck like glue with DJs who emerged from the scene itself, and promoters who loved to party. I knew all the main players and, more importantly, I got on with them all – and as I had a direct line of communication through my column, I felt it was the ideal scene with which to throw the biggest international club cruise to ever set sail from ol' Blighty.

Both Fevah and Fantic were up for it, but there was a fierce rivalry between them, and so I brought in a third promoter, a gently spoken Irishman called Derek from Omnipotence, who weren't as big as Fevah or Frantic, but he was well-liked and respected in the scene, and musically spot-on. I felt his involvement would reduce potential friction between Fevah and Frantic and give the event a bigger look: three promoters representing one scene, united on one huge boat, or 'an awesome antipodean armada' as I described it in my column.

I brought in John Delborello as a partner, he worked for TNT and sorted a sweet deal on advertising, and with the most dynamic promoters in London fully firing, and a nice preview I wrote in TNT Magazine, we'd sold out by 6 p.m. on launch day; 500 cabin beds filled! The ferry company had never seen anything like it.

The next part was winning over the ship's crew, whose officers were Danish with Thai service staff. Numerous ship visits took place to establish what we could and couldn't do. It soon became obvious that the production had to be beefed up, so we brought in a huge 20kW sound rig from Fearless Audio, who took it on as they liked a challenge and because, as they said, 'There's no work in Cornwall in April.' No lasers were allowed (as other ships may mistake them for morse distress code), and strictly no pyros on the pool deck for the same reason. Dry ice wasn't allowed as it was a vision hazard in the event of an emergency. Despite these restrictions, Kevin still managed to put together the biggest lighting rig yet to be seen on a ship. He really pulled out all the stops, and his three crew, all good Cornish lads, only slept when we reached Hamburg. Strictly speaking, all mini-cruise break passengers had to disembark upon reaching Hamburg, but when the Food and Beverages manager reported the record-breaking night's takings, word came from the bridge that they were allowed to stay in their cabins and sleep all afternoon, so they'd be able to work late the following night.

Safety was our overriding concern. When you're taking 750 hedonistic clubbers on a boat for a forty-eight-hour party, it's important to be prepared for all eventualities. So, in addition to the ship's own well-trained first aiders, we insisted on bringing our own medical team, including a GP. This was a significant extra cost as he was on duty all night.

So, that was the Friday and Saturday nights sorted, but what the hell were we going to do in Hamburg for the five hours on Saturday afternoon? I'd told the promoters it was the German version of Amsterdam: seedy bars, a red-light area...except with a Beatles museum.

However, I managed to persuade the Thomas Reade Irish pub at the top of the Reeperbahn to open early as I was bringing them 750 thirsty customers. They saved the day, preparing a buffet spread, pre-pulled pints of Guinness and even set up some decks in one corner for our DJs... result!

Impact! set sail from Harwich on 2 July bound for Hamburg, the sky was blue and, for once, the sea was thankfully calm.

Due to the nature of the event, we were expecting strict

searches from the customs guys on departure, but there was no more than usual, and the mood was very relaxed and welcoming – on this occasion at least.

As we didn't have the ship exclusively to ourselves, we had to fit in with the ship's existing entertainment programme. For anyone who'd dropped their pills in the queue for customs, this meant they came up whilst watching Billy the Balloon Twister create a dazzling array of animals.

Things got even more surreal when the puppet show took to the stage. Goggle-eyed ravers at the front table were transfixed as a bloke dressed as a pirate joined them and produced a white rabbit hand puppet which proceeded to sing Barbie Girl. He then produced a huge hairy caterpillar from his jumper, which disappeared into thin air.

When the ferry company mascot, a six-foot blue-and-white parrot confusingly named Jack the Pirate waddled in, handing out lollipops, it was too much for one chemically enhanced seafarer, who ran terrified from the Columbus Lounge head in hands towards a lifetime of parrot PTSD.

Then it was time for the ship's cabaret – a couple of leggy female dancers in sequined leotards and someone I recognised as the entertainments officer in a top hat, tails and cane deftly tap dancing his way through 'Putting on the Ritz'.

By now most of my crew were growing restless. They were here for hard house, not lame cabaret, and were primed to party.

As we made up ninety per cent of the audience in the Columbus Lounge I persuaded the entertainments officer to cut short the cabaret before it ended in Jack the Pirate being keel-hauled and balloon man being relieved of his nitrous oxide canisters, which were the focus of increasing interest.

At 6 p.m. we opened the red velvet curtains which had been

concealing the speaker stacks. A huge cheer went up as our first DJ started. There was no warm-up, it was a brutal all-out hard house assault. From zero to sixty in less than a minute. This caught the few members of the public who were still in there unaware, including an eightieth birthday party group from Billericay, and two tables of gingham shirts and cowboy boots heading to Germany for a line-dancing convention.

Both were up for the party, the oldies waving their hands to Spencer Freeland as they sat in their seats enjoying a glass of sherry, while the line dancers practiced their moves to DJ Misjah & DJ Tim's throbbing anthem 'Access'.

Everyone was smiling. No one judged and EVERYONE was welcome. Outside, floating on a calm ocean, oil and gas platforms glinted in the setting sun. The bars were doing a roaring trade, and as darkness fell the coast of Belgium sparkled on the starboard bow like a distant constellation guiding us to a new world.

By 2 a.m. the ship's officers were aware that this was unlike any party they'd ever witnessed. We'd draped all their glitter backdrops, turned off the mirror ball and added some serious rave lighting and strobes. Two huge stacks reached from the floor to the ceiling, tethered to the steel posts which supported the next deck to stop them toppling over in the event of choppy seas. We placed the decks on a sea of duvets which rested on a mattress-like contraption we'd made specially for the occasion, but it was so calm, we needn't have bothered.

The first Impact! was a huge success, and word soon spread around London and the ferry company inevitably had other promoters approach them, but my exclusivity deal meant that they were referred to Radical Escapes, and after putting a lot of work into this I wasn't going to let it be ruined by another crew I didn't know. So, we announced another Impact! in September, and once again had great weather... but the customs at Harwich appeared more interested, and when they found something on a few people the mood changed. I was called to the Chief Purser's office and told that undercover customs officers were onboard, and warned that if there was any evidence of drug taking the customs at Hamburg would be alerted to give us a 'personal welcome'.

*'It's better to be a lion for a day than a sheep all your life.'*
– Mussolini

I kept my log from the night:

*0127: rumours of a passenger wearing our wristband, growling and crawling around the Blue Riband restaurant on all fours, sniffing around a family who were sat eating dinner. Go to Blue Riband and see an uncomfortable-looking family of Germans talking about 'Lurve' but no sign of the growling sniffer.*

*0132: received call on radio from security. Guest on deck six is convinced he's a lion, accompanied security and medical team to cabin from which roaring could be heard. Guest refused to take instruction to calm down, persisted crawling around and making growling and roaring noises. Despite being advised otherwise, insisted he was the 'king of the jungle' and threatened to smash the window and escape.*

*Following numerous attempts to calm him, door was unlocked, he was forcibly restrained by Security A and Security B and given sedative by GP, who sat with him for the next few hours in his cabin.*

*0230: Called GP to check on sedated guest. Received the reply, 'No change in condition, sedation effective, the lion sleeps tonight.'*

The Danish later crew told me that *lowe* (which is pronounced 'lurv-e') is the German word for lion. Over breakfast the next morning, the doctor told me that the patient was suffering from clinical lycanthropy, a rare psychiatric syndrome whereby the sufferer thinks they can transform into or has already transformed into an animal.[4]

'We should count ourselves lucky he didn't think he was a dolphin, or we'd have lost him overboard,' he pondered in between bites of croissant.

Last I heard, he had moved back to New Zealand – hopefully to a Safari Park, rather than a zoo.

### Women and Women First!

Every now and then I'd patrol the outside decks to ensure no one was putting themselves in danger. It was a beautifully starry night, and as I sat on the steel steps taking a breather, watching the oil rigs napalm-like phosphorescence excite the night sky, I heard giggling. Along the deck I could make out two figures kissing beneath a lifeboat. As the sea was calm and the decks weren't out of bounds, I saw no reason to disturb them, and resumed my stargazing.

When I next glanced in their direction, they'd moved. Then I saw movement on the ladder of the lifeboat and watched as the legs of one of them scaled the upper rings and straddled the edge of the lifeboat. 'Hey!' I shouted, but it was too late,

---

4. In 2025 school-age children routinely identify as cats, dogs and koala bears, but back then being a 'furry' was considered highly unusual.

she'd disappeared under the bright orange tarpaulin cover.

When I got to the base of the boat, I realised that in order to climb the ladder, I had to stand precariously on the white metal rail surrounding the deck's edge. Rather than attempt this on my own, in the dark of night, in the middle of the North Sea whilst on a moving ship, I decided to report the incident to the crew and let them handle it. So, I went down the nearest stairs and told the Purser, who radioed for help, and a few minutes later I was leading them back up to the outdoor deck.

'Which lifeboat?' asked the burly Danish security man.

There were three. They all looked the same.

'This one I think,' I said, pointing to the closest.

One man climbed up and onto the ladder. Upon reaching the top, he lifted the orange cover and shone a torch into the empty vessel. 'No one here,' he called back.

This was repeated for the next one, and we moved on to the boat nearest the bow.

'Okay, so they must be in this one.'

'Hello, come out, please,' shouted the Purser.

No answer. So once again the burly fella climbed up onto the rail and to the top of the ladder and shone his torch into the lifeboat, and once again, shook his head and descended.

I was confused and concerned. Did this mean they had fallen overboard? I looked out over the ever-restless North Sea. The dancing lights of the oil rigs had disappeared, and although the ocean was relatively calm, at night time the water looked dark and foreboding.

Then the Purser broke the silence. 'Are you sure it was a starboard lifeboat?'

My lack of a sense of direction is often embarrassing. 'You mean there are more lifeboats on the other side?'

He raised his eyebrows and issued a cursory, 'Of course, there are,' like it was common knowledge.

We crossed the boat and sure enough there were another three large lifeboats hoisted in the same manner.

As the poor bloke searched the first two, the Purser told me that if all three were empty, we'd have to stop the party, do a roll call of passengers and, if the two lovers were still missing, follow procedure for person(s) overboard. This involved turning the ship around and launching the rescue lifeboat.

My concern growing with every passing second, I shouted up at the third lifeboat, 'Guys, if you're in there, come out now, or the party's over.' We waited for a few seconds. Silence. The security guard began his final climb. The mood was sombre. I felt responsible. How could I have let them out of my sight? All the detractors who said that holding a rave on a boat across the North Sea would be proved right. Those smug customs officers would be waiting for me with 'I told you so' expressions. And then there was the media, the port was sure to tip them off and there may be corporate manslaughter charges. But overriding everything was the sickening feeling that two young people had died at my event because of my slackness.

As our eyes followed him ascending the ladder, a hand holding a pair of high-heeled sandals appeared from beneath the orange cover. Then, a little further along, another hand appeared – also clutching a pair of clunky high-heeled shoes, narrowly missing the bloke's head climbing the ladder. He shone his torch at the lip of the lifeboat just as two pretty female faces appeared wearing that partly embarrassed, partly proud expression of someone caught having naughty fun in a lifeboat.

Over the radio, the Purser said something in Danish to the ship's captain, who asked him to repeat it. Silence. Oh, to be a fly on that bridge! The captain eventually acknowledged the message and confirmed he was increasing knots and proceeding on course.

The girls handed their shoes to the big Dane, whose mind was clearly boggling at what had been going on in the lifeboat. After descending safely to deck, the lifeboat-loving lesbian lovers were given a stern telling off, along with a final warning by the Purser.

As I walked back to the party with them, I couldn't resist asking them why they hadn't gone to a cabin like every other horny couple would, they glanced mischievously at each other. 'Ah, that's sooo boring! How often do you get the chance to have sex in a lifeboat?' one replied. 'Besides, we didn't want our boyfriends to find out!'

One thing I didn't mention was that it was a better boat – it possessed an open-air swimming pool on the top deck. This was so popular that we literally had to physically move people on arrival in Hamburg, and an hour after returning to Harwich there were still people splashing around and shuffling wide-eyed to silence, ecstatically unaware that not only had we reached Harwich, but that the music had stopped some time ago. On disembarking all boats it's essential that everyone is accounted for. There tends to be instances of someone, usually a sole traveller not being recorded re-entering passport control. A call is made to the ship, who will check the cabin. They'll typically find a holdall, passport and note on the bed which hasn't been slept in, and they assume they've jumped overboard in the middle of the night. This turns into a missing persons enquiry. Their bodies are rarely found. I'm thankful this never happened on one of my cruises.

## BEHIND THE BROCHURE

On a site visit in Ibiza to inspect the hotels we'd be using I was being shown around the restaurant by an eager-to-please hotelier.

'Have you got Gazpacho?' I asked.

'No... Gazpacho is Andalusian, Ibiza is Catalan. But we have Quiffy in the restaurant this year,' he countered.

'Quiffy?' I repeated.

'Si,' he nodded proudly. 'Free for all hotel guests.'

Ah, the regional equivalent. But was it a soup or a preservative I wondered?

'For breakfast?' I enquired.

'They can enjoy it all day, but only in the restaurant, not in their rooms.'

I nodded my understanding. This was reasonable, I could appreciate him not wanting his guests taking food back to their rooms. I made a mental note to relay this in my welcome booklet, and scoured the laminated menu card to confirm the spelling.

'Is it on the menu?'

Johnny pointed to the wall behind me. 'Here.'

I looked around, and spotted a sign that read FREE Wi-Fi FOR GUESTS, ASK STAFF FOR CODE.

# 8

# TRIPS AHOY!

*'You're gonna need a bigger boat.'*
*– Chief Brody,* Jaws

As I said, 'IMPACT: 2' was even messier.

Word had spread and this time we filled 732 beds. It was the biggest rave on the waves to ever set sail from a UK port.

There would've been another twelve people onboard had UK customs not detained them (mind you, there would've been a lot less if the captain hadn't informed the customs officers that they were taking so long searching our crew as they boarded that he was in danger of missing the tide, meaning the process stopped).

Despite these depletions, the crowd seemed fully rationed, and the action went on all night in three different areas, courtesy of Tony Price, Matt Clarke, Skol, Ian Mac, Phil Reynolds, Owen B, James Lawson, Steve Ryan, Chris Todd and Eamonn Fevah – all of whom were unknown to the London clubbing mainstream, but heroes to the Down Underground scene.

But despite the bars being busy, there was something strange about the way the senior officers acted. As they observed the party I detected they were hiding something. They exhibited a smugness which wasn't previously present. I needed to know what was going on and took a cake to the friendly Danish lady on reception, whose contract was not being renewed after twenty-three years of service at sea. She expressed her hurt at this and felt the company didn't value her. She particularly disliked one officer who she suspected had been instrumental in her having to leave the company.

'He hates your events as he has to stay up all night and doesn't get paid any extra. He'd rather be in bed tugging his tugboat,' she whispered wickedly in between forkfuls of chocolate gateaux.

She looked around before adding, 'He's been telephoning the German customs in Hamburg, he told me they've cancelled all leave tomorrow.'

So that was it. Despite their beds being filled and their bars busy, despite less trouble than they would normally get from Essex boys on a stag weekend, despite them being happy with my staffing and medical provision, they wanted to discredit my event in order just to go to sleep!

I called a meeting for some key people behind the amps where the officers couldn't observe us, and put the word out what was waiting for us in Hamburg. Within an hour everyone knew the score, and as we pulled into the port of Hamburg, we could see our welcome committee on the harbourside. A dozen or more armed customs officers and polizei with half a dozen snarling Alsatian dogs straining on their leashes were waiting.

The sign above the gangplank may have said, *Wilcommen im Hamburg*, but the pissed-off expressions of the police said, 'So you are the reason we had to give up our Saturday morning lie-in.'

We were made to leave six people at a time, so that everyone could be thoroughly searched. But it was our turn to look smug. No one was carrying anything incriminating, and after an hour we were all on the buses bound for the Reeperbahn, leaving behind baffled customs officers wondering why they were called into work on a Saturday morning when they could've been playing with their kids or enjoying sharing a bratwurst with their fraulines.

After a few hours in the Thomas Read drinking Guinness, playing pool and listening to even more hard house courtesy of Fevah DJs, we put the group back onto a fleet of ten buses and boarded without incident. In fact, there were no customs present other than two officers who regarded everyone who boarded with barely concealed looks of disgust.

All except three people were now onboard, and as I stood on the dockside, trying to persuade the authorities to give them another five minutes before pulling up the gangplank, my mobile started ringing. It was from my assistant (who I'll call Danny) who had already boarded. But the signal was poor. These were the early days of cell phones, and I couldn't make out what Danny was saying. Then a text pinged: ALL CABIN'S BUSTED! ASKING FOR U ON PA.

My heart missed a beat. This didn't make sense. If they'd found anything they would have arrested the occupant as they got back onboard, surely?

The officer at the gangplank interrupted my panic. 'We must leave now; the tide is falling.'

I reluctantly accepted and turned to walk up the gangplank.

'Hold the boat! Hold the boat!' echoed unseen voices from deep inside the covered corridor leading from the departures area to the boat. Staccato footsteps grew louder, and two figures came into view hurtling towards us.

I put my hand on the bloke who was closing the gate. 'Wait, they're here!'

Holding their Australian passports, they were waved onto the boat with no checks, searches or names given. The solitary-uniformed harbourside customs shrugged exasperatedly. 'I know their names, I'll add them to the passenger list at reception,' I reassured him.

Upon boarding, I heard my name being announced over the ship's Tannoy, and made my way to the reception area. My Danish friend behind the desk looked embarrassed and wouldn't make eye contact as she told me, 'The Chief Purser wants to see you in his office.' I walked behind the desk and into a small room where there were three large black bin liners. The Purser sat behind his pine desk and without looking up, gestured for me to take a seat.

'The Hamburg police and customs today mounted an exercise and boarded the boat whilst your group were ashore. They searched every cabin and only twelve out of the one hundred and seventy-two of your group occupy didn't contain drugs.

From outside the door I heard raised voices. Through the glass window I could see several of my guests holding torn shirts, ripped holdalls and slashed rucksacks, demanding to know what had happened.

'The confiscated contraband has filled the bags behind you.'

My head was spinning. 'If they caught so many people with illegal substances, why are there no arrests?' I asked.

'There aren't enough cells in the Hamburg city area for your people. The paperwork alone would take a week, and these guys want the rest of their weekend off. Your guests should count themselves lucky.'

I couldn't resist peering into the bag and sure enough, it was filled with small bags of pills, wraps, lumps of hash, a few bottles of poppers and a large pink, glitter bong.

He handed me the list of cabins. I was relieved to find mine was one of the few without a red asterisk next to it. I was sharing with my assistant, Danny, who I knew was a party animal and always sorting things out for people. Although I'd briefed him that when he worked with me he had to be whiter than white, I had no way of knowing if he'd brought a little something along to help him through the night.

I looked at the list. Over 700 people were alleged to have been found in possession of controlled substances, all Australian, Kiwi or South African. If the British press got hold of this, the Australian media were sure to follow. If names were printed, it could affect their future career prospects and their three-year working visa may have been revoked.

I explained this to the Purser, adding that it wouldn't look good that so many people had brought drugs through Harwich, despite the checks.

'The captain has a conference call with head office in fifteen minutes, I'll let you know the situation in an hour,' he replied tersely.

I left the office and placated the people in reception whose belongings had been trashed by the Hamburg polizei, explaining the situation. The damage appeared indiscriminate – like they'd spent a minute turning each cabin over and leaving clothes, make-up, cans and bottles all over the floor.

I went back to find my cabin relatively untouched. Danny was lying on his back on the top bunk and had a screwdriver in his outstretched hand which was inserted into a ceiling panel.

'Good news, they never found the acid!'

I was gobsmacked. Speechless.

'After the tip off, I offered to store a sheet of acid tabs in our cabin, as I figured they'd never suspect the organiser of carrying anything. Y'know, in plain sight, n' all that... in the event, they did, but no dog was ever gonna sniff this baby out!' The ceiling panel opened as the screw was loosened and a sheet of strawberry acid tabs floated down like a feather through the air, landing gently at my feet.

Now I'd seen everything. There was enough acid in my cabin to have me put away for three years. They would've also emptied my bank account thinking the money in there was drug money. For the sake of doing a favour to a punter who'd given him a few lines the night before, this idiot was putting my career and reputation at risk. I was incandescent and tore into him, explaining what could've happened. After thinking about it, he apologised and saw the bigger picture, but it was a shave too close for comfort and I never employed him again.

The more I thought about it, the more I started to question things. Starting with my new next-door neighbour, a clean-shaven guy in his early thirties who always seemed to leave and return to his cabin around the same time as me. I gave Danny express instructions not to engage with him, but to let me know if he was approached. Sure enough, as Danny was outside on deck having a Silk Cut, the guy walked up to him and asked him if he had any dope, 'Or anything else...'

I put the word out there were undercover German police on the boat, and within an hour we'd identified another three, either by the fact they never danced and just stood at the bar together with a drink which they never seemed to sip, or made their excuses and left when the gorgeous Aussie girl we sent to suss them out started asking too many questions. This is always a giveaway as any woman will testify, men just love talking about themselves on a first date. We also sent him a hunky surfer in case the suspected undercover operative preferred men, but he showed no interest whatsoever.

I was out on the deck getting some fresh air when he appeared out of nowhere and asked, 'I'm looking for something for the party... maybe you can help?'

'Something for the party?'

'To keep me awake. Sleeping is cheating!'

It was said so unconvincingly that I knew he was definitely undercover.

I had an idea but needed witnesses. 'Meet me in ten minutes in the Navigator's Bar on deck eight.'

'Is it the real deal?' he asked, handing me three crisp €20 notes.

I winked, 'Too right it is. I use it every time there's an all-night party.'

I went straight to the crew room where we'd loaded four trays of Red Bull, and five minutes later, returned with one of them (which was illegal in Denmark at the time} and a couple of Aussie rugby types.

'What's this?' he demanded.

'Something to keep you awake.' We left him seething, but unable to do anything about it.

At the appointed hour I walked to reception to hear my group's fate. The Chief Purser was brief: 'The drugs will be destroyed and there will be no charges. We've made our point and I think you, your guests *and us* can all have an early night tonight.'

Yeah, right! As the clock reached 5 a.m. the party was still going strong as the Danish crew looked on incredulously. I couldn't resist and as I walked past them, said, 'So much for our early night!' in a resigned, 'Kids, eh? What can you do?' manner. They glared, unable to comprehend how the crowd could continue to party so intensely without any 'fuel'.

What they didn't know was that the two latecomers who very nearly missed the boat back were late because they were doing business. Very lucrative business as it turned out, as the boat was dry when they finally got on! Aware that there was probably a welcome committee waiting at Harwich, they did their very best to shift the stock on the return leg... and by the look of the swimming pool area as the sun came up, they achieved their aim. I was of course unaware of this at the time and wouldn't have sanctioned anyone bringing large amounts of drugs onboard - which I guess is why no one ever told me anything.

No matter how hard we tried, they just wouldn't leave the outdoor pool deck, and an hour after arriving in Harwich were still dancing and lounging around in the hot midday summer sun. Like nodding, hunched Gollums, grown men sheltered from the strengthening sun in the kiddies' playhouses, refusing to come out while the music was still playing – even though it had finished twenty minutes ago. Having been there myself, I sympathised but this was getting embarrassing. Security was being ignored and an exasperated officer bellowed over the radio to me, 'Cut the power, then they won't be able to dance.'

'Well, the power was cut an hour ago, but they are still dancing, sir,' the Polish security bloke replied, scratching his head.

'What are they dancing to?' came the raspy response

'Silence, sir.'

Five minutes later, the customs officers appeared, dogs straining at their leashes, which was the cue for everyone to swiftly scarper from the pool area.

The delay meant that the area couldn't be cleaned or checked by my team. We had to leave immediately as the ship was due to commence boarding imminently and the boat train was due to depart.

On Monday morning I received the dreaded ship's report which read like a Grand Theft Auto charge sheet. In addition to possession, trafficking, bizarre behaviour of some group members in the shop involving large Toblerones and refusal to disembark, the report concluded that as copious amounts of discarded drugs had been found in the pool and children's play area, understandably the ship did not want to host the group again.

Whilst I could see their point of view, I pointed out that it wasn't unusual for passengers on their routes to misbehave; the Newcastle to Ijmuiden (Amsterdam) route is a well-known stag weekend option, hence the presence of no-nonsense security and holding cells (brigs). There were never any fights on my cruises. No damage was done to the ship, no staff were assaulted or threatened, and as far as I'm aware no complaints were made by the general public with whom we shared the ship.

But as we learned in 1989, people taking unlicensed, untaxed drugs rather than those sanctioned by the Government will always be persecuted on what they swallow and inhale rather than how they behave.

Though on noting the organisation and bar spend, the Harwich office was still keen to continue working with me, but asked me to put together a different concept as they were getting grief from the Danes in Head Office, whose interest had been piqued by the sleep-deprived senior crew members whose report may well have included an account of a wild same-sex orgy in a lifeboat involving eight girls and a group of marauding males thinking they were wildebeests, given the reticence to allow me back onboard.

With that kind of imagination, it's no surprise that the Danes had a thriving hardcore pornography industry at the time, after becoming the first country to legalise it in 1969.

Twenty years later, I was rummaging around in my loft looking for images to illustrate this book when I came across a Mini DV cassette. It was taken out on the deck around the outdoor pool at dawn and no words are needed as is evident; that Antipodean crowd really were 'all at sea' (watch it on www.kirkfield.net).

Top Tune: – Kick Ass! (Original Mix) {Zini & Kantini}

## BEHIND THE BROCHURE

Our sexuality is a lion on a leash, to the casual observer appearing controlled and tamed. Going on holiday is the equivalent of a lion slipping its noose. And when a wild animal senses freedom, they revert to type; making the most of their liberty while they can, knowing that the constraints of normality await, and they'll soon be back on their leash.

One way of guaranteeing 'What goes on holiday, stays on holiday' is to go alone; no one knows you, or can tell tales...

At the end of one welcome meeting for a radio station ski

holiday, a petite, pretty blonde girl approached our staff table. I asked her if she wanted to book any additional activities to make her time in the snow memorable. These included an overnight stay in a mountaintop pyramid, schnapps tasting, tobogganing and paragliding.

She hesitated. 'No thanks… but I'm hoping you and your reps can help me do something I've always wanted to do, but never had the chance.'

Suspecting she may be scared of heights and need help to take the cable car up the mountain, or need reassuring about the paraglider's safety record, I confidently replied, 'Well, you've come to the right place. We'll try our best, won't we, boys?'

They nodded. Looking at us all in turn, her tone was both earnest and honest, lest her words be interpreted as a joke and laughed off. Taking a deep breath, she slowly said in all seriousness, 'I've always wanted five men to stand over me masturbating.'

She was being serious. I was lost for words.

'Well… there's only three of us, so we can't really help you, I'm afraid,' I stuttered.

Turning around, she pointed to the two lads standing at the bar looking over at us expectantly. One of them gave me a hopeful thumbs-up.

'I've already got two, I just need three more.'

I genuinely care about my guests and do everything to try to deliver the best holiday for them. But there are limits to what my reps and I can do – who did she think we were, Club 18–30?

# 9
# COMPETITION WINNERS

'Win a free holiday!'

What a great marketing idea to promote a holiday... this is not. The lure of spending a week somewhere warm at no cost appears, at first glance, a generous promotional exercise. But in reality it's a fucking nightmare from start to finish, and in this chapter I'll explain why.

To begin with, if the aim of giving away a free holiday is to encourage sales, it's a flawed exercise from the off. Why on earth would anyone buy a holiday if they're in with a chance of getting one for free?

Every newbie travel set-up falls into this trap. As I did... and lived to regret it. As anyone who knows anything about tourism will tell you, competition winners are more trouble than they're worth. More entitled than Prince Andrew, more demanding than a spoilt child (Prince Andrew) and more time-consuming than binge-watching a box set. In slow motion.

My first experience with a competition winner was in 2004, when my company Radical Escapes was handed the contract to look after the winners of a competition a major mobile communications company ran in the *News of the World* showbiz pages over six weeks to 'Win a Clubbing Holiday in Ibiza!'

The winners would take their holiday at the same time as my Vibe FM in Ibiza package, meaning I was already in resort to look after them and could introduce them to other people – as the six winners were sole travellers.

Whether this was a budget constraint or an oversight I don't know, but it makes sense logistically for holiday competition prizes to be dual rather than singles. The cost of accommodation is not much bigger (as the shortage of single rooms in Ibiza usually means paying for single-person occupancy of a twin room, so it's virtually the same price), and solo travellers require more resort support than a couple.

'Win a Holiday for Two!' packs twice the punch of winning a single holiday, as you can then choose your holiday partner and never let them forget your generosity in every bar you walk into by reminding them 'It's cost you nothing to get here, you could at least buy the drinks,' which by night three they invariably do.

There should be a contract for anyone accepting a free holiday from a competition winner which would ensure they don't complain about anything whatsoever, buy lots of drinks and meals and show daily appreciation and, most important of all, don't even consider copping off with anyone and leaving the less attractive competition winner on their own for a night. You are there for company, not for copulation, remember.

But of course, there's no pre-flight agreement, and experience tells me the heavy debt associated with gifting a mate a free holiday fuels an imbalance between the duo involved, which grows like a cancer throughout the week. What starts as sharing a pan of paella in silence ends in them falling out forever. Rather than sit together on the transfer bus, one will typically make their own way back to the airport.

'Win a Holiday for Two, Lose a Friend and Return Alone' would be a more accurate strapline.

But I wasn't a consultant on the competition, I just had to deliver it.

One of the winners was a shady cockney character in his mid-thirties, a jack-the-lad type who knew it all and wouldn't look at you when you spoke with him. His face was familiar. I'd seen him somewhere, but couldn't quite place him.

He never turned up for the welcome meeting at which everyone received their event wristbands giving them admission to superclubs, so I went to his room to check he was okay. There was no answer. I was concerned. The first night in Ibiza often results in overindulgence. What if he'd choked on his own vomit, or overdosed on something he bought in the West End? This may sound overly dramatic but believe me, the first night in Ibiza can result in carnage. With bells on.

I checked with reception that the room was occupied and whether they'd cleaned his room that morning. They told me he'd refused entrance to the maid, so I went back upstairs and slid a note beneath his door along with the event wristband and my telephone number in case he'd lost his booking information and needed any help.

The week went by and he never turned up for anything. Each day I checked with the girls on reception if he'd stayed in his room. Each day they told me he'd refused the maid entry to clean.

On day six, one of my girl guests approached me to let me know her friend had been also staying in the room with Jack the Lad, and she felt he'd ruined her holiday, separating her from her mate and being quite controlling. She told me they'd both initially gone back on the first night for a drink, and he was initially charming, proudly showing them the framed photos of his kids which he'd placed on the bedside table. He talked one of the girls into staying just to keep him company as he couldn't sleep. That was three days ago. She'd responded to texts telling her friend she was okay, and comforting Jack the Lad as, 'His wife doesn't understand him.'

This was a difficult situation. Her welfare was not in question, she wasn't being held against her will and it wasn't my job to police people's infidelities. In this event, I didn't have to act at all. To my surprise, both the girl who'd raised the alarm and her previously incarcerated friend turned up for the boat party that afternoon. She was full of remorse at having had three days of sex in front of the photos of his children.

'He put them face-down, but just knowing they were there turned my stomach. How could he do such a thing?' she pleaded, failing to realise that she was the enabler, and that it takes two to tango.

'I told her she should sell her story to the *News of the World*,' gushed her friend over her blue slush puppy on the harbourside as we boarded.

I politely pointed out that just because he'd won a competition, it didn't make him a celebrity whose indiscretion was worthy of splashing across the front page.

'No, but he was a Premier League footballer, and used to play for...'

She went on to list all the high-profile teams he'd worn the shirt of...which explained why he looked familiar.

On returning to the hotel later that day I was relieved to hear Jack the Lad had left early and gone back to the UK. I urged the girl to put it behind her and enjoy the rest of her holiday with her friend. I also dissuaded her from selling her story to the tabloids, as she was being urged to do by others. I suggested that the cheque she would get would label her untrustworthy to future partners, and in the long term possibly ruin her life, forever branding her a 'kiss and tell' traitor. I was relieved to see she took my advice, and nothing ever appeared.

A few days after returning home, I received a phone call from the agency which had been employed by the mobile giant to manage the competition. They'd received a letter of complaint from Jack the Lad alleging his room hadn't been cleaned once, and stank to such a degree that he had no option but to fly home early. He was claiming £500 compensation, or he'd write to their client himself and tell his journalist mates how he was treated. I was gobsmacked. I'd been in business for five years at this stage and had never received a single complaint letter, refund or compensation request.

I told them the truth; his room smelled because he'd been shagging one of my guests senseless for three days and wouldn't allow the maid in to clean it. My contact at the agency knew I was responsible and a safe pair of hands and believed me, but had no choice other than reluctantly pay him the £500 to draw a veil over it. He knew that they'd have to cough up, of course. What a cheapskate! Some years later, he crops up on celebrity reality shows... and still looks and acts like a sleazeball.

Another group of competition winners I was looking after were staying in the Hotel Es Vive in Figueretas, a chic art deco hotel which was known for its after-hours parties which were frequented by minor celebrities and an older cooler clubbing clientele.

As the people carrier stopped outside, I used the few minutes the driver took to remove the bags from the hold, to brief the comp winners on etiquette:

'There may well be some recognisable faces staying here. They do so because the guests here are not likely to bother them. It's not the sort of place where you ask them for an autograph or selfie. So, if you do see anyone you recognise, please respect this, and just act cool, okay?'

They all solemnly acknowledged before leaving the vehicle, picked up their luggage and walked up the stairs into the main entrance and into the courtyard where the swimming pool is located. A slender female sat in a red bikini on a sun lounger rubbing sun cream into her legs. Her long ginger hair immediately gave her away. It was the actress Patsy Palmer, who played Bianca in Eastenders.

As one, the competition winners paused, looked at one another and shattering the chilled exclusive serenity, bellowed in unison at the tops of their voices, 'RICKYY!!!!!'

## Sucking Corporate Cock

A few years later in 2007, my friend and former editor and promoting partner Dan Prince and I put together an incentive trip for another mobile phone network and major retailer, which rewarded the six best salespeople in the UK in the month of June with an all-expenses trip to Ibiza. Looking back, we deserved all we got. The brief we were given was to put together and host an incentive weekend called 'PARTY LIKE A CELEB IN IBIZA'. This was a red flag we didn't spot. With the benefit of hindsight this was asking for trouble. We may as well have called it, 'Act like an entitled, self-obsessed asshole in Ibiza'.

In celebrity parlance, the budget was C-list, but we mistakenly went along with it thinking it could be the start of something regular

It was a lesson in what not to do when dealing with a big client.

The golden rules when Sucking Corporate Cock are as follows:

## 1. DON'T APPEAR TOO DESPERATE

With two children under five and having recently relocated to South Devon, it was essential I was able to continue working in Ibiza and remain on the radar of London media types. Dan introduced me to 'Mal'; a dance music fan who controlled the budget of a hugely popular phone manufacturer. This was an opportunity for me to move into the burgeoning corporate market. As a generation of former ravers attained budget-controlling positions in the companies they worked for, they knew exactly where they wanted to spend it – in the place they first discovered many years ago. This was a driver of the rise of concierge services and VIP culture. It wasn't *their* money they were spending; it was their companies.

We pitched how we'd deliver 'Party Like a Celebrity', outlining how the lucky winners would be treated like a VIP from the moment they landed, to the moment they left. The itinerary read like an Ibiza wannabe's bucket list: concierge service to a private villa, VIP tables at the best parties, private audiences with the DJs, dinner at the best restaurants, private yacht charter and a blowjob on the plane home. I'm only joking about the last one, but you get the idea. All food and drink paid for. The strapline was 'All you need is your passport!' They loved it – and why wouldn't they?

## 2. BEWARE THE CARROT OF CONTINUATION

We costed it up and Mal agreed, before reducing the budget by a few grand, which was, 'the norm in this process', as it made him look good to his accounts department, meaning 'more next time.' There was still ample profit margin in there, so we accepted. But this was another red flag, and one we regretted not heeding. After booking everyone's flights and paying the fifty per cent deposit on the villa, the budget was further reduced, this time considerably. We protested, of course, but as we'd committed to the flights and villa, we had no option but to swallow it. Mal reassured us, 'Don't worry, guys. Pull this one off and we can do five of these next year and there'll be a *proper* budget.'

The 'carrot of continuation' ensured we didn't reduce the quality of the product to reflect the lower budget. We saw it as a showcase, and retained every element in order to maintain the highest quality experience and show the standard to which we could work.

When we explained to Mal that the budget had been trimmed to such a degree that we were worried that we'd be operating at a loss, he reassured us that he'd ensure the guests wouldn't go too crazy, and he'd keep an eye on things.

He then reached for his company credit card and winked, 'Don't worry, lads. There's always the cavalry if needed.'

3. IF YOU SELL HEDONISM, EXPECT HEDONISTS

The winners of the incentive arrived in various states of disarray. John, a motormouth salesman from Merseyside looked and acted like a paunchy Poundland John Parrot, and was clearly going to be a challenge. Already full of himself from the in-flight drinks service, he began like he intended to continue.

Adding to every guttural utterance with the declaration, ''avin' it in eyebeetha, party like a sleb!' He'd then slap his fingers in that hip hop manner, before adding, 'Livin' the dream, la'.'

Upon arriving at the villa, and after arguing about who had the biggest room, the inevitable question was raised, 'Where can we get some gear?' This is always a sensitive one. My stock response is that I sort out everything else but this isn't my area, and that they won't have to search very hard to find sometime willing to help in Ibiza.

I wasn't wrong. Twenty minutes later another scouser turned up at the villa gates on a moped asking for John. It was the only thing he paid for the entire time he was in Ibiza.

There are a few things more obnoxious than an entitled, scouse competition winner in Ibiza. But one of them is a coked-up, entitled scouse competition winner in Ibiza

For late lunch we'd booked *La Ventana*, one of the oldest restaurants in Ibiza Old Town which offers views across the port. As it was the afternoon, we'd budgeted for the *Menu del Dia*, a set menu which is considerably cheaper than the *a la carte* menu. But this wasn't good enough for John. 'I'm here to party like a celeb, what's the most expensive thing on the menu?'

Of course, the other's followed him. Mal said nothing. What was supposed to be a light lunch cost us €2300. Dan, visibly twitching, paid on his card and we walked back down the cobbled pathway to the waiting Mercedes Viano, John emitting a punctuated fart as he walked, swigging as he swaggered from a large glass of *hierbas* he couldn't bear leaving behind. When I raised an eyebrow at him, he stopped, loudly farted and declared, ''avin' it in eyebeetha, party like a sleb!' and slapped his fingers in my face. 'Livin the dream, la'!'

His dream was rapidly turning into our nightmare.

That night, we'd reserved a table in the VIP section in

*Pacha* for Pete Tong thanks to Dan getting a good rate from his mate Danny Whittle who ran the place back then. Such are Dan's contacts that Pete had even agreed to come over and say 'hi' to the winners for us.

Later that evening we sat on the harbourside terrace at *El Divino* enjoying drinks – except John, who was inside the club buying the dancers drinks and charging it to our table. I went inside and asked him what he was doing. It was a stupid question, really. Predictably, the answer, delivered with open arms was, 'parting like a sleb in eyebeetha, soft lad,' before slapping his fingers and knocking a drinks tray from a passing waiters hand. The bill was double what we'd budgeted for, yet Mal's company credit card still remained hidden. Dan paid on his card, and we were all relieved to see our private motorboat chug towards the jetty to take us across the port to Pacha.

4. YOUR CLIENT WILL TRY TO BLEED YOU DRY

As I returned to the table from telling John we were about to leave, I overheard something which made my blood boil. Unaware of my proximity behind his shoulder, Mal was talking on the phone to a work colleague in London. 'Oh, it's well within budget, mate. I've absolutely rinsed them!' The guy was actually taking a sadistic delight in watching us struggle?

As usual, the club was packed as people paid through the nose to participate in an expensive game of sardines. We were shown to our table which overlooked the dancefloor, but after fifteen minutes there were still no drinks on it. When you book a VIP table it includes beers, a bottle of wine, bottle of vodka, water and mixers which cost €2000 back in 2007. I was aware that the drinks wouldn't be served until we'd paid the remaining fifty per cent of the bill. I found Dan at the bar, face white as a sheet, biting his nails.

The earlier extravagances meant his card was almost at its limit. This was embarrassing. I offered my card, despite suspecting that I must also be close to the limit after buying the flights for the entire group. To our relief, it was accepted, and the drinks duly arrived. However, within twenty minutes, the vodka was gone. John demanded more. I fixed Mal with a stare. He clocked it but before he could reach for his credit card added, 'Don't worry, Mal, Kerk'll sort it... won't you, Kerk?'

I ordered another bottle of vodka and carton of cranberry juice, and returned from the toilet to see John in full cokehead self-importance, magnanimously handing the bottle out to a group of girls on the next table who were all dressed from head to toe in white lace *Ad Lib* dresses which were popular at the time. Imagine a Persil ad with Pete Tong playing and you'll get the picture.

Upon spotting me, a scouse squawk rose above the sax intro to 'Destination Calabria', 'Kerk! Kerk! Champagne for the gerls, it's their berthday!' Dan had his head in his hands at the table. Mal stood eyes closed, glass in his hand, balcony rail in the other, swaying to the music above the dancefloor. The rest of the group were thankfully on the dancefloor, where they couldn't spend any money.

John thrust the empty bottle at me. 'Kerk, champagne, NOW!'

This was spiralling out of control.

What do I do? Buying strangers bubbly at €400 a throw wasn't in the budget, but wasn't this exactly what celebrities did in Ibiza? Budget considerations aside, the event was going very well; we'd delivered everything we said we would, and they were all blown away by the experience. To sour it for the sake of a few hundred euros seemed petty.

But before I could make the decision, John made it for me. The sweat-soaked white Topman shirt which stuck to his upper arms and strained to restrain his man boobs twitched in the flashing UV lights as the vodka-and-cranberry-filled gut it struggled to conceal exploded with a ferocity I've rarely seen. His head was thrown forward and upwards as the depth charge of vodka and cranberry detonated in his stomach. Funnelled to perfection by his oesophagus, a dark stream jettisoned forth from his open mouth, spraying anyone standing within range. The first heave subsided; he turned his head to the side. But it was a fragile peace; the calm before the sick storm – and the ceasefire ended as soon as it began – the second wretch bending him double as he vomited all over the virginal vodka Valkyries to his left, who screamed, causing Pete Tong to momentarily look up from his mix and snapping Mal out of his trance dance.

Footnote: In Norse mythology, a Valkyrie is one of a host of female figures who guide souls of the dead to the god Odin's hall Valhalla.

Dan just looked up, saw what was occurring, and slowly lowered his head back in his hands. But not for long... the third heave was the most violent of all, its force and projectile intensity causing John to simultaneously emit a rasping gurgly fart, which as we were to discover the following morning when we cleaned the villa, was not without substance...

A human Vesuvius of vomit and shit erupting from both ends. I manhandled him down some narrow steps to the ground level, where he cleared a path like Moses parting the Red Sea. Preoccupied with the sick scouse boy, I was unaware that Dan had to use his personal credit card to draw out a few hundred euros from the cash machine in order to settle the bill before we could leave.

Once in the seven-seater Mercedes John's head lolled from side to side like a ragdoll. A silver strand of saliva dangled from his mouth, briefly shimmering in the approaching car's headlights, 'Puke like a celeb in eyebeetha,' he slurred, before laughing and trying to slap his fingers. The smell of shit was palpable. 'More like shit yer kecks like a celeb in Ibiza,' a disgusted girl muttered under her breath holding her nose.

After dropping them off at the villa, we sat in silence. It was deafening. I had to break it. 'Well, that went well...'

But the silence only grew louder.

5. WEAR KNEEPADS WHEN CLEANING VOMIT FROM A VILLA FLOOR

The next morning, the incentive winners had been collected by the driver and taken to the airport leaving us to clean the villa. We'd cancelled the cleaner as we had no money left to pay her. It looked like Roman Polanski's gaff the morning after the Manson family called. Although my nose smelt cranberry, my eyes saw mass murder.

It took us four hours of hard graft to sweep up all the broken glass, wash the soiled sheets, burn discarded underwear, scrub the terracotta tiles and sift through the pool of debris. Under one bed we found a black vinyl Adidas shoulder bag with an LFC crest. It could only be John's. Dan emptied its meagre contents onto the bed. A pair of shorts, spare boxers, a fake Prada T-shirt and similarly fake Gucci toiletry bag.

Dan shook his head. 'The idiot's left without his stuff.' Normally we'd return it, but after the grief he caused us we simply threw it on the fire to burn with his shitty underwear.

When we'd finished we were utterly exhausted. Dejected and depressed and smelling of Domestos, we retired to the pool and crashed out on a couple of loungers watching blue dragonflies flirt and flit about its surface, reflecting on the disaster we'd brought upon ourselves in a shared, embarrassed, non-verbal void.

It was now the middle of the day, and a chorus of cicadas crackled the air like a million crisp packets being scrunched up. As I relaxed I drifted off into a semi-conscious state of relief and exhaustion.

I then became aware of another subtle sound in the chirruping cacophony. Also rhythmic, but lower in tone, it sounded like someone snoring. We were both so tired, I figured Dan must've drifted off. I kept my eyes closed and let him get on with it. He'd worked hard, and wasn't in the best of health. But then my lounger was nudged, and his voice urged, 'C'mon dude, we've got to be out of here, it's booked from 2 p.m.'

He was wide awake. 'I thought you were asleep?'

I wish! 'C'mon, let's do one.'

In the distance I could still hear the faint grunts.

'Shhh! Listen...'

Now Dan heard it too. It was coming from the shack at the end of the pool where the generator and filter system was housed.

We descended the steps and opened the rickety, sun-bleached wooden door.

There, laying on his side in the foetal position, naked and clutching a Liverpool Football Club man bag, was John.

I groaned. 'Fuck me! He's missed his flight.'

Dan was stoical, looking at him sleeping almost with affection, and said, 'Of course he has – that's what slebs do in eyebeetha, soft lad'

I bent down to wake him, but Dan put his hand on my

shoulder and fixed me with a mischievous stare.

I knew what he was thinking. 'It's tempting, but we can't...'

He raised an eyebrow.

'Dan, we *cannot* leave him here... can we?'

## Aftersun

As a result of our stint cleaning the villa, I was surprised to see we made a small profit of £270 on the trip. £135 each. Then a few weeks later, Dan's personal credit card statement arrived which showed a cash withdrawal of €300 at 4.07 a.m. in Pacha, Ibiza, which means we made a loss.

We weren't given any more incentive trips and Mal moved on to another job. John is now probably the regional sales manager for the retail chain he works for, if he ever got home that is...

---

**Top Tune: It's a Sin (Disco Remix) – Pet Shop Boys {Parlophone}**

---

## BEHIND THE BROCHURE

Be careful who you choose to go on holiday with. If it goes wrong, there can be no escape.

I recall one Ibiza guest, a Czech girl with short cropped blond hair who, according to her long-suffering roommate, loudly enjoyed nightly threesomes with a succession of men over the course of the week as her poor friend lay in the next bed with a pillow over her head to block out the sight and sound of the squelching. She barely slept a wink, and to make matters worse couldn't move rooms as all the hotels were full. By the end of the week, they were no longer on speaking terms.

Absent from the return airport transfer, the lady in question arrived there at precisely the same time as our bus, emerging from a sleek SUV with tinted windows, hastily adjusting her dress, while wiping her messy mouth with a tissue. As she was my guest it was my responsibility to ensure she was okay, and only right to check on her. 'Had a good week?' I enquired as she strode past me.

'Oh yes,' she purred, handing me the suspiciously soggy tissue, 'so much cock.'

'If her boss only knew', spat her roommate.

'Who does she work for?' I asked, intrigued.

Upon hearing the answer I froze, half in shock, half in mirth.

The thoughts, 'security risk' and 'international incident' flashed up on my mind's departure board. Both departed on time – destination: confidential (where they've remained ever since).

# 10

# BEATRIX POTHEADS

*'Damo and I both like to test the boundaries of clubbing. Our events push the envelope. We throw parties no one else has ever thought of. Everyone told us, 'Hotels are a waste of money 'cos in Amsterdam you don't sleep'…so we didn't offer one!'*
*– harderfaster.net interview, 2004*

I was at the World Travel Market in Earl's Court, blagging free schnapps from the Tirol tourist board, and was introduced to a sharp-suited bloke who acted as an agent for ferry companies including Stena. They'd heard about the numbers I was taking to DFDS, and were keen to develop the clubbing market for their new generation of high-speed superferries which sped across the North Sea in less than four hours as opposed to the nineteen it took on the route I'd been working on.

I was all ears as it meant there was longer at the destination to programme events, and in the event of bad weather figured the voyage wouldn't be as arduous. Onboard it felt like a cross between the StarShip Enterprise and a plush Heathrow airside lounge, complete with bar, burger bar, gaming arcade and children's play area. It represented the future of maritime travel. But then they said that about the Titanic…

It was a catamaran which was claimed to deliver a faster, smoother crossing.

The North Sea had other ideas, however, and in 1998, within months of coming into service, the *Stena Discovery* was travelling at full speed, when it was hit by a freak wave. Sea water hit the bridge windows and ripped through the underside of the nose. It was later discovered that this was beyond the boats design capability. Small air holes were fitted on the underside of the nose to prevent a repeat incident and sailings cancelled if there was a particularly severe storm.

When I questioned how regularly this happened, the cruise agent shrugged dismissively, saying, 'We do over 700 sailings each year, a couple are affected. The chances of being affected are 350-1, not bad odds, eh?'

Stena were keen to develop the clubbing market, but while their route from Harwich to the Hoek of Holland worked well for freight traffic and families looking for an arrival for their self-drive holiday, the Hoek of Holland wasn't a strong enough hook on which I could hang a clubbing package.

When I discovered Amsterdam was around ninety minutes up the road, it became slightly more palatable. I figured that even with a couple of hours on the bus after the four-hour crossing, it was still preferable to the nineteen hours toil on the North Sea boil we'd suffered on the north German routes from Harwich.

Amsterdam. If Europe was a comprehensive school, Amsterdam is either the smoke-filled boy's toilet at lunchtime, or the recess behind the bike sheds; somewhere boys gravitate to in order to get intoxicated or an erection.

Amsterdam has the personality of the prettiest girl in the school. She has the pick of the boys, is supremely confident and desirable – but boy does she know it. Amsterdam's popularity and sense of self-worth explains why its hoteliers got together and agreed on a minimum three-night stay at the weekend meaning that if you want to stay in central Amsterdam, you'll have to book three nights. The number of empty hotel rooms which have been paid for on a Sunday night in Amsterdam is proof that this is a rule which benefits the hoteliers rather than the guests.

Stena offered me a really fair group price, but their time-table (going out on Saturday morning and returning Sunday afternoon) meant we were only in Amsterdam for one night, and no hotels wanted to know – even though it was early November. I was learning that Amsterdam was an all-year-round destination.

Despite hiring the biggest club in 'The Dam' for the group, the lack of accommodation meant it just wasn't possible to run the trip. This was a real shame as I knew the Aussie club crowd were up for adventures, and with Heat UK and TNT magazine, I had the strong promotion and marketing partners in London I needed.

'Heat' started as a yard party in Acton Town. Together with his business partner Anton Marmot, promoter Damian 'Damo' Gelle had a house rental business giving them direct access to around 80–100 backpackers. Damo's approach to promoting a party can best be described as leading by example. Like all the promoters back then, he organised parties because he wanted to party. These days they study Event Management and Marketing before launching their 'brand' and regard it as a career rather than a lifestyle.

The following Thursday I met Damo in the Retox bar and gave him the bad news. He thought for a moment before fixing me with an intense inquisitorial stare. 'Do we need to include a hotel, mate?'

I was incredulous. What was this guy on?

'Of course we do!'

He looked at me intently, almost squinting. 'Why?'

I started to doubt myself. 'Well… it's somewhere to sleep for starters.'

This drew a raised eyebrow. 'Really?' He leaned forward and stated earnestly, 'Mate, my crew don't sleep.'

'Okay, I'll concede that. Not that many do. But they can't just hang around the station for hours after the club closes at 5 a.m. in mid-November. The buses don't leave until 10 a.m. They'll be freezing, and easy prey for the pickpockets and scum who hang around Centraal Station, not to mention the Dutch police.'

He took a swig of his Rolling Rock. 'Are there any after-hours venues?'

I was warming to his madness. 'Let me check.' I stood up and put my jacket on.

'We can't let one tiny thing spoil a great concept, mate.'

Only Damo could call an absence of accommodation for a weekend city break a 'tiny' thing.

Damo was always at his best when faced with an impossible task. He hated being told he couldn't do something, and I'd just revved him up bigtime.

One of the golden rules in package travel is that if you can't get the beds, you haven't got a product. But Damo didn't know about the golden rules – and even if he did, he would've probably broken them like every other rule he came across as he blazed a trail across London's nightlife. His questioning was like cold water in my face, bringing me back to my (non) senses; I didn't form Radical Escapes to follow rules, but to do things differently. It was time to walk the talk!

So here he was, talking me into putting together a weekend city break without any accommodation... in the depths of winter. Was I crazy?

I bade him farewell and strode away, but he wasn't finished. 'There must be somewhere which'll take in 400 people from 5 a.m. to 10 a.m. It's Amsterdam, for fuck's sake, they're supposed to be liberal and there's nothing more liberating than staying up all night?'

I couldn't disagree. My friend Terry who lived in a canal boat in Amsterdam suggested a place near the centre called Hooters which would open for a private party, but wanted an extortionate hire fee 'as the topless waitresses couldn't just rely on tips'.

I made a clean breast of it and told them clean breasts weren't really what we were looking for, and called up my old pal Henk who ran the Rotterdam Dance Parade. He knew of a basement in the Victoria Hotel right opposite Central Station. Miraculously, they agreed on the understanding I'd leave €2,000 as a bar guarantee. The Aussies drank like fish and as they didn't have anywhere else to go, would easily spend €5 each, so I knew my money was safe.

But how would we get 400 people from The Powerzone, some six kilometres away in the northern outskirts of the city to Central Station at 5 a.m.?

No bus company was interested, they all wanted to charge a full night rate and a minimum hire of four hours. It simply wasn't worth it for what would be a fifteen-minute journey.

I started to get cold feet and called Damo. 'Mate, on reflection, I don't know if it's a good idea to take four hundred of our crew to Amsterdam for twenty-four hours without giving them a bed.'

There was a pause. 'That's what we'll call it: "Twenty-Four Hours in Amsterdam!"'

Resistance was futile. I embraced it. It truly was a radical escape.

So, we span the lack of accommodation and turned it into a badge of honour. He continued, 'In years to come people will talk about the group who spent twenty-four hours in Amsterdam without sleeping. Mate, it'll become legendary!'

There was nothing stopping people from booking a hotel room in the suburbs which accepted one-night stays, but the few who did have never lived it down (as Phil Reynolds can testify).

I turned my attention to solving the problem of sourcing the transport between the venues. As I poured over the map, I noticed a canal ran right outside the Powerzone.

I traced the canal south and found it led to… Central Station!

A canal cruise in Amsterdam is hardly radical, but what better method of transport in the middle of the night for 400 saucer-eyed clubbers? Maybe I could book some clog dancers and hand out complimentary Gouda cheese as well?

I knew that each narrow boat could take one hundred people, but how would I persuade four captains to get out of their warm beds in the middle of the November night and be waiting for us outside the venue at 5 a.m.?

I called the Amsterdam Tourist Board, and after some persuasion they agreed to help. This was in their interest as I told them the alternative would mean 400 flouro'd-up hard house heads wandering through quiet residential areas at dawn with air horns and whistles. They didn't have air horns and whistles, incidentally, but the tourist board never knew this.

I jumped on the next plane to Schiphol and met the fella who owns all the Perspex-covered tourist boats in the city. A chain-smoking Johann Cryuff lookalike whose fingers wore tobacco smoke like a jaundiced glove and hooded eyes which suggested an aversion to his bed.

Although reluctant to assist me, he was clearly under orders to help, but insisted on full payment in advance – in cash. I was anticipating this and handed him two thousand Euros, realising that if they didn't turn up at the right place at the right time, I would be thrown in the canal by some very cold and pissed-off Australians.

The journey out from Harwich was swift and calm; flat seas for once. Stena even kindly pre-recorded the rugby international which had been played down under for the Aussies to watch as live entertainment. The Powerzone club venue worked well, but I couldn't relax until everyone had boarded the canal boats… which at ten minutes to five were nowhere to be seen. I stood shivering on the canalside, dwarfed by the surrounding industrial units, shivering. My teeth started chattering. I felt so lonely. I heard the swirling, kaleidoscopic anthem 'Stardancer' by The Martian fade to cheers. I called the number the canal boat boss had given me, but my flip top Nokia refused to work. Then, around the bend came one… two… three… four long dark shapes. Their reassuring collective chugging floated over the dark water like a chorus of cats purring.

It was a serene, surreal, dreamlike journey. We slipped through Amsterdam in silence like a series of stealth torpedoes silently scything through suburbia like we were being sucked into the heart of the city.

People were simply awestruck. Like children in an alpine cable car, they stared wide-eyed at the ever-changing vista. The contrast from a banging warehouse party to a still winter's night on a canal resulted in an atmosphere of hushed reverence.

Thirty minutes later the boats arrived a block away from Centraal Station, from where we led them into the basement of the Hotel Viktoria. Pretty soon it was throbbing away to the bonkers Tidy Trax anthem Bits and Pieces. Smiles abounded, and people thanked me as I walked through the packed labyrinthine rooms. I couldn't believe we'd pulled off the weekend without a hitch. Someone handed me a beer. I accepted.

I started to relax. It had been a stressful twenty-four hours, but all the hard work had been done. All that remained was the straightforward task of loading them on the buses which would stop right outside the front door of the hotel, drop them off at the ferry terminal and we'd be back in blighty by late afternoon. Job done!

As I unwound in the cacophony, people were smiling and shaking my hand. We'd done it, twenty-four hours in Amsterdam without a hotel. I congratulated myself, we were almost home and hosed. Almost...

Then, half an hour before we were due to board the buses, Heat UK resident Marc French appeared across the room munching on a cone of what he called 'Bukkake Fries': chips smothered in mayonnaise – one of a number of the group who'd spent the morning relaxing in The Bulldog Coffee Shop, smoking strains which gave them Stan Laurel smiles.

He sought me out and I could see from his expression that something was up.

'Have you seen what's happening outside?' he asked.

As I'd been in the windowless basement for the previous four hours, World War Three could've broken out and I'd have been blissfully unaware.

I ushered him into a corner so I could hear over BK's 'Bad Ass', as conversation was challenging when the Hadron Collider's being hoovered.

'What's up, Marc?'

'All the roads have been closed to traffic. Crowds are building up and armed police are fucking everywhere. It took ages to get back in, and I was only a minute's walk away.'

I could tell from his girlfriend's worried reaction that this wasn't a wind-up.

Was it a raid? Had we been set up by the tourist board to send out a signal to other UK promoters?

I raced upstairs to the main entrance on street level, my heart beating with every step. The pavement was six deep as people stood around. I edged through the crowd to the corner of Damrak where the buses were due to pick us up. My phone rang. It was my booking agent Nick from Vacation Club, 'Fuck me, at last! I've been ringing you for hours—!'

'What's going on?' I interrupted.

'Ahh, you've seen, then. This is why I've been ringing you. Stena called to tell me Queen Beatrix is attending an awards ceremony in the Royal Palace just up the street from where you are. The route passes right outside, so all the central roads will be closed to traffic for an hour from 9.30 to 10.30 a.m., just our flamin' luck! There's a different pick-up point for the buses.'

'WHAA-AT? WHERE?' Someone turned my tinnitus up. At the same time my heart did a snare roll.

'Apparently there's a coach park somewhere behind Central Station. I'm on my way there now, but the traffic's so horrendous I'll be surprised if the coaches are even there. They were a bit vague with the directions, but you'd better set off with them now. I'll update you to the exact location as you walk.'

'Set off now?'

Andy Farley's 'Out of Control' had just crept into the mix and was taking no prisoners. It never did. I had zero chance of getting them out while that was playing. Then the music stopped momentarily, and a female voice declared, 'There's a problem here,' before the track snarled on once more.

No shit, Sherlock.

'Kirk... Kirk...?'

Shit, I was still on the phone to Nick. 'Sorry, go ahead,' I said.

'I was saying that you need to set off now as the buses only have a forty-minute window before the boat leaves. The tide is rising and the Captain's said he's leaving with or without us.'

'Really? After breaking their bar records on the way across?'

'Yes, considering all the business we've given them, but there you go. Not a lot we can do really.'

'Nick, there's no way I can get four hundred fully charged insomniacs out of the venue, through the crowd and locate and load those buses in the next half an hour. We'll lose them in the crowds for starters, and as no one knows where the hell they're going. It'll be a disaster. The buses will have to come to the group – or get as close as they can.'

Nick, now exasperated, said, 'They can't get to you, Kirk, the roads have been closed.'

'Similarly, I can't get the group to the buses for the same reason. We must keep the group together at all costs.' There was a pause, followed by: 'Including missing the boat back?'

My trusty rep Macey appeared at the bottom of the stairs and held his finger in the air like a cricket umpire giving a batsman out. This is clubland sign language for 'one more?'.

I drew my finger across my throat to indicate absolutely not. He nodded and as he turned to pass it on to Ian M, I bellowed, 'No encore, buses won't wait. Clear the venue... clear the venue.'

'Hello... hello...?'

I'd forgotten I was still on the phone. I took a deep breath and said, 'If they won't fucking wait they can put us on the midnight sailing instead. People can crash out in the terminal until then. It'll be messy, but at least we won't leave anyone stranded in Holland.'

Five minutes later he called back. 'The drivers are refusing to move and say they'll give us fifteen minutes before setting off.'

By now the music had finished and my stewards were rounding everyone up and shepherding them outside into the bright sunshine, blinking and shielding their faces like vampires at the onset of dawn.

The pale trail of zombies emerging from the bowels of Hotel Victoria provided a stark contrast to the wholesome fresh-faced classes of Dutch schoolchildren and fresh-faced flag-waving families who'd gathered to get a glimpse of their Queen.

Somewhere a clock struck ten. At the same time, my heart missed ten.

Five minutes went by, then Queen Beatrix came into view in an open carriage, waving to the adoring masses. When her gaze met the Antipodean zombie nation, for the briefest of moments, her smile dropped and her mouth gaped open.

My phone was ringing again, probably to tell me the buses have left, and we'll all have to get the train to the ferry port.

I answered, and Nick said, 'They're over the road from you. They said they'll wait five minutes for you but then they have to leave as they're needed to pick up the incoming passengers.'

I peered into the low sun. Over the shoulder strap of a short-handled submachine gun, across the glinting metallic tramlines, beyond the Royal procession and above the politely applauding crowd lining the far side of the road, I could make out a line of pale blue buses. Or could I? Was it merely wishful thinking? My eyes were tired from lack of sleep and still adjusting to daylight.

'Can you see them yet?' Nick asked.

'What colour are they?'

'Sky blue,' he replied.

'I can see them! We're coming over now, tell them to open the doors.'

I briefed my stewards and told Damo to ask for volunteers to act as a decoy group. In exactly one minute we were going to rush the Royal procession and get on the buses. It was our only hope.

The clip clop of hooves on tarmac was receding as the horse-drawn coach procession passed by. I realised they would wait until the royal family were out of sight and safely at their destination a few blocks away before opening the road to traffic. But we couldn't wait another ten or fifteen minutes.

I counted down from sixty in ten-second gaps. When I got to 'ten', some of the group who had booked accommodation (as they planned to continue their stay) broke through the unsuspecting cordon of police and stewards keeping the crowd back from the road. Crucially, there were no barriers. This distraction worked, drawing the attention of all nearby stewards and leaving a gap for us to rush through. On the other side of the road, the shocked cordon started advancing towards us. A brief game of British Bulldogs then took place; a rugby match without a ball played on slippery tramlines on a pitch peppered with steaming horse shit commenced. We outnumbered them fifty to one, and once I'd told the burly policeman who was restraining me round the waist that we weren't anarchists, anti-monarchists or terrorists, just stay-awakes who were shit scared of missing their bus back to the ferry, they showed their libertarian liberal side and let us all go.

The drivers remonstrated with the chief of police in Dutch about something or other, before the reassuring sound of coach doors hissing closed allowed me to start breathing again.

As we left, I could see motorcycle outriders in front of my bus, the driver explained that as technically the road was still closed, we were afforded a police escort to the city limits.

When I announced this over the mic it particularly tickled a couple of the boys who some years later approached me in Ibiza to thank me for getting them a police escort that day, adding, 'If they knew what we'd just picked up, they wouldn't have been quite so obliging!'

Damo was spot on: 'Twenty-Four Hours in Amsterdam' quickly became legendary. To this day anyone who attended regards it a badge of honour, but I suspected it may be something people only wanted to do once.

I persuaded Damo to provide accommodation and so 'Forty-Eight Hours in Amsterdam' was conceived with the strapline: 'Twice as long, twice the fun *and* a bed!' As straplines go, this must be up there with my finest: 'The World's Greatest

Show on Snow' (Snowbombing) and 'Cross over to the other side' (my North Sea cruise break which featured spirit medium Derek Acorah, which you'll hear about later).

The prospect of a weekend in Amsterdam in November with the 'down-underground' scene's finest DJs obviously appealed, and we sold out within days.

Once again, Stena had given me a date in early November... but even if the seas were rough, the Superferry hydrofoil would glide over the waves in a few hours. Or so I thought...

I'd been watching the weather all week and sure enough a huge storm was brewing which would hit the North Sea on Friday. It looked like a particularly strong one, but back in those days they didn't give storms names. But I did. It was 'twat' – and by the end of the next couple of chapters you'll understand why.

## Blade Runner

But before the next Aussie event, I put together a thirtieth birthday celebration weekend for a well-known London DJ and promoter. The prevalence of sheepskin coats and flat caps at the pub in Liverpool Street indicated that this was a different crowd to any I'd worked with previously. Some were already steamed by the time we boarded the train to Harwich, still two hours away.

Things were lively on the boat, like all the best promoters, the host was at the centre of the party action and enjoying his birthday weekend. But the mood gradually changed, and I was aware that one of the guests appeared to have an issue with him. By the time we'd reached the Hook of Holland there were rumours that he was carrying a knife and was threatening to 'skank' the promoter in the car park as I was about to load the bus. I asked him not to get on the bus until I'd asked the driver to help me conduct a 'drinks search', giving us a chance to check people's pockets. The guy in question hovered a few yards away, aggressively pulling on a cigarette and staring at the fella whose birth he was supposed to be celebrating, appearing to psyche himself up. He was clearly charged on coke, and after flicking his fag away, pulled something from his pocket which he concealed behind his back.

By now everyone was on the buses waiting to depart for Amsterdam except the promoter, his would-be assailant and me. People were getting restless and wanted to leave, but I couldn't leave the promoter there, or allow the bloke to get on the bus with the knife. I stood between them, separating them like a boxing referee. I asked the promoter to get on the bus, and calmly told the coked-up knifeman that if he wanted to board, he'd have to hand me the weapon.

'And if I say no...?' he frothed.

He came closer, swaggering towards me like a Del Boy Liam Gallagher, slightly taller than me, the peak of his cap now touching my quiff, '...are you going to stop me?' A wave of cigarettes and alcohol washed over my face. His glazed eyes blazed with the threat of violence. I was aware we were being watched by half the people on the coach and he wouldn't want to lose face. If I let him on, it could be a green flag for murder and I'd lose all authority over the group, as well as being open to a charge of corporate negligence.

My insides were churning. Was this how my life would end? Bleeding to death in a dark and windy Dutch ferry terminal? How would my wife explain this to my son when he asked where his Dad was?

As calmly as possible, I replied, 'Well, I'll have to try, which means you'll stick it in me… which will result in the driver closing the doors and calling the police… who are only over there.' I nodded to the terminal building, before continuing, 'You'll miss your weekend in the Dam and face a twenty stretch in a Dutch prison. Is it really worth it?' As he kept staring into my eyes, my guts were turning somersaults, and involuntarily, I farted. Although silent, it was vile.

Without averting his stare, he sniffed a few times, and said, 'Have you farted?'

I guiltily nodded, and did that Gary Lineker at Italia 90 expression, you know, when he was signalling to Bobby Robson that Gazza had crumbled after receiving a yellow which would keep him out of the World Cup final should England get through. It broke the ice.

'Fack me, that's disgusting! What've you been eating?'

I thought for a second. 'Let me think,' I said. My mind was blank. I farted once more, this time an audible gurgling rasp, which drew a look of incredulity from the coked-up knife boy.

'I, erm… had a Big Mac at Liverpool Street, but I think it's more to do with the fact I'm shitting myself you're threatening to stab me, and I'll miss my boy's third birthday party next week.'

Maintaining eye contact, he continued his interrogation. 'What sauce?'

'Sauce?'

'Dipping sauce: Honey Mustard, Sweet n' Sour, Tangy BBQ…?'

'I can't really remember.'

He continued staring at me. I could see the knife being raised in my peripheral vision.

'Oh, I think I remember now – it was Sweet Curry.'

'Oi fackin' knew it!'

His face broke into a smile. He raised the knife and waved it between our faces, using it as a fan to waft the fart away. Behind its glinting blade I could see his face screwed up as he continued to be consumed by my gastric expression.

'It's like the saying.'

'Eh?'

Pointing meekly at the blade as it wavered before my eyes I offered, 'Y-You could cut the atmosphere with a knife…'

He thought for a second, paused the knife whose trajectory my eyes were following like a centre court tennis crowd sat near the net, then roared with laughter. 'Nice wun! Jesus Christ! If that's what yer insides smell like, I ain't opening *you* up.'

Handing me the knife, he climbed up the stairs and staggered down the bus to the back seat to drunken jeers. By the time we'd reached Amsterdam an hour later, he was best mates again with the birthday boy and all was forgotten. It was a top weekend in fact, with no more issues. But if I was to work without security I needed to find a crowd which didn't carry knives.

---

**Top Tune: Out of Control – Andy Farley {Vicious Circle Recordings}**

---

## BEHIND THE BROCHURE

At a student event at a holiday park in Cornwall there was no Wi-Fi and we had to notify each chalet of a last-minute venue change. One chalet had been transformed into a sex dungeon. A plentiful PVC-clad student-turned-dominatrix sat on a chair as two lads wearing only socks knelt before her, licking her boots.

Another lad stood behind, looking quite confused in handcuffs and a chef's apron with the words 'Proper Job!' emblazoned across a Cornish flag.

After discreetly establishing that they were there by choice and not being held against their will, I left them to it. As we walked away, my colleague Ian shook his head and said, 'Theology students, they're all the same.'

# 11

# AMSTER*DAMNED*: OUTBOUND

*'There is no past or future, only the present.'*
— Hector Garcia

Have you ever imagined what it feels like to fall from a great height to certain death? It's something I often ponder. I'm intrigued whether I'd be able to savour the last few seconds of life and enjoy the sheer exhilaration of falling through the vast empty sky in beautiful freedom, or fail to make the most of the adrenaline junkie's ultimate rush and amazing view because I was preoccupied with what was coming next.

This is why freefall and 'Poundland parachuting' (aka bungee jumping) took — or rather stepped — off: all the thrill of the fall without the SPLAT! I've never done it. Truth is, I'm fearful how it will end. Not of the elastic snapping or jarring my back, but if it did, ascending to the spiritual realm resigned to the fact that 'One, two, three, BUNGEE!' would've been my last words. Anyway, back to the scenario of falling. The challenge would be making the most of every moment, rather than being worried about what was coming next.

Then, one night on the dancefloor, during what the Sann-yasin sect call Dynamic Meditation and we call raving, I had an epiphany. A universal truth was revealed; being born is, in effect, falling from a great height. We're all hurtling to our deaths – and although we may choose to flap our arms to slow our descent, or hold out our hands in front of our face to protect our teeth, resistance is futile. The ground is looming for us all. The challenge is to look at the horizon and not below, to breathe in the air and feel the sun on our face, to live in the moment and savour our brief but beautiful time alive.

As Eckhart Tolle put it: 'Realise deeply that the present moment is all you have. Make the NOW the primary focus of your life.'

This is easier said than done. One example springs to mind...

As usual, the ferry company had given me a date. Yes, you guessed it, in November. So, it was no surprise when the weather warnings started building in midweek warning of a large storm.

The 2005 Atlantic hurricane season was the most active on record and the fact we were using the HSS catamaran rather than a traditional vessel made me nervous.

I sold it like this: *The world's largest and smoothest superfast ferry will be transformed into a floating club! We'll be programming the music through an immaculately crystal-clear sound system surrounded by a huge Toshiba 24-cube video wall, intelligent lighting rig and bars selling drinks at pub prices. It's the only way to travel!*

After watching the late-night weather on BBC1 the night before we were due to depart, I didn't sleep very well, and my worst fears were realised when my phone rang at precisely 8.30 a.m. as I was eating my Coco Pops whilst flicking through the free local newspaper, which I referred to as 'The Enfield Murderer' due to the weekly catalogue of violent deaths within its pages.

It was my booking agent Nick Cade from Vacation Club. Whenever anyone starts the conversation with the question, 'Are you sitting down?' you know it's not going to be a chat about the weather. But that's exactly what it was about.

Nick explained that as suspected, the wind was too strong for the HSS catamaran, and the day's sailing had been cancelled with our group being booked on the Eurotunnel instead. My head span. What should've been ninety minutes on a bus to a swift crossing on a spacious ferry, followed with another hour or so on the bus into 'The Dam', was now a torturous eight-hour drive from London via Folkestone, through France, Belgium and Holland, before reaching Amsterdam some 360 miles later. This is like driving from London to Glasgow for a night out.

*I was aware that my feet were no longer on the ground...*

There was no time to tell everyone who'd booked, as we only had contact details for the group leaders, and we figured it would only cause confusion and, if I'm honest, cancellations. As we'd already paid our suppliers (Stena, the coach company and venues) we would've been unable to give a refund, and as the event wasn't cancelled it would've been their decision not to go. Whilst this was all above board, it would've caused resentment and effectively torpedo any credibility I had in the scene. So, from mid-afternoon, people arrived at Liverpool Street expecting a relatively short bus ride to the port of Harwich.

When we told them the score, they hastily dispersed in search of essentials to sustain them throughout the long nocturnal journey ahead; alcohol, cigarettes and sandwiches.

As we got caught up in the Friday evening rush-hour traffic, leaving London took an age.

In a trading estate on the outskirts of Rotterdam, a middle-aged man sets the burglar alarm and locks the office for the weekend. Before he enters the code he pats his breast pockets to check he hasn't forgotten the tickets for the Saturday night performance of *Night of the Proms* at Rotterdam Ahoy. He's so preoccupied with these, he forgets his glasses, which sit forlornly on his desk.

## On the Buses

At the back of my bus, I was aware people were smoking, which wasn't allowed. The driver, a middle-aged Roy Kinnear looka-like called Cyril, theatrically sniffed, 'Samwune's smawking.'

This was before the smoking ban, and back in those days it was up to the driver's discretion whether smoking was allowed on the coach. Each seat had ashtrays. As did seats on planes and (unbelievably) in doctors waiting rooms. London tube trains even had smoking carriages and my corner shop sold schoolkids a Players No. 6 with their lunchtime meat and potato pie or 3p lucky bag.

Cyril theatrically coughed. Twice.

I had to act. 'It's a long journey, Cyril. Could we perhaps arrange something?'

'It'll mean cleaning the ashtrays. That takes toime... and toime is maney.'

I announced over the mic that if we had a whip-round for the driver people could smoke, and proceeded to collect around fifty quid for him in a Sainsbury's bag. I heard other buses did the same.

I also handed out black bin liners for empty cans which people used diligently.

Eventually, we made it to the Eurostar terminal at Folkestone. I was somewhat disappointed to discover that it wasn't the swish art deco passenger train we were booked into but the grim freight service. For those not familiar with 'Le Shuttle', allow me to explain. Your vehicle is carried on a train. You're urged to remain inside your vehicle for the duration of the crossing; a noisy sub-oceanic rattle which is in the same category in the Unpleasant Noise Olympics as roadworks outside your house, dentist drill and MRI scan. Although the crossing only takes half an hour, it feels much longer. No toilets were available on the train, meaning the bus toilets got filled much quicker than was planned.

This led to the drivers, already mightily cheesed off at having to drive through the night, to lock them – which of course caused people to use empty cans as urine receptacles. Have you ever tried pissing into a can? The hole is so small that you have to be absolutely still and your aim true, or your stream hits the edge and sprays all over the place. This would explain the shrieks from the back of the bus and the aroma of wee as we eventually neared Amsterdam the following morning.

It was probably my mistake that the permission to smoke earlier didn't specify what people could inhale, and inevitably the heady aroma of spliff snaked its way to the front of the bus. I glanced nervously at the driver, who appeared oblivious, tapping out the beat to an Anthony Pappa Mixmag CD I'd slid into the player on leaving Liverpool Street, appropriately called The Journey. I did Anthony's first interview and gave him his first UK show at Brixton Academy in 1997. He was up there with Sasha and Digweed as far as I was concerned, and remains to this day the finest DJ Australia has produced.

The smell of weed grew stronger. A glance behind told me the guys in the seat immediately behind the driver were smoking a huge cone. Jesus, it was pungent. A wispy blue plume curled and coiled around Cyril's neck like Kaa the snake in Jungle Book. He was enveloped in skunk and so was I. As we made our way north through France, the road signs read like a list of famous battles: Dunkirk, Waterloo, Ypres, Ghent, Antwerp...

The dreamy trip-hop emerging from the CD provided the perfect soundtrack to the neon motion passing our eyes. Sven Vath's 'Blue Spliff' may have been written for this moment; repetitive loose jazzy vibes within a pulsing beat.

The concave front window of the bus reflected the cats' eyes, rhythmically zipping upwards across the glass as we scythed through the night, a seemingly eternal stream of fairy lights ascending before my eyes, escaping the asphalt like souls leaving the body at the point of death.

A voice muttered something about lights. I snapped out of my stoned daydream.

'Pretty white loights,' Cyril said, smiling beatifically at me. Oh shit, the driver's high.

Next thing I know he's pulling into a service station and reciting EU law, 'After five hours n' thirty minutes of droiving, the rules state that droivers mast take a break of at least thirty minutes.'

Although my instinct was to get to Amsterdam as soon as possible, I welcomed a chance to get some fresh air and my guests an opportunity to pee in a urinal rather than a beer can.

Another one of our buses pulled up next to us. This became known as the 'Braveheart bus', named after the only DVD onboard. For the planned ninety-minute ride from London to Harwich this would've been fine. But on repeat (at this point we'd been on the buses for over six hours), the full-bloodied action epic had become a nightmarish *deja vous* with blue war paint and dodgy Scottish accents.

Rob, aka DJ Beamish, who was repping that coach (and who, with his wild ginger hair, could've well been an extra in the film), joined me as I helped a visibly wobbly Cyril into the services, my arm linking his.

He disappeared into the shop desperately looking for a DVD to buy while I ordered the coffees. Cyril really was quite out of it, babbling some nonsense about a home for blind cats, where all the cats who'd had their eyes removed for road markings lived out their final feline days.

As we sipped our coffee and munched on a stale sandwich, through the window of the café area behind the driver's head, I watched our bus judder before driving off. I continued to sip my coffee, thinking the driver was probably using the break to refill with fuel before we got back on.

WAIT A MINUTE – I'M SAT WITH THE DRIVER?

Evidently, I was also a little hazy.

'Er, Cyril, have you got the keys with you?'

He patted his pockets and shrugged. 'Damn, I must've left them in the ignition. Not that it's going anywhere, mind. They aren't easy to droive.' His words were punctuated by the screech of tyres as the bus disappeared past the window. Upon hearing this, he spun round to see his bus reappear into view as it snaked and juddered across the thankfully deserted coach park. We all ran outside and began comically chasing the hijacked bus around the coach park. Mercifully, they couldn't find second gear. As the door was still open, screams could be heard from inside as the few passengers who hadn't disembarked, probably because they'd been asleep, lurched from side to side.

It was reminiscent of that scene in Dirty Harry when the baddie Scorpio hijacks a school bus. All that was missing was a forced rendition of Old MacDonald. Instead, the soundtrack was Tiesto's 'In Search of Sunrise 3'.

In search of sanity would've been more appropriate.

As the bus lurched towards us once more, now on its fourth lap, Cyril struck an exasperated pose at the entrance to the services; hands on head and mouth open at what he was witnessing. I had to do something. This time I tried to flag down the bus by standing in its path. It drew closer, growing in size. As it bore down on me, I could see a couple of lads at the front clearly having the time of their lives. Thankfully they hit the brakes, which exhaled their relief. TSSSSHHHHH!

I scrambled up the steps and whipped the key from the ignition. Cyril appeared below, framed in the doorway. 'They get off here, or oi do. Oi'm not driving them any further.'

The lad in the driving seat stood up and held his hand out to Cyril, saying, 'We wuz only 'aving a larf, fella. We went up to change the music. That trip-hop was doing me 'ead in. Awl we wanted wuz some trance. But when I sat in the driver's seat and saw the keys in the ignition... Well, it'd have been rude not to, wouldn't it?'

Time for diplomacy. Whilst I could appreciate Cyril's point of view, I didn't feel good about leaving two pilled-up trance heads at a motorway service station in Belgium at 2 a.m., but Cyril, still incandescent with rage, wasn't having it. Harrumphing with folded arms, he said again, 'It's me or them. Your choice.'

By now the rest of the passengers had reached the bus and were keen to get to Amsterdam. They started having a go at the hijackers, making them feel unwelcome. They got the message.

'Where are we, anyway?'

'Belgium, eight kilometres from Bruges,' Cyril snorted.

'Any clubs in Bruges?' one of them asked, jiggling to 'Touch Me' by Rui da Silva. This was my chance.

'Too right there are! Bruges is proper having it these days.'

That was it, they were sold on the idea. One recovered their bags from the bus, whilst the other ran inside to call a cab from the stickers on the public pay phones.

I checked they'd got their passports and enough cash and left them there dancing in the coach park to trance music they couldn't possibly hear anymore as they waited for a cab to take them to Bruges.

Rob, who'd been searching for DVD's returned empty handed, resigned to another three hours of Braveheart. We loaded the buses and moved off as the bus hijackers rolled a spliff as they waited for the cab they'd just called, blissfully oblivious to the 'wankers' and 'fuck off' hand signals emanating from my bus.

Some hours later we finally arrived in Amsterdam. It had taken twelve hours and the coaches, as you might imagine, smelt like an alcoholic's breath laced with stale smoke. In a pissed-in phone box. Next to a cannabis farm.

Bus four, which my colleague Nick Cade was repping, arrived just after mine. The doors opened to expose a very loud, very fast, dustbin lid kick drum pulsating as Minnie Mouse on helium sang 'Just a Feeling' over and over again. Nick staggered from the bus, hands in his blue jacket visibly twitching. His forehead was covered in beads of sweat and since leaving Lille appeared to have developed a facial tick.

'Everything okay, mate?' I enquired.

He stood there trembling and fixed me with a thousand-yard stare. 'No more Gabber, I can't 'andle anymore Gabber, I'm telling ya.'

He wasn't putting it on. He was genuinely struggling. We'd made CDs for each coach to reflect the group's musical tastes, and Nick had drawn the short straw as his was bus four: Gabber. As the radio on his bus was broken, he was forced to listen to twelve hours of Rotterdam's most hardcore sounds. Gabber has been described as a punch in the face. It's the most raw, angry, visceral genre in dance music. And twelve hours of being punched in the face is enough to break any man.

Another bus arrived. As it came to a halt, I could see the passengers weren't wearing very much. Girls sat in bras while the entire back seat crew were bare-chested. My mind boggled at what had been going on. This was Tommy's bus. He emerged in a vest, red-faced and exhausted. He had an eye for the ladies, and they had an eye for him. I feared the worst. The door opened and I was hit by a wave of warm air. It was like opening a sauna door or walking off a plane into a sultry Spanish summer's day. Except this was dawn in November in Amsterdam.

'Tommy, why are the passengers undressed? Put your shirt on please.'

'The bloody driver wouldn't turn the heating down. It was on full all the bleedin' way.'

I looked at the driver, who, unlike those emerging from the bus, appeared to be unaffected and explained, 'The A/C is faulty. It was either a warm charabanc or a brass mankey bas.

With my circulation I feel the cold, so I chose the warmth. I'm not paid enough to be cold in my workplace environment.' A picture was building up of a militant, work-to-rule bunch, who clearly resented having to do the job they were being paid well for.

More buses arrived; a stream of vomit comets which had blazed through the night, each one with tales of how uncooperative and miserable the drivers had been. My guests would stagger off them and wander around in a dazed state. 'I feel like I've been hung, drawn and quartered,' rasped Damo. Coming from someone who suffers for their art of partying, this illustrated just how challenging the journey had been.

We checked everyone into the hotels and I finally got to bed around 6 a.m., utterly exhausted. Except for The Hijackers, everyone was present, and the storm was subsiding, hopefully meaning we'd be able to take the five-hour HSS ferry back on Sunday morning rather than trouble Belgium again. I fell asleep telling myself we'd got through the worst of it.

As I slept I was unaware that wasn't the case – and another, much more damaging storm was brewing which would have potentially catastrophic repercussions for us all.

In a high-end villa affording spectacular views of Table Mountain in Cape Town, South Africa, an overweight middle-aged man reclines beside his infinity pool receiving a massage from a young, attractive dark-skinned woman. He is talking to one of his employees who is in Amsterdam.

'Not at all, Cyril, thank you for letting me know. Don't worry, I'll deal with it.'

The man gestured for his masseuse to pause while he ended the call to his driver in Amsterdam, before checking with Sandra in accounts that they'd already received the full amount for this job. When she confirmed they had, he smiled and punched in the number of the group leader who was asleep in Amsterdam.

'Urgh, hello, Kirk speaking...'

'My name's Nigel. I own the coaches your animals have just trashed, and I want to know what you're going to do about it?'

Rapidly waking up, I blurted out, 'Well, I wasn't aware of any damage to the buses. We had to go via Folkestone, so my group was on them longer than expected, but we'll get them cleaned up, no problem.'

'According to my drivers – one of whom now has shingles after listening to that dreadful music they forced him to listen to – two of them are damaged beyond repair. I heard one was stolen in Belgium, and another driver couldn't sleep after the music you insisted on playing.'

'Hmmm, that must've been bus four. Let me explain; the so-called hijackers never got out of first gear, and it was only possible because your driver left his keys in the ignition. Those responsible were ejected from the bus immediately and they apologised. As for the mess, we'll get the coaches cleaned today, I can assure you.'

'Too right you will. And only then will I decide whether to tell the drivers to return to Harwich at the first available sailing.'

'What, and leave 400 of your guests stranded in Amsterdam?'

'They're not my guests, laddie. They're yours. Now get those buses cleaned, sharpish.'

The balding, red-faced man clicked the button and smugly gestured for his poolside massage to continue.

*My limbs flailed wildly. I was now aware I was falling...*

In that minute, my consciousness had gone from fast asleep

to full-on trauma. Tinnitus screamed and whistled loudly in my head like someone had just turned it up to eleven. I splashed water on my face to check it wasn't a nightmare but still felt nothing, so I took a cold shower. Not out of choice, there was no hot water. I stared at myself in the mirror of the cramped attic room where I wanted to remain, hiding from it all. My head span. A nearby church bell started ringing, but not as loud as my ears were. I was Anne Frank on amphetamines. It was a nightmare, all right. But one I was experiencing whilst being awake. To make matters worse, my favourite pair of boxer shorts I pulled out had been mixed up with the coloured ones, and instead of being white were a horrible yellow. Even my underwear was jinxed.

An hour later Nick called from the coach park. He was checking the damage and to my relief confirmed that despite the vehicles being messy and smelly, which you would expect given the length of journey they'd just undergone, it was nothing which a clean wouldn't rectify. There was certainly no lasting damage as the owner had been led to believe by the fishwife drivers.

Nick priced up a thorough valet which cost us €1,200, but I wanted to ensure the buses were returned to a state I'd be happy to let my guests travel home in. I didn't believe for one moment the threat which had been issued.

How could a coach company leave 400 people in Amsterdam? That wasn't only irresponsible, but reckless and very unprofessional. The travel industry has a duty of care to those who place their trust in it. This has always been important to me.

When I used to travel and get into all sorts of scrapes there was no one on hand to help me. An important part of the inspiration when I set up Radical Escapes was to be there for my guests when their hedonistic shit hit the fan of reality. In the same way it takes a thief to catch a thief, only a raver (or in my case ex-raver) truly understands another raver. If someone's struggling and its substance related. I hope I've got the experience and their trust which fosters honesty. Maybe they wouldn't tell a 2wentys rep they'd done too much ketamine or dropped a microdot, fearing repercussions, but experience has shown me they trust me with that information. After witnessing the hopelessly out of touch major tour operator 'youth' brands in the mid '90s, I was aware 'The E Generation' needed a travel company who understood and didn't patronise or judge them.

The coach company may not have been set up to deal exclusively with clubbers, but it was unheard of to leave a large group overseas, and after speaking to Nick over breakfast, I was confident Nigel was merely sabre-rattling from his poolside villa in the sun before his happy finish.

'Is he really going to leave 400 guests stranded in Amsterdam now we've cleaned his bloody buses?' Nick reasoned over breakfast.

Later that afternoon, I was in the basement of the Hotel Viktoria setting up the party when Nick called to tell me that someone at the port had just informed him that seven empty buses had just boarded the late afternoon sailing to Harwich...

*My speed has increased, my face is distorted by the gravity, the noise in my ears is a deafening WHOOOSH!!!*

The fuckers had waited for us to clean the buses before driving off – leaving me with 400 people in Amsterdam and no way of getting back.

What's more disgusting is that they never told us they were

leaving, and if the port hadn't told us, we'd have turned up at the meeting place on Sunday morning wondering where the buses were.

This was one of those moments I wanted the ground to open beneath me and swallow me whole. This was the stuff of nightmares. My shirt was rippling from the impact of the kick drum. Then I realised the sound guy was still setting up and it was my own heartbeat.

Four hundred people stuck in Amsterdam. Some had jobs to go to on Monday, others had flights to catch. All expected to be back in their beds in blighty on Sunday night.

We appealed to Stena, who told us that they would allow us to cross as foot passengers. This wasn't good enough. The returning buses had used our booking without our consent. We also pointed out that had their Superferry really been so super, we wouldn't have had to go three hundred miles out of our way in the first place. They claimed they couldn't supply us with buses to pick us up from Amsterdam as they were being used for other passengers, and advised us to tell everyone to take the train. This was far from ideal as many people:

A: just didn't have sufficient funds for two train tickets (Amsterdam to Hook of Holland and Harwich to Liverpool Street);

B: hadn't the foggiest clue where to go. Can you imagine shepherding four hundred off-their-chops Aussies to the correct platform in Amsterdam Central?;

C: were scattered all over the city and were mostly uncontactable.*

*as this was the pre-smartphone era, by this time most people's phone batteries were flat.

As it was a Saturday evening and outside business hours,

we were unlikely to find any coach company to step in at short notice with seven coaches and drivers, particularly as they were needed for 11 a.m. the next morning.

Damo walked into the DJ booth looking stressed. I tried to speak with him,

'I need a word, we've got a problem, Damian.'

He stared at the decks and, without looking at me, curtly replied, 'I can't deal with this now, mate. I've got one of my own.'

'This is important, pard'ner.'

'So is the one I'm dealing with. The DJ who's supposed to be playing is having a bad trip and is hiding in a cupboard, and no one wants to play the warm-up.'

Oh, if this was the only problem I had to deal with!

Only when we are presented by a big problem do the ones we previously thought of as issues shrink. Nothing puts things in perspective as a real problem. A proper problem – and boy, was this a proper problem. If we left everyone to get themselves back to London, both my company Radical Escapes, Nick's (Vacation Club) and Damo and Anton's (Heat UK) would be ruined. None of us would ever work again. Our reputation would lay in tatters and our bodies probably swinging from lamp posts in the Red Light District.

I stood next to him, staring straight ahead. Realising I wasn't going away, eventually he leaned over. 'What is it, mate?'

Speaking slowly into his ear I calmly said, 'The buses have driven back to England without us.'

He stared at me in disbelief. 'Say that again.'

Calmly, I repeated, breaking up the sentence as Michael Caine might do, 'The buses (pause) have driven (pause) back to England (pause) without us.'

He threw his head back and burst out laughing. 'FUCK! Now *that's* a problem!'

He later told me that this was the moment he realised how fragile clubbing travel is. 'It's always the things you can't control which fuck you up' is one of my mantras, and for good reason. You can bag the best venue, put together the strongest line up on the planet and design a flyer Rembrandt would be proud of, but if a volcano in Iceland erupts, a storm blows up in the North Sea, a pandemic explodes, a ferry route changes or an airline goes bust and people can't get there, you're stuffed.

Former British Prime Minister Harold Macmillan was once asked to identify the greatest challenge for any statesman. 'Events, dear boy, events,' he replied. He wasn't wrong.

---

Top Tune: Falling – McAlmont & Butler {Chrysalis}

---

## BEHIND THE BROCHURE

Daytime clubbing started in Germany in 1989 with Love Parade, a street procession of sound rigs on trucks attracting one hundred and fifty people. A decade later a million people would witness the annual event, spawning other cities to do the same; Zurich, Geneva and Rotterdam, the latter of which Radical Escapes were UK official travel partners. This led to me running trips to Dance Valley and Sensation White after I told promoters ID&T they weren't truly international parties without British clubbers. I pioneered going for a Saturday night out in Paris or Amsterdam using Eurostar – a new train company. I realised while Fridays and Sunday evenings were busy with weekend breakers, Saturday and Sunday morning trains were empty. The staff had never seen anything like the Italian psy-trance crew Antiworld brought with them. It was clear from their behaviour that the 'Sensation White' party crew I was accompanying, who were all dressed in virginal white from head to toe, were self-sufficient when it came to mood modification. So animated were they that I was concerned they may draw the attention of the customs at Waterloo station. When they were waved through without any body searches, even receiving 'good luck' wishes, there was general surprise... until I explained I'd told the customs they were a special needs amateur cricket team representing Southern Counties in a European tournament...

# 12

# AMSTERDAMNED: RETURN

We walked outside and called Nick, who was frantically searching for Dutch bus company telephone numbers. No progress had been made.

Every fifteen minutes I repeated this procedure until it got to 8 p.m. when I asked him to come to Hotel Viktoria so we could decide when to break it to the group that we couldn't get them back.

*The ground was looming, but there was nothing I could do about it, so I decided to feel the rush of air and enjoy the view.*

We found an Indonesian restaurant on Damrak and ordered huge amounts of food like condemned men enjoying one last meal before their execution.

As I crunched into a prawn cracker Nick's phone rang. He walked outside. I could see him through the window talking and nodding. Ten minutes later he strolled back in like he'd just simultaneously won the pools, lottery and EuroMillions draw whilst picking up Liz Hurley's car keys at a swinger's party.

We sat speechless as he sat down, raised his glass of beer, and solemnly proposed a toast, 'To Leo Ringelberg.'

'Who the fuck is Leo Ringleberg?'

'The Dutch gentleman who's sending seven of his finest coaches to Rijksmuseum Square tomorrow morning to take us all to the ferry.'

'You fucking beauty! To Leo Ringelberg – and to you!'

*I feel the reassuring tug of a parachute opening above me. My descent is now a gentle dangle.*

Unbelievably, Leo had called into his office on Saturday evening on his way to the theatre to pick up his glasses, and upon seeing the answerphone light flashing, momentarily checked his voicemail messages and heard Nick's plea from a few hours earlier. Despite us not being able to pay so much as a deposit, and having never met us, he heroically agreed to supply seven drivers and luxury buses to pick us up at 11 a.m. the next morning to take us to the Hook of Holland. A huge weight lifted from my shoulders. We were going to be able to get the group home after all!

But at the back of my mind there were doubts. Surely it was too good to be true - why would he take such a risk? What if he contacted the port and heard why the other bus company drove off. Or worse still, called the UK bus company and they told him we trashed their buses? Bus companies knew each other as they were all members of the RDA, the International Coach Tourism Federation. I wouldn't be able to relax until everyone was on the buses en route to the port.

I needed to make sure everyone was on their best behaviour for the return leg. Damo and Anton called several influencers together and briefed them what had happened. The word soon went round that any mischief on the buses would lead to us all being left in Amsterdam. As a precaution, we'd considered moving the departure time forward by an hour to give people the extra time to make their own way home by train or plane if Leo's chariots didn't show for whatever reason, but it was too late. We couldn't just message everyone back then in a WhatsApp group.

The group had a choice of attending HQXL in the docklands, watching a stellar line up of hard dance royalty and Ed Real: The Organ Donors, Nick Sentience, Proteus v Kevin Energy, Dark by Design, Alex Kidd and The Tidy Boys mercilessly pulverising 60,00 Dutch ravers into submission, or staying local and enjoying downtown 'Dam in the cellar of our accommodation, The Hans Brinker Hostel where we'd booked 300 bunk beds.

I was going through the rooming list with the girl on reception when my assistants Rob Beamish and Macey emerged from the party which was happening downstairs in what they called The Brinker Bunker.

'How's it going, many in?'

They looked at one another and grinned. 'One or two of note,' quipped Macey, with one hand on his hip and the other holding a can of coke.

What did he mean? They beckoned me to descend. As I emerged into the dank, low-ceilinged basement, I was surprised to see the bus hijackers bouncing off the walls. I called them out for a word. Having failed to get into any club in Bruges, they hailed a cab and told the driver to take them to Amsterdam. €700 later they pulled up outside the hotel. I asked if they were okay, and after filling them in about the driver's desertion their behaviour had contributed to, told them that they'd have to make their own way back as we couldn't risk another incident on the return leg. They were more than happy to get a flight back and had adequate funds to do so.

I finally got to bed around 5 a.m., laid awake for a few hours trying to focus on the horizon and not the void beneath my feet.

A few hours later I watched a dazzling sun climb above the red brick clock tower next to my attic room. I showered and ventured out into the crisp, peaceful morning. Amsterdam was serene, sensible and sunny.

Today would seal my fate in the clubbing travel business. If I pulled this trip off it would be the talk of London clubland, but if 400 souls had to find their own way home, I wouldn't be able to set foot in a London nightclub ever again, let alone run anymore overseas events. Furthermore, as my TNT readership were Antipodean and I'd promoted the trip in my weekly club section, I couldn't credibly keep the job. Coupled with the financial impact of having to refund disgruntled guests seeking compensation for having to get themselves back to the UK, and the cost of cleaning the buses whilst still having to pay the DJs and venues, I'd be financially and reputationally ruined. I thought about smug Nigel on his Cape Town sunbed and the offer of a few of the Aussies to start a fire in the yard where he parked his buses overnight, but although it appealed, emotionally and karmically I felt that it wasn't my style to get others to act on my behalf in this manner. It somehow didn't feel right. No, if his malicious, inconsiderate over-reaction ruined me, I'd bloody well torch them myself.

Sunday morning: I arrived at the meeting place, the Museumplein half an hour before the group was due to board the buses. Although there was an after-party taking place, people were already waiting, nervously standing around in silence. All wore grave expressions. More disturbingly, all were sober. It felt more like a funeral gathering than a clubbing weekend in Amsterdam.

One girl grabbed my arm and pleaded, 'Are the buses

really coming? I'm having an operation tomorrow; I must get back tonight.'

Another group of older lads were laying bets that they'd have to take the train or plane back.

As the clock struck quarter to eleven, the crowd swelled in number. Hundreds of pairs of eyes followed me everywhere. I called Nick again. Worryingly, he'd heard nothing from Leo since last night, but said this was expected as he'd told him he would be in church on Sunday morning, and that everything had been organised. And reassured me the buses would be at Museumplein near Rijksmuseum for an 11 a.m. departure as requested.

'Do you believe him?' I implored.

'I always believe the Dutch, actually. They sound so sincere,' was his reply. He had a point. The post-match interviews of Dutch football managers are always reasoned, and I'll watch nodding in agreement. It's the accent I think; a laid-back drawl which suggests impartial intellect and a reassuring honesty at work.

Usually, private buses arrive at least fifteen to twenty minutes prior to departure time to allow for boarding and loading luggage, yet it was now ten minutes before the designated departure time and there was no sign of any buses. Although I was shitting myself, I did my best to exude confidence. Despite trying to conceal how nervous I was, my constant pacing up and down probably gave it away. I was aware people were eyeing my every move.

*'And I looked, and behold, a white horse.'*
– Revelation 6:2

Then I saw it! A white bus pulled into sight. I heaved a huge sigh and smiled. My sense of relief spread around the assembled group like a Mexican wave. The group who'd been laying bets exuded both cheers and groans.

Another bus entered the square. Everyone picked up their bags.

'Where are the others?' asked Rob.

'Probably stuck at a red light around the corner, let's load these and get off, you and Macey can take one each, I'll wait for the others,' I replied.

But to my horror, as they drew level with us, they didn't slow down but kept on going. The livery read Groen Heart. These weren't the right buses – or were they?

*My parachute harness comes loose. Once again, I'm freefalling...*

In order to escape seasickness, a customs operation or listening to Gabber, Nick was flying back to the UK. He was at the airport about to board his flight, but I just managed to catch him. 'What colour are the buses? It's nearly five to eleven and I'm getting worried, please call Leo NOW!'

Then the clock struck eleven. ALL the clocks struck eleven; a bright jarring jangle rang around the cobbles amplified by the still morning air. Notes clashed, creating a chaotic metallic discord which perfectly reflected my state of mind.

Rob took a drag on his rollie and exhaled, solemnly declaring, 'For whom the bells toll.'

I didn't appreciate his gallows humour and grimaced. The bells continued their painful clanging cacophony. I suffer from hyperacusis – sensitive hearing – and wanted to block them out like Quasimodo in The Hunchback of Notre Dame.

Two irate Aussies approached me. 'Where's the fucking coaches, dude?'

'Yeah, how're we getting back. We've got no cash? You better deliver, hey?.'

Beside myself with worry, I called Nick again. 'THEY'RE NOT HERE!' I shouted, alerting all around me to my panic.

I could hear his flight being told to board, he had only moments before he had to turn off his phone. 'One of the drivers has just called me wondering where you are? They've been waiting since half past ten, Kirk. Seven white buses with Leo Ringelberg written on the side. You'd better get to them sharpish as they think it's a wind-up. If you're not there by eleven, they'll leave.'

WHAA-AT? I frantically looked around and in desperation beseeched them, 'Can anyone see any white buses?' Scores of eyes scoured the square, but there were no white buses just like there's no Santa Claus, tooth fairy, unicorn, Loch Ness Monster, honest politician or a retributional God with a beard. *Everything* I'd believed in up to that point had dissolved, leaving my life less magical, enchanting and wondrous than I was told it was when I was a wide-eyed child. At this moment in time, as a squinty-eyed forty-year-old, I wanted so much to believe in the existence of Leo Ringelberg's seven white luxury buses more than any of these other things. Yet here I was again, being let down and feeling like a fool for believing in the first place.

*I'm hurtling once more to the earth, desperately clawing the air, but time is running out…*

KLANG!

The clock struck one, another ten of these would be the cue for the buses to depart, stranding us.

KLANG!

I had a scary thought. What if they've gone to the wrong

meeting place? Was Nick still on the line? I put the flip-top Eriksson to my ear. I can still hear the Final Call announcement.

KLANG!

'Where *exactly* did they say they were waiting?'

'The coach park at the Rijkspalace.' Click, his phone is switched off. I'm on my own. On my own with 400 people looking for a lift home.

KLANG!

'The coach park? Where the fuck's the coach park?' I ask the phone.

But no one is there. Although large, the square was mainly pedestrianised with but no parking. There was nowhere for a single coach to park, let alone seven of them.

The worried girl who'd spoken to me earlier approached me again. 'Excuse m—'

KLANG!

'Not now, please, I need to find the coach park.'

KLANG!

'Is that it?' She pointed to a simplistic depiction of a bus on a blue sign with an arrow pointing down a ramp. I had been standing next to it for the last half an hour.

KLANG!

I ran down the ramp. But at the entrance (which I later realised was the exit), the barrier's down. I dip underneath it.

KLANG!

Descending slope after slope I can hear everyone's footsteps echoing off the roof as they pursue me down below the city. I really hope this is the right place...

KLANG!

The screech of brakes. I run around a corner and nearly

under the wheels of a small flat-bed council truck

*The ground looms. I can make out the hard grey concrete, instinctively, I put my hand out to break my fall...*

My outstretched hands slap against the windscreen like Ewan MacGregor in Trainspotting. The driver is naturally shocked. I apologise and dart around the side of the truck and shout, 'ONCOMING VEHICLE!' to those behind.

KLANG!

I keep running down the seemingly endless ramp and a thought enters my mind that there may be more than one floor; a multi-story cavern of torment. That would be unthinkable on so many levels... I banish this thought from my mind as I inhale fumes...

*The ground is getting closer, I can make out I'll hit an expanse of concrete, my life is almost run...*

What's that smell? I pause and breathe in, and the acrid aroma of diesel fills my lungs. It was the sweetest breath I'd ever taken.

Diesel fumes must mean buses, right? Whether it was the lack of oxygen in my lungs, or the intoxicating promise of the waiting buses which exuded them, I inhaled the fumes like they were a freshly opened sunflower or bottle of poppers – a long deliberate breath. I was now physically at one with the seven chariots of salvation. For a split-second I was Orpheus in the underworld, leading a heroic quest, Indiana Jones outrunning a giant boulder, James Bond escaping the villain's lair, before I exhaled the poison and morphed back into my true persona, a clueless travel and rave promoter who couldn't find where the fucking buses were.

Silence.

It had been at least ten seconds since the last KLANG.

The peace and quiet is deafening. Breathlessly, I run around one more corner and the sight which meets my eyes I can still see now when I close them tightly. They're there when I'm told to 'focus on nice things like holidays' when I'm under the dentist's drill, or in an MRI scan.

*Inches from the concrete I'd fallen 13,000 feet to stare at, I'd suddenly stopped and pushed myself backwards, arching my back in order to manoeuvre my legs into position…*

There in front of me are seven pristine, virginal white coaches in a perfect line, each one bearing my favourite word RINGELBERG signed like a movie star's autograph. Has there ever been three syllables more satisfying to speak in succession? Just saying the name massages the mouth and tantalises the tongue. RINGELBERG: a post-coital cigarette of a word, oozing satisfaction. RINGELBERG: a meditative incantation which'll get you to nirvana swifter than any other mantra *and* with seatbelts, air conditioning, a toilet and a DVD player. RINGELBERG: say it loud and there's music playing, say it soft and it's almost like praying. RINGELBERG: I'll never stop saying RINGELBERG.

The drivers were huddled around on the pavement, smoking and looked somewhat surprised to see me.

'Kirk?' one asked.

'YES! We're here.' At that moment, the stampede spilled out of the ramp behind me, a noisy stream of British, Australian, Kiwi and South African clubbers carrying holdalls and expressions of glee, chests heaving from the subterranean sprint. They kept on coming until four hundred of them were assembled in the cavernous concrete womb.

*I stepped down onto terra firma like a freefall display team calmy stepping onto the large bullseye at an air show. The ground had never felt so good.*

Once aboard the buses I briefed all reps to let everyone know that word was out and warned them the border officials at Harwich were expecting them. This was code for them to jettison any 'leftovers' from the weekend. But instead of throwing it in the black bin liners we passed around, they of course decided to swallow anything they had left and make the most of the return ferry crossing for which we'd programmed DJs to play. The ferociousness of the dancing was an indication that no one had anything left in the locker, which visibly disappointed the UK customs.

There was only one issue: one group of eight had pooled their passports, handing them to the group leader to take care of on the ferry, before redistributing them on arriving at Harwich. For this to work, everyone must be able to recognise their own passport. This particular group were so far out of it that they didn't even know their own names, and subsequently presented the wrong ones to the customs. They were gibbering wrecks, unable to comprehend what the problem was.

One thick-set, dark-haired, olive-skinned Kiwi guy kept pointing back and forth at the open passport photo and back to his face as if to say, 'It's me, right?'

The photo he was pointing to was of a female with long blonde hair.

The ferry company had lined up transport from Harwich back to London. The rate we were charged was extortionate as it was a Sunday evening, and the bus company they'd approached had insisted on two security staff accompanying each bus due to our 'reputation'. There would also be a police escort from the port. We were made to feel like mafia bosses being taken to the Old Bailey, when they close all the roads and post snipers on the rooftops in case an escape attempt is planned. It was totally over the top and hysterical, but we had to accept it. The train wasn't an option, as they'd allegedly refused to take us as they couldn't source adequate transport police on a Sunday evening in November, as they had all worked extra shifts because it was a big football weekend.

*'When He opened the seventh seal, there was silence in heaven.'*
– Revelation 8:1

Security wouldn't allow music on the coaches. For once, no one cared. Everyone either snoozed or giggled their way back to Liverpool Street. As we disembarked, the drivers all expressed surprise at the politeness and good behaviour shown by the group.

To make matters worse, the coach company who deserted us had been in touch, warning them off the job. 'We wuz expecting a bleedin' riot, but they're all pussycats,' one driver told me.

The London based Aussie and Kiwi hard house crew may have all had eyes like saucers and bellyfulls of sweets, but they were well brought up, decent people and were always a pleasure to take anywhere and certainly didn't warrant the treatment from Nigel's coach company who shall remain nameless.

I finally got home around midnight, after just managing to catch the last train to Enfield Town at Seven Sisters. My wife had gone to Devon for the weekend, meaning the house was exactly as I'd left it on Friday. A half-drunk cup of coffee stood next to a dirty cereal bowl. A high tide of dehydrated Coco Pops clinging to the bowl, stranded like sailors clinging to a life raft. The local newspaper, littered with toast crumbs, lay open. I threw my holdall down and collapsed onto the chair, and resting my elbows on the table, held my head in my hands. I was staring at the horoscope page...

**Gemini** *(May 21 – June 20) Hold tight! With Mercury retrograde, expect crossed wires and confusion. Travel is on the horizon, so pack that bag! There are challenges ahead, but with a Leo's encouragement, you'll persevere and emerge stronger. Geminis are social butterflies remember, so use your wings! Wear yellow for luck. The number seven is significant.*

Henceforth 6 November is Leo Ringelberg Day; I watch Braveheart whilst eating Coco Pops (but pass on the Gabber).

---

### Top Tune: The Bells (Original Mix) – Jeff Mills {Purpose Maker}

---

## BEHIND THE BROCHURE

The sunset in San Antonio, Ibiza, is the most photographed and hyped nightfall anywhere on the planet. It has made the bar owners millionaires and is the reason why they can charge €40 for a Caesar salad. So, it's not surprisingly that it's on every Ibiza virgin's 'bucket list'.

I remember one newly arrived couple who told me how they'd sacrificed their first night out on the island in order to get to bed early. They rose at dawn and were thrilled to find Sunset Strip practically deserted, allowing them to get a front table on the terrace at Mambo – where they sat for two hours, facing the west, excitedly waiting to capture the iconic 'Ibiza sun over the ocean #livingthedream' shot to post on their socials.

Their tale culminated in the woman dismissively declaring, 'We can't see what all the fuss is about. When it did finally appear, it was from over the bloody building behind us, not the sea like we've seen in all the photos. Should we have come in June?'

# 13

# SHUDDERING HEIGHTS

'In the midst of winter, I found there was, within me, an
invincible summer.'

– Albert Camus

Like many in grey Britain, I dread the shorter days and
longer nights and spend hours wandering amongst skeletal
trees mourning the summer. As a kid I used to envy my pet
tortoise (which, along with racist jokes, celebrity paedophilia
and coronation chicken vol au vonts, were deemed acceptable
in the 1970s). In November, upon Blue Peter's command,
we'd put Fred away in a cardboard box with shredded newspaper and then wake him up around Valentine's day, when
Blue Peter woke Freda.

I knew that despite the sun being no hotter or the sky
bluer in Ibiza than it was in neighbouring Mallorca, when
it came to clubbers choosing where to spend their summer
holiday, Ibiza would always win hands down (or in the air,
to be more accurate). I felt it only a matter of time before
skiers and snowboarders would similarly select their winter
holiday destination based on the quality of music and venues
in a resort.

Having spent two winters as a singer and DJ in the lively Austrian resort of Mayrhofen, I had witnessed, first-hand, the energy and exuberance of partying surrounded by mountains and how après ski was, for many, as important as 'ski'.

So, when the familiar face of my former boss appeared at the guest-list window of Raindance's 'Indian Summer' party in autumn 1990, I was gobsmacked.

Owner of the Strass Hotel in Mayrhofen, Erich Roscher was in town to check on this new youth culture and what he saw that night, convinced him to build a venue beneath his car park. It would be the first club in Austria to showcase house music and host the next generation of superstar DJs and acts. As he told me at the time, 'Clubbing is massive and impossible to ignore – and will define the next decade. They rave back in England and want to rave on holiday, at the Arena they can do this every night!'

Erich invited me to come and see his vision; a split-level, state-of-the-art 1,500-capacity subterranean superclub in the snow. Roman pillars framed a central staircase which led to the dancefloor. With bars in each corner, a VIP cocktail bar above the stage and a DJ booth boasting more technology than the bridge of the Starship Enterprise. The Arena was to alpine raving what the Grand Ol' Opry was to country music.

It's a bluebird day in early January. I'm in a cable car with John Digweed, Crescendo's Jon Crosse (Are You Out There?), Guru Josh and Bill (aka Altern 8's robot). The robot is on stilts and the local's eyes are on stalks.

The previous day we walked around the medieval centre of Innsbruck where Bill's twelve-foot metallic laser-firing creation stopped the traffic and caused an old lady to faint, believing aliens had landed and were there to steal her schnitzels.

My Mixmag feature in Jan '91 led to interest from the anarchic TV show, 'The Word,' which was hugely popular at the time, going out live every Friday evening on Channel 4.

As it was The Arena's official opening party some of us decided to celebrate by dropping a cheeky half, minutes before the live interview was due to take place, to ensure we wouldn't be in full gurn mode when the cameras were on us. Then the Location Producer took a call on his walkie talkie. Presenter Katie Puckrick had slipped on the ice making her way across the frozen car park to where we were filming and had to return to her room to change her clothes as she'd fallen into a dirty, slushy puddle.

The satellite link was rebooked for fifteen minutes later... by which time our eyes were the size of saucers and we were chewing gum for Great Britain.

The interviews were conducted at the speed of light by a flame-haired Katie wearing what looked like a Friesen cow amidst a crowd of jiggling, shimmering and shuffling ravers who were clearly under the effects of more than just glühwein. So many people saw that interview that I began to wonder if anyone in the UK was watching anything else that night. If it was on any other programme I'm sure there may have been more press interest, but The Word was known for controversial content, and so by the next week it was forgotten... with no evidence cropping up on YouTube either, which is probably a blessing.

The Arena's first season was a huge success with a different show every week gleaned from my list of contacts in London. Dancers from the Hippodrome, angle-grinding fire breathers from the Camden Palace and PAs like Maxine Harvey who sang on the KLF hits and Eurovision scouse songbird, Sonia.

## Maxi on the Mountain

Some years later I found myself back in the Alps. This led to me being asked by the Mayrhofen Tourist Board (TVB) to programme a mountain-top concert in 1997.

They'd seen how high-profile annual end-of-season shows took place in Solden. But whereas Solden had a budget bigger than the Matterhorn and could afford Elton John, Tina Turner and Robbie Williams – I had a somewhat smaller budget and had to follow a brief which was one act to appeal to the youngsters and one for the oldies.

I thought Faithless would be perfect, and mentioned it to Jamie Cato when I interviewed him a few days later in London. He was intrigued by the prospect of playing at the top of the mountain and as luck would have it, on the date the show was scheduled, they had a rest day between Munich and Milan shows. To drive from Munich to Italy, you go through the Alps, meaning Mayrhofen was en route – result!

After engaging my mate Neil O'Brien to deliver what remained of ELO for the oldies, I focused on the mountain top show, which involved building a festival mainstage at the top of a mountain, which in winter is only accessible by helicopter or cable car.

The weather on the morning of the show was stunning. Sun-kissed 'chocolate box' peaks against a clear blue sky. Not a breath of wind. I pulled on a T-shirt and board shorts and bounded downstairs... where I met David 'Jurgen' Stock, who was a double World Champion paraglider at the time. I pointed to the bluebird sky and smiled.

He looked at me ruefully. 'Now, yes, but later, no.'

This wasn't good news. As anyone who's ever spent time in an Alpine resort knows, the weather is the number one topic of conversation. Will it snow? If so, how much? For how long? To what level? As paraglider pilots only fly when the weather is benign, they have the most up-to-date info and a local knowledge of the mountains and microclimate in each valley. So, if you want to know what the weather's going to do, ask a paraglider pilot – and like the pope and Roy Keane, Jurgen was never wrong.

Sure enough, the pale blue sky grew paler, gradually turning milky white, before the mountain tops disappeared in a veil of dark grey. An hour later a blizzard was raging. Snow stung my eyes and tickled my nose as I emerged from the top station of the Penkenbahn, ushering the shivering band into the caterpillar-tracked piste bulldozers which would transport them the few hundred metres to the stage.

Through the snow I could just make out a red LCD sign mounted on the wall of the lift station. *-5 grad,* then *-6 grad,* before dropping to *-7 grad.* Despite the atrocious weather there were still around a thousand people gathered. But then the wind changed direction, and the entire stage moved like it was thinking about taking off. Instructions were swiftly issued to remove the backdrop, which was acting like an envelope, trapping the air and extra anchorage was added to weigh the structure down.

I reassured Jamie everything was fine, and lent my hat to a shivering Sister Bliss. But it was Maxi Jazz I was most concerned about, wearing only a thin Harrington lightweight jacket and no hat or gloves, he was clearly suffering. Insomnia was the least of his problems; he was on the verge of hypothermia. After three songs I decided to act, grabbing a tray from the Pilz Bar, and filling it with six glasses of Jagartee – 'hunters tea'; a hot brew which contains tea, inlander rum and schnapps. It's the best winter warmer I know... but very strong.

When the song ended, I caught Maxi's eye and gave him the tray, telling him to pass it round to everyone. Five songs later I repeated the exercise, but also gave them a Schnapps. I can close my eyes now and see Maxi standing centre-stage, hands cupped around the mug of Jagartee, smiling benevolently as the nectar worked its magic and saved the day!

After the show in the SMT ski school kindergarten room which doubled as a dressing room, I joined the Burgermeister, the head of the tourist board, the town's most senior policeman, the boss of the cable car company and the band around a large table and waited for the warmth to return to our extremities, cradling mugs of hot chocolate while snuggling up against the radiator on the wall.

I caught the eye of the boss of the ski school, whose room we were in and ordered another five ruby red steaming mugs, which I delivered on a tray.

Maxi sipped it and exhaled sharply. 'What IS this stuff, man?'

I explained and he took another approving sip. 'It's liquid Ganga!'

I could see a joint was being passed around between the band. It gradually got closer and closer and was now in Maxi's mouth. Weed has never been my thing and as I never smoked, except on special occasions, I wasn't particularly desperate for a drag, but the fact the great and the good were stood in the room and unable to do anything about the joint which was being smoked in their presence was too much of a temptation to resist – besides which, I'd worked bloody hard on the show, been through hell with the weather, and was not going to pass up the opportunity of sharing a spliff with the sunken eyed holyman MC Maxi Jazz – one cool Buddhist (when he wasn't tearing off tights with his teeth).

So, when it was offered from the left-hand side (as is tradition according to *the Gospel of Musical Youth*), I accepted, inhaled and passed it on. At this point, the VIPs walked out and a few minutes later, I was asked to join them in a room next door.

Here we go. Having delivered a top band to their resort and keeping them in drinks from my own pocket, I was now for the high jump for a few puffs of weed, offered by the artist.

I walked into the room, and they were all sitting down, real formal-like. It felt like a hearing. I was asked to sit down in front of them. The boss of the Tourist Board stood up and cleared her throat, while the others watched me intently.

'On behalf of the Tourist Board, the Chamber of Commerce and townsfolk of Mayrhofen, I'd like to present you with the Silver Award for Tourism.' She handed me a large silver certificate and a cut-glass Schnapps decanter and six beautifully etched shot glasses.

'Really? I thought you were going to talk to me about smoking a joint with the band.'

She paused before continuing, 'We weren't... erm... aware of that. It's great how you relate and interact with them, culturally. We appreciate that this has given us the possibility for today's show, many thanks.'

A few months later, Jamie sent me a copy of their next album. The sleeve notes read, 'The last twelve months has seen us play seventy-eight shows in twenty-three countries. We've played in festivals, stadiums, arenas, theatres, clubs and even at the top of a mountain in Austria!'

> **Top Tune: Insomnia – Faithless (Monster Mix)**
> **{Arista}**

## BEHIND THE BROCHURE

Lunchtime on the first day of a dance music radio station's ski holiday. I was having a beer with some of my local mates in a mountain top bar, when a popular ski instructor's class filed through the door.

'How was your lesson,' I asked an attractive blonde girl, who'd just placed her helmet on the barstool next to me.

She looked at my lanyard and recognised me, probably from the welcome meeting. 'You're the bloke running this, right?'

'Yes, it's all my fault!' I grinned cheesily, holding my hands up in a surrender gesture. But she didn't smile.

'Good, can you come with me please?'

She asked me to join a group of frowning girls who were huddled outside the bar.

'We want to make a complaint about our instructor,' declared one.

'Yes, he's out of order!' interjected another

'Who is your instructor?' I asked with trepidation, despite already knowing the answer.

'That Austrian guy over there.'

She pointed to my mate Mike. Spotting me across the bar he waved and flashed a smile.

I drew the girls closer and asked them to describe very clearly what he'd done to warrant their wrath.

'Well, we were on the chairlift about twenty minutes ago,

and he said we were going to do one more run and then all take all our clothes off.'

'Sorry? Are you sure?'

Another girl jumped in. 'Yes we are! I heard him too. He was sitting on the chairlift with three of us, he said he was sure we were all going to get "totally naked" after one more run. It's disgusting. We want to change instructors.'

'Yes – and report him for sexual harassment,' added another.

The sponsors were also in the bar and had overheard everything. This was serious.

My head was spinning, Mike was a good instructor and someone I'd known for fifteen years. Whilst I was aware he had always been popular with my female guests, there had never been any unwanted advances made, or any complaints raised.

I walked over and asked him for a word in private. When we were outside, I asked him what he'd said on the chairlift to my guests.

He thought for a while, looked confused and then recalled the conversation.

'One of them, Nina, the one in white, asked how long to go before lunch as we'd been riding hard all morning, and I could see they were tired. So, I told them, "We make one more run and for sure you will all get totally naked".'

'Hmmm… and what did they say to that, Mike?'

'The fat one on the end said, "Speak for yourself. Not me!"'

'I told her the run was a black, and that by the time she finished the next run, for sure she would be completely naked, one hundred per cent.'

I thought for a while, then looked at him.

'Mike, I think you may have meant to say "knackered"…'

# 14

# DESTINATION: IBIZA!

Having been banned from Hamburg, I felt it was time to introduce my Aussie, Kiwi and Saffa mates to Ibiza.

June 2001: Destination: Ibiza! featured the leading 'down-underground' London club nights Fevah and Frantic and was the first package holiday (or 'tour' as those from down under called them), to the white isle tailored specifically for Aussie clubbers.[5] Traditionally, they'd be taken to the running of the bulls at Pamplona or Oktoberfest. But I figured they were ready for Ibiza. And I wasn't wrong.

This group helped me redefine the clubbing holiday package. Along with return flight and transfer, seven nights of accommodation, an outdoor foam party at Kanya and a club pass, we also included a free breakfast. At the end of the week Johnny from our host hotel the Florencio was sitting on over a thousand uneaten sausages as no one had turned up.

'Maybe give them to homeless charities or the hospital?' I suggested.

---

5. Not including the ground breaking Special Branch clubbing packages Nicky Holloway put together from 1986 which were the first Ibiza clubbing packages.

Uncomfortably, he explained, 'The Spanish people will not eat them... even the homeless. They call them "dedos de las lepras" ...leper's fingers.'

We included clubs in the package and gave everyone an event wristband. It was the best aspects of a package holiday; affordably priced with everyone in the same hotel and a rep on hand for when the shit inevitably hits the fan, but without the cringey stuff; welcome meetings, cheeky chappie, clean-cut reps in uniforms upselling over-priced excursions and promoting parties which weren't the best, but which gave them the biggest kickbacks... following the Ten Commandments of Clubbing Holidays I'd written down back in 1997.

I was aware that even though the clubs didn't open until midnight, no one would arrive for another hour or two. I spotted an opportunity. I had DJs who, although were capable of playing these booths, were never likely to land a booking there. I also had a large group who were used to going out at 10 p.m. and who were more interested in hitting the floor, rather than arriving fashionably late. They were also familiar and comfortable with being taken by bus around their itinerary, meaning I could confidently guarantee the venue large numbers of people at a specific time. This, in turn, allowed me to ask for a generous group ticket price whilst justifying my request that my own DJs played the opening sets. Whilst this model worked for the venue and promoter, it also benefited the product; I could include a number of clubs in the package and in return for booking the package and bringing their mates, could offer my DJs the opportunity to be heard in some of the best clubs on the planet.

We didn't know it at the time, but this was an early example of affiliate partner marketing.

There was still the element of quality control to navigate. The first set was supposed to be a warm-up and the all-important second set also required brakes applying as this is when the tempo shifts and paves the way for the following name DJ. Whilst most DJs followed the script, there was invariably one each week who couldn't resist bangin' out anthems to his mates on the dance floor. In principle there's nothing wrong with this – unless it's twenty past midnight, which it usually was. As a result, I had to vet the DJs who played, and in the case of the more discerning nights like Cream Ibiza, send a mix from those I was putting forward to play. After a few years I was trusted to choose the right people for the job, and looking back, this has been the most satisfying aspect of my contribution to clubbing travel. To watch damn good DJs, get the chance to show what they can do in Pacha, Amnesia, Space or Privilege was a joy; they never let me down, and would find me afterwards and hug me, cry, or tell me it was the best day of their life. It was a sweet reward and gave me the incentive to persevere with this unique aspect of my Ibiza packages.

This altruistic aspect to Radical Escapes was what set us apart from every other bandwagon jumper. I had to fight for those slots like they were for my own sons. Ibiza is a challenging place to work. Everyone's out for themselves and looking after number one. What they'll agree in May and confirm in an email in June, will, by late June, have changed. I had to use every tool in my box to hold the venues to the deals they'd agreed when their pockets were empty in May, and I transferred the cash for 400 tickets.

This model was revolutionary at the time and was based on an awareness that clubbers aren't stupid and deserve better, coupled with a desire to show the best of the island to people, so that they'd return and spread the word.

But it couldn't have started any worse. Ibiza has legal crackdowns like kids have playground crazes. Things which have gone on unnoticed for years are suddenly deemed forbidden – with a gusto usually reserved for cop killers.

So, it was just my luck that unknown to me, the authorities chose the day of arrivals for Destination Ibiza – when Radical Escapes would be welcoming its first ever guests from Fevah and Frantic to the island – as the time to clamp down on unlicensed taxi drivers at the airport, issuing on-the-spot fines of €5,000. As my guests excitedly emerged from the baggage carousels into the arrivals hall, following instructions to 'look for the Ibizan Heat signs', I was being held against a wall by two people in uniforms and hi-vis vests, who'd confiscated the *Ibizan Heat* sign I was holding up on a clipboard, who were formally charging me with being an illegal taxi driver. This was so embarrassing. In full view of my guests, it looked like I was being arrested.

My Spanish was limited to a handful of useful phrases, but 'I'm not a fucking taxi driver, you jumped-up jobsworths. If you don't believe me, there's four coaches waiting outside' wasn't one of them.

Eventually Juan, one of the bus drivers, a six-foot Celtic warrior from Galicia, with long ginger hair and a short temper wandered into the terminal building and saw what was happening. He strode over and began castigating the officials holding me. They immediately released me, and I began loading the buses. I thanked Juan for telling the police that I was a bona fide tour operator. He laughed. 'I told them that Celta (Vigo) are on TV in an hour and if I missed it I would eat their balls!'

'Wow! That's some way to talk to the police, Juan.'

He roared with laughter. 'La policia? No, funcionario del consejo.'

It turned out they were only jobsworths from the local council!

Hundreds of hard house loving, hard partying, fluoro-friendly antipodeans who drank the bars dry wherever they went hit the island like a dose of smelling salts. Although things got inevitably messy, there was never any trouble; this was a crowd who could hold their drink – and whatever else they swallowed.

As there was no template for a group holiday orientated around the music, rather than getting pissed, laid, or lining the pockets of the reps, we made it up as we went along. I hired the boats for eight hours rather than the three which is the norm these days. We'd board at 1 p.m., cruise briskly across to the unspoilt island of Formentera, where we'd spend the afternoon. Formentera is considered upmarket: Ibiza's chic little sister. Ses Illetes is where Barcelona footballers moor their yachts and millionaires eat lunch. The Spanish Royal family owned the only house on the neighbouring isle of Es Palmador. The beach is very popular with celebrities. They'd never seen anything like it when one hundred and fifty hard house loving Aussies rocked up on the glass bottomed boat! Italians in budgie smugglers stood with hands on hips as we trooped onto the white sand, their exclusive turquoise paradise stained by Stussy boardie's and Frantic T-shirts. They really weren't happy at the exclusivity being ecstatically enhanced by the great unwashed masses from Ibiza.

By the following year they'd stopped party boats docking in Formentera altogether, but my antipodean friends grew up in water, and after a chat with the captain, it emerged we could stop at a small rocky outcrop 100 metres from the beach, which wasn't technically Formentera. So we waded in, holding our valuables over our heads as the water was only chest deep. Once again, the lobster loving French and Italians shook their heads at the hoi polloi walking ashore. The following year, I learnt they'd put a stop to that also, and imposed a 500-metre exclusion zone for party boats.

'No worries, we'll swim in,' was the response when I broke it to my group. I couldn't resist a wind-up. I called Juan y Andrea to reserve tables for fifty-two people who would be arriving from Ibiza the following day on a party boat.

'No permission for party boats,' the maître d snapped.

'We'll be docking outside the exclusion zone and swimming in,' I breezily replied.

'It's 500 metres offshore. Who are they, the Australian Olympic Swimming team?' he scoffed.

'Yes - and a few divers from South Africa.'

This was only the start of the war on party boats which for many visitors, is the highlight of their week: cruising around the spectacular South West coast of the island in crystal clear waters, with DJs playing and drinks at sensible prices. Sometimes dolphins swim alongside, attracted by the vibration of the engine and undulating throbbing house basslines. On a few occasions, I've even seen flying fish pierce the surface, extend their 'wings', glide for up to five seconds before disappearing once again, piercing the surface. The rise in popularity of the party boats proved problematic for the superclubs, who resent anyone spending their money anywhere else except their discotheques.

As I was forbidden from docking in Formentera, I needed

to find somewhere else, and one blissful early May morning, I went exploring on my trusty white Vespa, discovering coves and beaches I'd never been to before. Spotting a wooden jetty on an unfashionable side cove near Cala Tarida, I stopped, jerked the scooter back onto its stand and walked into the nearest restaurant. It was a humble family-owned concern. Twenty minutes later, I'd got a new shore leave destination and the legendary Ibizan Heat all-day boat party was back on.

As we pulled into the cove, the music subsided and after docking at the jetty, 250 of us filed into the restaurant.

We stayed there for four hours, a few ate lunch, some played volleyball, some swam, and others sat in the pool in plastic chairs keeping cool as our DJs played on the terrace, before we left and headed for Es Vedra and Atlantis. It was a resounding success.

## Macey's Missed Departure

There's always ten per cent no-shows for boat parties; people overdo it the night previously or don't fancy a day on the ocean. Even though the departure time is 1 p.m., some will inevitably sleep in having only hit the sack a few hours earlier. One year we were serenely sliding out of the harbour when Damo approached me with a panicked expression. 'Macey isn't here!'

'I can't knock on everyone's door, mate. Did he say he was definitely coming?'

Damo stared at me intensely. His blue eyes wide and piercing. 'Oh, he was coming for sure, lots of people are waiting for him.'

Just then my mobile rang. It was Macey telling me he'd just woken up and was asking if we'd left. I told him we had.

'Aw, fack, I'll have to rendezvous on that island we go to, how do I get there?'

I told him to forget it as it was quite a schlep and not cheap, involving a cab ride to the Ibiza town port, jumping on a ferry to Formentera and then getting a cab to Ses Illetes, where he'd have to walk to whichever restaurant we were eating at. And even then he may not get there on time to make it before we left Formentera for the return leg.

'I'll throw some clothes on and leave now,' was his response. I bid him godspeed and finished the call, only to look up to see a group of guests stood around me hanging on every word. I knew Macey was popular, and thought it was nice to see his absence was being felt.

The outbound journey wasn't as wild as it usually was, which I put down to the searing heat and people's tiredness. Every twenty minutes someone would ask for an update on his progress. I was imparting information to Macey in a series of calls as back then Lord Macey was in a somewhat cognitively challenged state which rendered him incapable of taking in more than one instruction at a time.

'I'm at the cab rank, where do I go?'

'The port.'

'In San An?'

'No, the port in Ibiza town.'

Twenty minutes later my phone rang again.

'I'm at the port, which ferry do I take? Denia?'

'No! That's mainland Spain. Take Formentera.'

Thirty minutes later my phone rang once more.

'I'm on Formentera, where the fack are you?'

'In Juan y Andrea, in Ses Illetas. Get a cab.'

'Where?'

'To Ses Illetes. Just ask the driver for "Sez Eeyetis".'

Ten minutes later my phone rang a third time.

'I'm at that place you said. Where the fack are you?'

'At the restaurant with the yellow Pacha flags.'

I didn't realise that ALL the restaurants on that beach flew Pacha flags.

It was 4 p.m., and there was still no sign of Macey. He was on the island somewhere, desperately looking for the restaurant we were in. People crowded around me like they do a transistor radio in a tight Test Match on the fifth day. I was talking to Macey, giving him directions, guiding him in like an amphetamine-fuelled air strike.

BOOOOOOORRRRRRR!

The captain sounded the ship's horn; the signal for us to reboard for the return leg to Ibiza. Then my Ericsson P900 flip-phone died.

All around me, people sank to their knees. A collective groan rose like a cloud of disappointment and hung in the sultry air. I felt somehow responsible. 'I... I did everything I could for him,' I blurted.

A girl embraced me. 'I know, we all saw you did your best. You couldn't have done any more.'

It felt like a death in the family.

People began to trudge down the beach to the waiting party boat.

'Wait! Who's that?' someone loudly exclaimed, pointing to the brow of the hill behind the beach. We stopped and turned around, peering into the sun. Through the shimmering heatwaves something pierced the horizon. We stood in silence. Could it be...? No one moved as the shape grew bigger, first a wide-brimmed hat, then a brightly coloured coat which billowed in the breeze. A silhouetted figure came over the ridge. There, like a fluoro galleon, all guns blazing, was Macey; slight but formidable, like a cyber Lee van Cleef bringing salvation and goodness knows what else.

A spontaneous cheer went up. The sort you hear in public squares when England score a World Cup goal. It blasted the cloud of dismay and alerted the restaurant management who urgently dispatched the in-house paparazzi to check which world-famous celebrity was responsible for causing such a commotion.

The journey back was much livelier than the outbound leg. I made a special announcement welcoming Macey, who I said was so keen to join us that he'd swum over from Ibiza to Formentera through shark-infested waters – a distance of twelve miles.

Inevitably, some addled souls believed this, and it only served to reinforce the regard he was held in, especially given that he'd done it in a purple fedora hat, long zebra-skin coat and clumpy platform trainers!

As we chugged serenely past the strange rock formations in the southwest of the island known as Atlantis, the whole boat was rocking with peak euphoria, mass hugging in the breakdowns and pumping arms in the drops: HMS Bliss with bells on. The captain looked at me knowingly. 'The coffee at Juan y Andrea must be strong, yes?'

On my recce trip the following May, I called on Pedro and Margarita to confirm my date for late June, but instead of being met with smiles as I expected after the success of the previous party there, instead I received frowns. The family told me that other groups had followed my lead, and the rival restaurant further up the beach had pressured the council who amended the licence to a café concerto classification, meaning no more than just sixty-eight people could be admitted. I could barely hear him as all around us staff jangled cutlery which was placed on crisp white tablecloths. At the far end of the room a muffled, dry repetitive, 'Uno, dos... Uno, dos,' indicated a sound check was underway.

'A show?' I asked.

'Banquette de Bodas – a wedding. 200 guests.'

'But your licence allows only sixty-eight people?'

'We can apply for wedding licenses, but no more than one each month.'

Placing my hand on his shoulder and with my most earnest expression I began my pitch. 'Pedro, in my group there's a boy and girl who get married the morning they fly to Ibiza at an office...'

'They get married in an office?' he replied. Catholicism runs deep in Spain, remember.

'Oficina, a registrar office. Not a church wedding.' Pedro made the sign of the cross for their lost souls.

'After the wedding, both they and over eighty of their friends will fly out to Ibiza. They've asked me to arrange a wedding reception for them, so I was looking for somewhere suitable. Could we do it here?'

He thought for a moment before beckoning Margarita over. She wore the garb of a fantasy sit-com waitress; tight white blouse and tighter black short skirt. Very Vicky Michelle in the Ibizan version of 'Allo Allo' ('Alioli, Alioli', perhaps).

After sharing an incompressible exchange, they appeared

to concur, nodding their agreement.

'Si, we try.'

A pen and notepad appeared. 'What are their names?'

'Their names?'

'We need their names to apply for the wedding licence,' he explained.

Oh shit, there weren't any names. I'd made the whole thing up.

'It's...Kylie.'

The sound of scribbling followed by the sound of silence.

'Si...'

'And, er, Jason.'

'Their full names?'

'Donovan and Minogue. Kylie Donovan and Jason Minogue.'

Miraculously, they submitted the names and received the licence, but were told to expect a visit from the local police who would be calling in to congratulate the bride and groom!

The June trip was acclaimed as a great success, so I decided to run another one in September. With my wife heavily pregnant and not in great health, I was the sole breadwinner and with a mortgage to pay on our first house there was a lot riding on my September trip. I'd put all my savings into the second instalment of *Destination Ibiza*: bought one hundred and fifty flight seats and hotel beds, paid a fifty per cent deposit on Manumission and Cream tickets and a holding deposit for the boat party. It was the biggest financial risk I'd ever taken – but it was a risk based on a proven product, and with my routes to market strong and established partners in Fevah and Frantic, I was confident I'd hit the numbers.

The highlight of the trip for the DJs was to play at Bora Bora. I mischievously told Eammon from Fevah that it was a themed day, and all the DJs would be playing in drag. Undeterred, Eammon played a blinder – dressed in a grass skirt and bikini!

As I mentioned earlier, a condition of getting an overdraft facility with the bank (essential in the travel industry as deposits have to be paid leading to cash flow issues) was to use my house as a guarantee if I defaulted. But with the trip almost sold out and less than a week away, the considerable money I'd put on the trip looked safe as houses – meaning my house was safe from HSBC. Or so I thought...

### Afterglow

Mo Chaudry left the party far too early in 2017. Ibiza is less exciting without him. He was a great ally and friend, and I was honoured to be asked to write his obituary for Mixmag. May he rest in peace.

> **Top Tune: Planet Funk – Chase The Sun (Extended Club Mix) {Bustin Loose Recordings}**

## BEHIND THE BROCHURE

I'd just collected the Cream tickets to distribute to my group from the promoter Mo Chaudry's villa in the hills near San Juan. I was riding down the bumpy country lane on my Vespa, my handset around my neck on a lanyard. I suddenly felt the scooter handlebars jolt. I'd hit an unmarked sleeping policeman which caused me to recoil like I'd fired a rifle, shaking my body, causing the phone to fall from its plastic casing onto the road. I braked to a halt and turned round... to see the dustbin lorry I'd passed a minute earlier run over my handset. The dust settled, exposing broken blue plastic shards scattered across the road. This was a disaster; without my phone I couldn't operate. In these pre-internet days, it was the only way of communicating with the venues and buses, and was the emergency number for my guests. I was fucked, basically.

I stood there holding the bare metallic unit like a clumsily dropped wrap retrieved from a toilet, examining the damage and mourning my loss amidst a loud chorus of cicadas. I didn't know where my tinnitus ended, and the insects began. Then, miraculously, the cell started vibrating! The glass screen, which although scratched was still intact, showed the word DAMO. I couldn't answer it as the keyboard was smashed to smithereens around my feet, but within half an hour I'd bought another casing from the phone shop and was back in business... and playing Snake2!

So, hail the Toyota Hilux of handsets: the indestructible 3310!

Black box flight recorders are more fragile. If only Nokia made hearts...

# 15

# THE PARTY AT THE END
# OF THE WORLD

*'Earth-shaking flames from the world's centre roar /*
*And make the earth around a New City quiver.'*
— Nostradamus, Centuries, quatrain 187

By early August I was well on my way to a sellout of my Destination Ibiza Closing Parties package. We only had five seats left to sell. I recall they were bought by someone in an 'internet café', which were springing up in high streets at the time offering access to the ever-expanding menu of coffees with Italian names and the 'information superhighway' which people were saying would change every aspect of life, including how people booked their holidays.

Around the same time my remaining five flight seats were snapped up, a young Egyptian guy also bought five seats on an American Airlines flight from Boston to New York in another internet café in Las Vegas.

SEPTEMBER 11, 2001: the trip was four days away.

I came downstairs, boiled the kettle, buttered some toast, and went back upstairs to my small office to check if I'd received any new email messages, which were becoming ever more frequent. Most days I had one. Usually something from AOL or an offer of virus software, but increasingly someone I knew would contact me and tell me they were now online!

I then got to work. After writing the welcome letter and allocating the DJ set lists for the week, I broke for lunch. That afternoon I had to go into the West End for a meeting with Adam Lockhart from Ministry of Sound to discuss a ski product for their new *Clubbers Guide to...* brand, and was preparing a PowerPoint presentation in my office. My wife Catherine suddenly appeared at the door frame, her expression serious. 'You'd better come down and watch this...'

We stood and stared in silence at the TV. Something was happening in New York. Smoke spiralled spoiling an otherwise perfect blue sky. Over the next few hours, I watched open-mouthed, yet speechless, as the biggest news event in my lifetime so far dominated all channels.

The Egyptian guy who'd booked those five seats a few weeks earlier wasn't using any of them. At 8.46 a.m. he was sitting in the pilot's seat when it hit the north tower of the World Trade Centre.

First there was one, then two, then three and then four planes involved. They closed the skies. I thought it was a temporary thing, but twenty-four hours later no white lines scarred the empty hazy sky above my back garden. No jets circled above Enfield waiting to land at Heathrow. All was quiet. And as they say in cowboy films when the distant drums cease their throb, it wasn't just quiet, it was too quiet...

I couldn't sleep. I lay awake staring at the ceiling as my wife slept soundly beside me, blissfully unaware I'd put the house as guarantee for my business loan. How long would this go on for ?

I had all my money tied up in flight seats and hotel beds. Without the former, the latter were useless. A quick call to the hotels informed us that there would be no refund, as the hotels were still open, and the beds were being held as we'd requested. The fact there were no planes to get people there didn't seem to be of any relevance!

I suggested moving the booking to the following week, but this was impossible as the beds were reserved for other guests.

My booking agent Nick Cade called to inform me that ATOL, who issue licences to tour operators to sell flight seats had informed him they'd received no indication from the CAA (Civil Aviation Authority) when the skies would reopen. This was unprecedented. Understandably our guests were contacting Nick to ask if the holiday was going ahead, and if it wasn't, were requesting refunds.

In travel its always the things you can't control which fuck you up. This was another example. In the aftermath of 9/11, as Manhattan smouldered and blame was laid which would forge foreign policy for the foreseeable future, as Osama Bin Laden emerged as the Big Bad Wolf, and any questioning of how on Earth Tower 7 fell were dismissed as unpatriotic, my 150 flight seats paled into insignificance. Strangely, Tony Blair failed to mention them when he hot-footed over to the Ground Zero as it was now known for a photo opportunity. Similarly, George Bush, full of righteous revenge 'n' retribution, was so preoccupied with 'smokin' 'em out', that he failed to confirm if we'd get to Ibiza in time for We Love… Sundays at Space. It was almost as if he didn't care that David Morales *and* Carl Cox were playing.

Surely BBC2's *Newsnight*, which could usually be relied

on to uncover the story behind the headlines, would mention my precarious financial predicament? But despite devoting an entire show to the attacks on the World Trade Centre, they too failed to recognise the impact it was having on my closing parties' holiday.

Almost 3,000 innocent people lost their lives on that morning, many thousands more would develop respiratory problems[6]. Geopolitically, the Earth shifted on its axis, yet the most important thing to me was whether my trip to Ibiza was going to happen. Nature is a healer and so I went for a walk around Forty Hall in Enfield, where Greater London meets the countryside, and beneath the empty skies reproached myself for being so selfish. People had been vaporised, leaving no body to bury or remains to pay final respects to.

I felt selfish and shallow. It's an inconvenient truth that we really only care what happens in the world if it directly affects us in a negative way.

As regards travel, the sky would never be as blue again as it was when dawn broke over Manhattan on the morning of September 11. It was year zero for the industry. Things we'd taken for granted like taking liquid on planes, going to the cockpit to chat to the pilot, and waiting on the tarmac to board a plane were no more.

Looking back, it was the end of an age of relative innocence and the start of a new darker era. The time before it now seems carefree and almost naive by comparison. Since 9/11 (as the North Americans call it – and let's face it, it was their baby to christen, both in terms of conception and birth), the world has

---

6. An estimated 400,000 people were exposed to 9/11 toxic dust in the aftermath of the attacks,

been a different place: wars, regime change, terrorism, pandemics and increased surveillance are the legacy of that morning.

FRIDAY 14 SEPT. Civilian flights resumed… but all the aircraft were in the wrong places, and the airline couldn't guarantee any flight for the following thirty-six hours. People were told not to turn up to the airport unless their journey was 'absolutely necessary'. All this information we passed onto our guests, prompting the response, 'Going to Ibiza IS absolutely necessary!'

Furthermore, in the event terrorist activity increased, they offered no guarantee we'd be able to get back. If anyone still harboured any doubts about whether to go to Ibiza, this dispelled them. The prospect of being stranded in Ibiza at the airline's expense was the clincher.

FRIDAY 15 SEPT: British Airways announced they were resuming flights from Gatwick and Heathrow, albeit subject to long delays. Nick called each group leader and warned them that they would probably get to Ibiza, but we didn't know when, and that they may not get back when they expected to. This gave the package holiday an element of adventure and risk.

All Aussies and Kiwi's love risk. They grow up with it. At the beach they can get eaten by sharks. In their gardens they can get bitten by snakes. When they use an outside toilet, they run the risk of being lethally poisoned by spiders. Even a Sunday afternoon drive in the country can be life threatening if they run out of fuel. If the snakes, spiders, or crocodiles don't kill them, the weather most certainly will.

Come to think about it, they go out of their way to embrace risk. Their version of football involves more violence than is good for an unprotected scrotum, and their idea of a city break involves being pelted with tomatoes or being pierced by the horns of a bull. Not content with admiring the view from a bridge, antipodeans aren't happy unless they've jumped off it on the end of a large rubber band. This is the part of the World who invented bungee jumping, remember.

So, telling an Aussie they may get stranded in Ibiza was the best marketing angle I've ever come across! Suddenly it was potentially hazardous and there was a sense of unpredictability. What was previously a holiday, was now an adventure.

We gave people the option to cancel but were reassured by the promoters that no one would. They were right. Not one person asked for a refund -in fact, others even called up wanting to book the trip! Everyone wanted to be at the party at the end of the world it seemed.

As I arrived at Gatwick I was aghast to see tanks parked outside. Soldiers were everywhere. Those who'd booked were told to turn up four hours before the departure time to allow for the new security checks which had been brought in. From this point on, all hand baggage would be scanned, and passport details provided to the airline in advance.

The flight to Ibiza was due to depart at 10.40 p.m. on Saturday. The screens simply read 'DELAYED, AWAIT FURTHER INFO.' At midnight they surprisingly closed the cafes and bars, even though the place was heaving with passengers. My guests had already bought enough beer to see them through the next few hours, and more importantly the electricity supply was still on, allowing the boombox stereo one of them had brought to pump out sounds long into the night. Just as importantly, the water in the toilets was both cold and free, an increasing rarity in turn-of-the-century London, as unscrupulous venues realised the preferred beverage of those on pills was water, turned the cold water taps off. Additionally, the presence of a raver-friendly vending machine selling snacks including chewing gum and Ribena meant the party had everything it needed to flourish. And flourish it did! People danced on tables, arms in the air like they were at the Astoria or Camden Palace rather than Gatwick South. Bemused military police toting sub-machine guns stood close by in two's, yawning as the late night dissolved into early morning, driven by the BOMP! BOMP! BOMP! of hard house.

The departure boards kept blinking their instructions to wait, so after issuing my sleep averse assistant Macey instructions for me to be woken should they announce the departure, I decided to get some sleep. I inserted a couple of foam earplugs and strapped on an eye mask I'd bought from Boots earlier. Occasionally, I'd wake from my slumber, lift the eye mask to see the silhouettes of my group, fist pumping and shimmering in the half-light beyond the balcony on the upper level, before turning over to get more shuteye.

At around 0330 I was roughly prodded awake, and pulled up my eye mask to see the black shiny barrel of a sub-machine gun and bullet proof vest. The fella was talking to me, but I couldn't understand what he was saying. He gestured to my ears. I removed the plugs and sat up.

'I understand you are the group leader of the group having a party. If you are, please do us all a favour and tell them to turn the music off, as their flight to Ibiza is thankfully ready to commence boarding.'

'Hasn't it been announced?'

'They can't hear the announcement because the music is too loud and when we tell them, they just shake our hands and continue dancing.'

It's never an easy job stopping a party. There's an unwritten rule that DJs will play until they're unplugged. It's a pain in the arse as it means I've got to play the party pooper. However, this was one occasion where I had a very good reason to stop the music and one which would be acceptable to those partying – or so I hoped

I walked upstairs to find the party in full swing; sweat-soaked T-shirts clung to saucer-eyed table dancers, girls sat on the floor next to the soft drinks vending machine, one massaging the other's hands, causing the recipient's head to sway, eyes closed in bliss. Clearly the holiday had already started.

I located the stereo which vibrated on a small round table, but rather than hit the OFF button, slowly turned down the volume. As Steve Thomas's mix of Bells and Revolution subsided, it was replaced by a chorus of jeers.

I took a deep breath and said, 'Ladies and gentlemen, your flight to Ibiza is now ready for boarding.' The jeers turned to cheers. I walked through the crowd to recover my hand luggage downstairs. But as I reached the top of the stairs, the music suddenly started up again. People dropped their bags and ran back to the party. I was incredulous and stormed back upstairs to the stereo to find the gangly frame of Skol stood over the stereo, tweaking the bass.

'What the fuck?' I exclaimed, exasperated.

Aaron Feveh stepped between us like a UN peacekeeper, with his hands in 'surrender' mode and pleaded, 'One more tune, pal?'

Twenty minutes later we'd taken off and finally were on our way to Ibiza! As we left the ground, I breathed a huge sigh of relief. No matter what happened now, I'd deliver the trip and my business would survive. The cheer when the plane touched the tarmac in Ibiza was never as loud as it was the morning of Sunday 16 September 2001. We landed over five hours late, yet no one complained – even when the bus taking us from the airport to the resort broke down in the middle of the countryside and we had to wait for another to be sent out to rescue us. It all added to the sense of uncertainty, and only amplified the sense of achievement when we finally took a first sip of San Miguel at Kanya a few hours later. If you've ever seen the movie *Ice Cold in Alex* you'll get the picture. If you haven't, Youtube it.

On the last night, I'd usually invite the promoters out to whichever club they wanted to go as my guests: Pacha, El Divino, Privilege, Amnesia, wherever they chose they wanted I'd sort out the guestlist. Fevah promoter Wayne Hart chose to go to The Blue Rose, the island's premier strip club which was in Figuretas. So, I obliged. As it was late season and the night of the Cream closing party, we were the only ones there. I'd also put us on the door at Amnesia, but the lads wouldn't leave the Blue Rose, and as the guestlist closed at 1.30 a.m., I told them they'd missed their chance to witness the sheer *sweat*actle of Cream's curtain closure. But I was wrong. At 4 a.m., when the Blue Rose closed, the girls invited us all to join them in Amnesia, and we waltzed through the doors with a girl on each arm after one of the door staff mistook me for the owner's son!

Another memory from that trip was the VIP area at Manumission with Wayne Hart and Fevah resident Riksta, when I bumped into Paul Oakenfold's wife Angela, who I used to keep a protective eye on when she was his teenage girlfriend and used to sit alone at the bar, waiting for Paul to finish his residency at my club Flirt! back in the early '90s. She recognised me and walked over to our booth with a striking blonde lady who I recognised as, the model, aristocrat, and socialite Lady Victoria Hervey. Riksta immediately turned on the charm, telling her how he was a DJ and had a new record out called 'Don't Touch Me'. His pitch ended with an offer to put them both on his guestlist at Fevah's show at The Tube, just behind the Astoria that Sunday. She politely declined saying she had a prior engagement at the Italian Grand Prix as a guest of Ferrari. Angela demurely wished him well with his record and his DJing.

Never knowing when he was beaten (which wasn't often, to be fair), the boyish shock of bleached hair made one last pitch, 'Maybe the following week, eh?'

Afterwards he was mortified when I told him he'd been talking to Paul Oakenfold's wife girlfriend and urged me to keep it to myself, which of course I agreed to do unless I ever wrote a book...

World War Three never broke out that week, and we all got back when they said we would – which some of those who attended were quite disappointed about, as I recall.

Well, I say all of us. One lad didn't make it home with us. He was staying in the Hostal Valencia and like many Ibiza virgins, struggled to find their way back to their hotel in the early hours. I'll regularly come across them as I walk home, they stand puzzled in the middle of a junction. I'll ask them where they are staying. 'Well, it's a big white building with balconies,' they'll almost always reply.

Back to my guest. On the fateful night he disappeared, the fella in question had taken a water taxi across San Antonio bay to meet some mates in a club there. Returning to San Antonio town in a cab at 5 a.m. for a few pints at The Ship... which he stumbled out of an hour later. In his addled state, he'd forgotten he'd returned to San An, and thought he had to get the water taxi back over the bay. He turned up at the port with no shoes and socks and approached what he thought was a water taxi telling them he was lost and had no money.

They asked him where he wanted to go. After struggling for a minute, he blurted out, 'Valencia!' and pointed across the bay

The crew looked at the pathetic creature with pity, they'd all been in similar states in their youth and had been working in Ibiza long enough to understand how someone could lose track of time – and their wallet.

'Valencia? Are you sure?'

'Si, señor, Valencia, it's definitely Valencia.'

As soon as he got onboard, the exhaustion kicked in and the lad passed out, blissfully unaware he was on a fishing boat and would wake up eight hours later – and some 200 kilometres away in mainland Spain, in the port of... Valencia. With no footwear, ID or cash, he relied on the Australian Embassy to buy him some flip flops and put him on a ferry back to Ibiza.

## Aftersun

Post 9/11, many charter airlines went into receivership or downsized, cancelling orders. This presented an opportunity for Ryanair which, in January 2002, was able to secure an order for one hundred Boeing 737 aircrafts – more than double the size of its fleet at the time – at an 'exceptionally competitive' price. So, its Osama bin Laden's fault!

> **Top Tune: Spanish Guitar (Original Version) – Groove García {Cassagrande}**

## BEHIND THE BROCHURE

A few years ago, I approached a promoter who was taking big numbers to Lloret de Mar to entice him to Ibiza, extolling its superior clubs, boat parties and sunsets. It was effective; he agreed to try Ibiza, but on the condition I could deliver a party at a water park like he threw in Lloret.

'Of course I can!' I gushed, having previously privately hired Aguamar in Playa d'en Bossa. But this was late September and they closed for the winter the day the group arrived. No amount of money could persuade them to stay open for one day extra, it had been a long, wet season and they'd had enough.

Then a friend told me about another water park which was right at the end of the bay road in Port Des Torrent, San Antonio, so I jumped on my white Vespa to check it out.

It was late afternoon, and I hadn't eaten anything since the night before, missing the hotel breakfast and lunch after spending the last few hours sorting out an incident with a profusely bleeding Geordie and some paramedics. I was unshaven and washed out after a week of late nights and not eating. But, by luck I'd parked my scooter outside a sweet shop – sugar rush!

I eagerly filled a large pink and white striped paper bag with all things Haribo, and strolled into the hotel nearest to the water park vacant-mindedly chewing on a jelly snake. Following excited shrieks, I made my way out onto a terrace overlooking the waterpark so I could assess its suitability for my group. I noticed there only appeared to be children using the slides and chutes. I started counting them in an attempt to estimate what the capacity of the park was, whilst gnawing on a jelly snake which stretched from my mouth like an bright green elastic band.

A firm hand gripped my shoulder from behind.

'Are you a hotel guest?'

I turned around to see a stern man in a white shirt and black trousers.

'No, I'm just here to look.'

'Come with me,' he led me firmly by the arm inside.

'W-where are we going?'

'To the hotel manager.'

We arrived at a small office behind the reception desk. They exchanged a few short sentences in Spanish, before the manager addressed me. 'Juan tells me you were watching the children with caramelos.'

'No, I was on my own.'

He gestured to my bag of sweets.

Idiotically, I offered him it. 'Would you like one?'

'Caramelos... Candy,' he replied, dismissively waving it away. 'Why were you watching the children?'

Then it hit me: an unkempt, dishevelled stranger wandering in with a big bag of sweets, appearing to be taking an interest in children... I was mortified. How could I have been so dumb? I earnestly started explaining why I was there, showing him my business card and giving him the names of a number of local hoteliers who I'd worked with for twenty years, suggesting he call them for a character reference. Two of the people I mentioned were his cousins, which is exactly what I'd hoped, San Antonio being a small town. He called one, and after replacing the receiver visibly relaxed. He explained there'd been recent complaints about a nonce taking photos of the kids as they played. He didn't match my description, but my behaviour was spotted on the CCTV. After establishing the water park was for hotel guests only and not an option for a few hundred ravers, the security escorted me and my bag of sweets from the premises. Sheepishly, I offered him one. 'Tangfastic?' He just looked at me like I was a pillock. Which I guess I was.

The following year I threw the party in a water park for the group in question, complete with DJs, MCs, foam, a $CO_2$ cannon and free Gummy Bears... in Lloret de Mar.

# 16

# VOYAGE TO THE BOTTOM OF THE STRESS

*'It's not the destination, it's the journey.'*
— Ralph Waldo Emerson

With a dozen club cruises under my belt and more bad weather tales than an Oklahoma storm chaser in my locker, by the time I came to do 'The Voyage' in late 2004 I had the confidence of an old sea dog and thought I'd seen it all and felt I could handle anything the North Sea threw at me.

How wrong I was.

Things were looking good; we had the line-up booked and had sold over four hundred tickets.

But as you know, this was the cue for something to go wrong. And right on cue the ferry company called to say the route had changed. They'd stopped sailing to Hamburg and instead docked at a place called Cuxhaven.

'It's been a port since the Middle Ages, and today is a quiet little seaside town – and what's more, the journey time is shorter, giving your group more time there,' was how it was described to me by the group sales lady at the ferry company.

Now in summer, this would've been a destination I could easily sell to my antipodean friends. I would've organised a beach party, rustled up some BBQ's and a small sound system, but there's not many more forlorn places to be than an out-of-season seaside resort in November.

I went over on a recce trip to check it out, and was dismayed to discover that for a seaside resort it was lacking a few essentials; a pier, a funfair, gaming arcades, discothèques, nightclubs and a concert hall I could use for an afternoon rave. I was aghast to find Cuxhaven consisted of dainty beach huts, a few small bars, and one huge freight and fishing port – home of Europe's largest fish finger factory.

It looked – and felt – like the unloved bastard offspring of a drunken one-night stand between Frinton-on-Sea and Grimsby.

The flyers were hastily reprinted and described the new destination as 'A medieval harbour surrounded by cobbled streets hiding small shops, cafes and bars where you can sample the local delicacies, renowned regional brews and traditional music'. Despite my flowery copy, Damo saw straight through it. 'So we're selling them frankfurters, sauerkraut and oom-pah basically? I'm not convinced, pardner.'

Damo was the best promoter I had ever worked with. He didn't just promote a product, he possessed it, riding the campaign like Frankie Dettori in the final furlong. He would eat, sleep, shit, piss (and now I come to think about it, probably ejaculate) an event until it was sold out. Cut him and he'd bleed belief. And because he always has such commitment in his events, this doubt was somewhat of a problem.

We met one afternoon at his modest first-floor flat in Clapham, Club Damo. He got straight to the point as Aussies do. 'Mate, how are we gonna sell this shithole they're taking us to?'

I took a deep breath and cited the wisdom of Buddha. 'In Buddhism, the path is the goal.'

He looked at me, raising an eyebrow. 'Go on…'

'Buddha said, "It's better to travel well than to arrive".'

I could see his mind whirring. 'So there's no destination?'

I shook my head and continued, 'Like life itself, our next trip will be about what happens on the way; not one, but two nights at sea with great DJs and all your mates. Why, the Saturday afternoon is merely incidental, a few hours to soak up the culture, chill out and maybe eat.'

I could see I'd landed a punch, but he was still standing. 'It could work,' he said, continuing, 'but I'm still not buying the sauerkraut, sausages and oompa-loompa angle. We need to find somewhere to take 'em, even if it means getting on buses. Find a venue and I'm in, pardner.'

I agreed. How hard could it be to find a venue in a port town?

A bold strapline was added to emphasise this event was about the passage, and if anyone was in any doubt we rather grandly called the event 'The Voyage' invoking transatlantic seafaring odysseys to exotic new worlds – which I suppose it was, as you couldn't get sauerkraut in Stockwell back then.

On the flyer there was some deliberately vague mention of 'partying' in a 'special place', which could've meant anything. I always prided myself on promoting my trips accurately but on this occasion, I had no choice but to leave it ambiguous.

To make matters worse, the journey time was a few hours less as we didn't sail along the river to Hamburg, the 'shore leave' was longer. What on earth were 500 ravers going to do in Cuxhaven for six hours?

To be fair, the ferry company offered me the opportunity to cancel the event, but with artist and production deposits paid and promotion already out there, we were looking at a £12,000 loss even if we cancelled, and more importantly, losing face. Clubs are only as good as their last event and if Voyage didn't happen both Radical Escapes and Heat UK would suffer fatal reputational damage. Again. With the event less than two weeks away, I *had* to find a venue in Germany... and I had to find it fast.

We printed 100,000 flyers and took full page ads in TNT which proudly proclaimed, 'It's all about the journey, not the destination.' What it didn't say was, '...because, as it stands, there isn't one.'

These were the early dial-up days of the internet. Surfing was in slow motion as pages took up to a minute to load, gradually revealing themselves from the top down like a burlesque lady on one of those tip-and-strip novelty pens. Night after night I searched for a venue. The two late night bars in Cuxhaven didn't respond, probably closed for the winter. It became clear that there were no niterie's within a thirty-kilometre radius. A geek friend told me about a new satellite website called Google Earth which had just launched. I typed in Cuxhaven Germany, and it eventually showed a tiny port surrounded by miles and miles of featureless countryside. Hamburg was over two hours away by road, and the only other town was an even uglier port called Bremerhaven an hour's drive away. Considering the time needed to load the buses at each end, this would mean another two hours on a bus – which is quite a schlep for a few hours in *Kim's Karaoke, DeeJay Tommy's Roller Disco, the Erotik Establissement Bremerhaven,* or the bewildering *Bjorn's Spasskeller,* all of which were too small and would've meant using multiple venues, and in the case of *Tommy's Roller Disco,* the local casualty department, too.

Then, three nights before the event, during my ever increasingly desperate nightly slow-motion surf of northern German farmland, I stumbled across a brand-new website called *Jannsen's Tanzpalast.* The site was still under construction. There were no images, just a paragraph talking about state-of-the art sound and light and a *riesig tanzfläche* – a huge dancefloor!

I sent an email asking about capacity and if they were prepared to open this coming Saturday at noon for '500 thirsty Australians'. No reply was forthcoming, so I resent it. Time was running out. We were two days away from the event and I had no venue. I kept resending the email with the same logic you use when you keep pressing the button when standing at a zebra crossing and it hasn't changed from red within ten seconds. Hoping against logic for a different outcome.

The lovely Tara Hawes interviewed me for harderfaster. net intrigued about this new concept. Harder Faster was the biggest underground online clubbing platform at this time and very influential in London. This was supposed to be when I unveiled where we'd be taking everyone to after docking in Germany. Instead, this appeared:

*Can you tell us what happens when the boat gets to Germany?*

KF: Ahh, that's a mystery! Let's just say people may be very surprised where they end up on Saturday afternoon!

The day before we set sail, I booted up my computer and an AOL notification binged 'You've Got Mail!' Receiving an email in those days was a novelty. Excitedly, I clicked the speech bubble notification.

'Halo, Kurt, is this a joke? We open at 9 p.m. on Saturday!!! Our opening party, but we are already full (invite only). Sorry, but we have no room for 500 people, even thirsty Australians!!!'

I immediately called the number at the bottom of the email and explained that we needed a venue on Saturday afternoon, not evening, as we were on a mini-cruise break and it would be a super preparation for his opening party later that night, and a chance to test the sound and lights and for the staff to get familiar with their new workplace.

'500 people, really? How can I trust you? Maybe you pay a deposit?' This I wanted to avoid at all costs. I had no spare cash and it would've cost extra to make a same-day transfer. Instead, I provided a contact telephone number of the boss of the ferry company to verify the numbers. To my utter amazement, he called back a few hours later and told me he would be waiting for me, with dry ice, lasers and eight bar staff and that if I didn't turn up with the numbers I'd promised, he'd come to the port and find me.

It was on! I booked a fleet of buses and began bigging up the 'secret venue' to Damo and the group leaders. I still hadn't seen it, remember, but it was the only alternative to spending six hours in *Bjorn's Spasskeller*.

For once the crossing was relatively smooth compared with the previous tempests we'd braved (except for having to persuade the captain to delay departure for our headliner Fergie to finish recording his Radio One show and get to Harwich). By the time he arrived he'd been hitting the Jack Daniel's and coke with Damo and his most (un)trustworthy lieutenants.

This was foretold in an interview he'd done with harder-faster when he was asked if he was a good sailor or did he get seasick, to which he replied, 'Nah, I'll be fine, it's just like being pissed isn't it?'

He was then asked, 'Do you plan to take advantage of the duty-free booze?'

'I'll take two record bags: one with drinks and one with records because they always tend to keep the rations a bit low.'

It was refreshing to see a thoroughly refreshed Radio 1 DJ – but challenging. He went missing before his set. I found him in the children's play area, submerged in the ball pit; only a solitary arm protruding from the sea of primary colours holding aloft a bottle of JD like the Statue of Liberty.

An officer walked past, saw the outstretched limb and spotting the wristband around its wrist said sternly, 'Your guests should be watching the DJ, not playing in the children's area.'

'This is the DJ...' I weakly replied.

Over in the Columbus Lounge K90 delivered a scintillating set, climaxing as everyone had hoped with Red Snapper. There was the added surprise in the form of Damo and his mate Ragdoll's live act 'Rage With the Machines' who shamelessly stole the show in a blur of wigs and performance pique.

On arrival on Saturday morning, I was relieved to see the customs in Cuxhaven weren't interested in my group, meaning we could board the waiting buses without delay. Five minutes later, a convoy of coaches crawled along country lanes slicing through featureless muddy flat fields. A drizzly grey mist only reinforced the miserable November light. As we peered out, an Australian voice behind declared, 'Jeez, it looks like the fackin' Somme.'

He wasn't wrong. After another ten minutes of bland country lanes and one-street hamlets we found ourselves stuck behind a tractor, the only vehicle we'd seen since we left the port.

'Where the fuck are you taking us?'

'Yer 'avin a laugh. There's no superclub around here.'

The wizened skull of Macey appeared on my left shoulder having walked down the bus to the front where I was sitting in the front row behind the driver.

'Er, Kirk, the natives are getting restless. I hope for your sake this club is all it's cracked up to be, hey?'

Next to me, Damo sat with his hands folded, looking straight ahead, muttering something about always doing a recce trip in future. Even he was worried. But not as worried as me;

we'd been driving for twenty minutes through flat, feature-less countryside.

Outside what looked like a barn on the edge of another group of agricultural buildings we slowed down and stopped in a farmyard.

TSSSSSSSSS!

The sound of compressed air as the driver applied the handbrake never sounded so sinister.

I jumped out onto the damp ground and told the driver to keep the door closed until I gave the signal. Manure and puddles pockmarked the ground. A large black crow hopped three times across the rough ground and landed on a small wooden fence. I walked towards the door, hoping to hear the heart-quickening THUD of a kick drum. But instead I heard nothing. In fact, the silence coming from the building in front of me was deafening. Unseen in the mist, a cow mooed from an adjacent field. Somewhere in the gloom an invisible tractor chugged, my nostrils told me the farmer was muck spreading.

It was the most unglamorous, unfashionable, and unwelcoming place I could imagine to bring seven buses of party-seekers and a Radio One DJ.

As I approached the large steel door, I could feel hundreds of pairs of eyes burning into my back from inside the coaches. There were no signs or indications that this was anything except an unremarkable barn in the middle of the north German mud. I swallowed hard and pounded the door with my fist.

No reply.

What was I thinking? Bringing five hundred of the biggest party animals in London town to a fucking cow shed. I had no contract, no guarantee... and no escape.

'Caw! Caw! Caw! Caw!' from atop the fence post the crow was laughing. A large drop of cold water fell onto my head from the ridge of the wooden roof above.

I knocked again, but after thirty seconds knew the game was up. I took a deep breath and turned to face the buses. The crew at the back were now banging on the windows. They'd been cooped up for long enough and were understandably demanding their freedom. Instead, I was about to condemn them to another hour on the bus as the driver wound his way through the lanes before depositing them to wander the streets of the German Grimsby, where they'd forlornly and fruitlessly search for somewhere to shelter from the rain which wasn't a petrol station or kebab shop. I was staring at disaster.

The clumsy clunk of a lock interrupted my regret.

'Kurt? Wilcommen! We are ready for you!'

I spun around to see an attractive brown-haired fraulein-framed person in the door, silhouetted in smoke and red light like that bit on 'Stars in their Eyes' when Carol from Crewe says, 'Tonight, Matthew, I'm going to be Kate Bush.'

I gave a wild thumbs-up to the driver in the first bus. People literally exploded from the buses. I proudly held the door open for my guests, most of whom passed me with me with an appreciative grin, before coming back up the stairs a few minutes later to shake my hand and mutter, 'Legend.'

It took the best part of fifteen minutes to move everyone from the buses into the cavernous club beneath the barn, meaning I was the last person to set eyes on the venue I'd taken them all to! Upon reaching the bottom of the stairs I was amazed to see a heaving dancefloor being peppered with strobes and smoke as beautiful azure laser fingers 'blessed' the congregation, fanning over hundreds of heads like a benign Freddie Krueger glove.

Someone shouted my name. It was the guy I'd spoken to on the phone. He was entertaining Damo and some of the DJs in an upstairs room which overlooked the dancefloor. He was a generous host and clearly loved the fact a large group of the fiercest London clubbers had christened his brand-new club.

The word soon got out, and locals started arriving in the late afternoon gloom.

Even the farmer arrived dressed like Super Mario in blue overalls and cow shit-stained wellies to observe the carnage with frothy beer in his hand, it was most bizarre!

This was not only the biggest party the area had ever seen, it was the *only* party the area had ever seen. The DJs were really firing and the crowd making the most of the fact they were raving in a foreign country on a drizzly Saturday afternoon in November. The bars were busy, the sound was pumping, and when we left at 5 p.m., we did so with a heavy heart. But we had a boat to catch, and the tide was rising.

The owner grabbed me and insisted I do a shot of Jagermeister before asking how much bar commission I wanted. I was just happy he'd opened and told him not to worry, but he insisted and bunged a couple of €50 notes into my hand. 'Same time next month, ja?'

The coach's horn blared. They were waiting for me.

'Sure thing! I'll call you on Monday. Auf Wiedersehen... und danke!'

I shook his hand, gave the cute bar manager a peck on the cheek, and sprinted up the stairs, jauntily hop-scotching my way through the puddles and cow pats, bounding up the steps of the leading bus to an appreciative cheer and round of applause.

I took a bow and sat down, closing my eyes in relief.

The bus back to the ferry terminal was an envelope of elation. Everyone loved the club. I'd pulled it off. Without this internet thing I'd never have found the place. Maybe it was a game changer like my geeky mates had been telling me after all.

All we had to do now was deliver the return leg. But the North Sea had other ideas...

After a few hours the ship reverberated to a huge BOOM! The ship violently lurched to one side, causing me to stagger across my cabin.

I opened the door and ran straight into Mark Doggett and his wife Jane who had similarly left their cabin after hearing the impact.

'Have we just been hit by a wrecking ball?' he asked, the colour drained from his face.

Just then another door opened. A dazed and confused Damo dressed in a T-shirt and boxer shorts emerged.

'Was that a submarine or a whale we just ran into?'

Whatever it was, we ran into it again as a horrible metallic CLANG! Which caused the corridor lights to flicker and us all to strike crucifixion poses; arms outstretched with a hand on each wall as the vessel tilted alarmingly to one side.

Although the subsequent impacts weren't as violent, we were being tossed about like a plastic duck in a hyperactive toddler's bath.

We staggered and scrambled around the lower decks like a paralytic Leonardo di Caprio and Kate Winslett in *Titanic,* eventually reaching the cafeteria where people clung to tables as wave after wave struck the boat. Fifteen minutes later, four plates of sausages and chips lay untouched, as they slid spookily from one side of the table to the other, paused, then slid back again: possessed frankfurters with a life of their own. This was too much for Mark and Jane, who by now had turned green. They staggered off muttering, 'Never again.'

Just when I thought things couldn't get any worse they closed the bars. This is never a good thing no matter where you are. But at sea, it's a confirmation that you're in a pickle. Boosting the onboard spend was the very reason the ferry company entertained the idea of my groups. For them to decide it wasn't practical or safe to keep the revenue stream open, meant it was particularly rough.

Not that the dour security man wolfing down a huge plate of chips at the next table was concerned.

'This is nothing, if it was really rough, they'd batten down the hatches,' he said, his Polish accent only reinforcing his lack of concern. By the time he'd emptied his plate, an announcement was made to batten down the hatches. The security fella merely shrugged and shovelled the final chips into his mouth. Crew were to lock all exterior doors. No one was allowed out on deck. No one wanted to leave their cabins in any case. Around midnight, the sea became calmer as we emerged through the storm. The bars opened and some DJs got to play to the handful of stay-awakes and die-hards who were still up for it and not covered in vomit.

Despite the drama of the homeward crossing, the word around town the following week was that the weekend was overall something special, and the lure of spending Saturday afternoon clubbing in a subterranean superclub in another country in between two nights at sea raised the possibility of running one of these cruises every month.

I had the best promoter in London, an up-for-it crowd, a keen ferry company and a fantastic club. Finally, my hard work and bravery would pay off.

But incredibly, shortly afterwards the route ceased to operate, meaning there were no longer any direct ferries from the UK to Germany.

I was scuppered and it was back to the drawing board. Again.

---

**Top Tune: K90 – Red Snapper (Original Mix)
{Recover}**

---

### Afterglow

We found out the collision was a rogue wave, which some-times in The North Sea can reach a staggering twenty-five metres high. They occur in the winter months and are the by-product of a Polar Low – a trough of low pressure over from the arctic. A Stena HSS Superferry had to return to port after being hit by a rogue wave the previous winter. Fergie has been sober since 2018, holds a residency in Las Vegas and is as popular as ever. At the time of writing, K90 still hasn't played at sea again.

## BEHIND THE BROCHURE

San Antonio, Ibiza. My phone was ringing. I knew it was serious as no one calls you before 10 a.m. in Ibiza unless they need to. It was the concerned father of a nineteen-year-old guest we'll call Piers, whose son was on a student holiday in Ibiza I was providing consultancy for. He'd just received a call from his son who claimed he was being held against his will in a private medical clinic.

A call to the clinic provided the other side of the story. Piers had been thrown out of three bars in the West End and collapsed on the street in a drunken heap. The door staff called an ambulance... which explained why a shirtless Piers was plugged into a rehydration drip and refusing to pay the €380 for the ambulance and treatment he was receiving – whilst also refusing to produce his passport before they let him leave.

I relayed this to Daddy, who reluctantly accepted this version of events, thanked me for my assistance and apologised for the inconvenience his son had caused. 'Not at all, that's what I'm here for. I'm a father, too, and have it all coming! These things happen when kids go on holiday,' I replied, 'and it's not just limited to kids, grown men can be worse!'

He agreed to wire me the money, which I collected and returned to the clinic to pay Piers' bill after buying him a cheap T-shirt to wear. Newly liberated, but ungrateful, the posh boy looked at me with disdain, and said, 'If there's one thing nobody likes, it's a grass.'

I smiled. 'If I was a grass, Piers, I would've told your daddy about the blowjob you paid for in a doorway last night from that rotund Ghanaian lady... the photos of which are being shared on phones around the hotel pool as we speak.'

He froze.

I pulled my crash helmet on and walked away. '...enjoy the rest of your holiday.'

*Front and centre! Air cadet summer camp 1976,*
*RAF Lossiemouth*

*My waxwork boards the QE2 in 1988 bound for America*

*An Englishman in New York: Quentin Crisp.*
*(Keith Beaty/Toronto Star via Getty Images)*

*Clare Fray and Tara MacDonald:*
*enough to send any man overboard.*

*Rave on the waves, Impact 2000*

HeatEvents presents

radical
**24-HOURS IN-AMSTERDAM**

RAPTURE TV

StenaLine | THE POWER ZONE | 020 | **SAT 15/SUN 16 NOVEMBER 2003**

# 48 HOURS-IN-AMSTERDAM
## PARTY ACROSS THE NORTH SEA TO THE WORLD'S MOST LIBERAL CITY!

ITINERARY:

**FRI: 1600 LIVERPOOL STREET STATION:**
Board convoy of executive coaches (air con, our choice of music & films on cd / video / dvd, toilet, fridge, reclining seats) for Harwich Intl port.

**1900- MIDNIGHT STENA HSS DISCOVERY**
The worlds largest and smoothest super fast ferry is also a floating club! We'll be programming the music for the crossing through an immaculately crystal clear sound system, surrounded by a huge Toshiba 24 cube video wall, intelligent lighting rig and bars selling drinks at pub prices... the only way to travel!

**MIDNIGHT – 0130**
Our convoy glides past canals & windmills and into the 'Venice of the North'...Amsterdam!
Check in to the Heat Hotel - centrally located budget accommodation with club venue in basement! We have over 300 beds reserved here.

**SATURDAY, ALL DAY:**
Free time to explore a place, which every scholar & clubber should visit. Home of Twente, of pounding Dutch dance events such as HQ & Dance Valley, 'The Dam' is city of tolerance and a city built for life's little pleasures; eat international cuisine, drink the world famous local brews, explore the red light district, check out the coffee shops & myriad of museums exhibiting everything from Van Gogh to Hemp!

**SAT NIGHT 1900– 0300**
HeatUK hosting 'the Bunker' (basement of Hans Brinker hotel). Admission is limited to '48 Hours in Amsterdam' wristband wearers; cheap drinks ( small draught beer £1, spirits from £1.50, Red Bull & Vodka £2) & an intimate party vibe with both a hard & funky soundtrack.

[OPTIONAL EXTRA] £100-0200
HQXL – 6,500 hard dance followers & 17 DJ's in Amsterdam docklands.
Nick Sentience (live),
The Organ Donors, Proteus vs Kevin Energy, The Tidy Boys, Steve Hill vs JP, Gaz West aka Dark by Design vs Alex Kidd, Danny D vs Jay Pidgeon,
Ed Real vs the 'TING',
Tom Harding vs Fausto & MC Da Silva.

**HQ XL**

**SUN MORN 0700-1100**
CLUB ZYON centrally located in Dam Square. A legendary Amsterdam party haunt. Formerly called, Time & 020, it has hosted everyone from the legendary 'I Love Hardhouse' parties, and was both Tiesto's first residency – and our after party venue for last years '24 Hours in Amsterdam' trip. £2 million pounds later it has been joined with next door, to create a two-roomed treasure chest of suspended sound system & spraying dancefloor. Free admission with wristband.

**SUN: 1100**
Convoy armada at our canal cruisers transport you from Club Zyon to Heat Hotel - last chance to chill in the coffee shops & bars, or maybe enjoy a traditional Dutch breakfast.

**SUNDAY: 1300**
Coaches depart from near to Heat Hotel for Hoek of Holland.

**SUNDAY: 1530 - 1900**
The return crossing doubles as a film premier. We're showing the 3 hour upstate epic, 'HEATUK... THE MOVIE' all the big scenes. Music wise, we take control of foliage as darkness falls, and rig our lights to ignite. You may want to take advantage of the amazing duty free superstore deals (up to £5 a bottle) or 24 personal allowances!?!!

**SUNDAY: 1900 – 2100**
Coaches return to London Liverpool Street.

**HARD DANCE DJS:**
PHIL REYNOLDS / SPENCER FREELAND
NEIL MURPHY & PHIL WONG (IRELAND)
BRAD THATCHER / MACEY / DEX
SHAF DE BASS / TREVOR MCLACHLAN
JARED V / NUMATIX (IRELAND)

**HOUSE DJS:**
MIKE WALSH
SI
PHILL NODA
NATHAN LARKIN
CLAUDE LYONS

HeatEvents
radical

*There may be trouble ahead...the storm which meant we had to do a 331-mile diversion.*

*Behold the Saviour! The Great Leo Ringleberg with one of his heavenly chariots.*

*Happiness is...a white scooter on the white isle.*

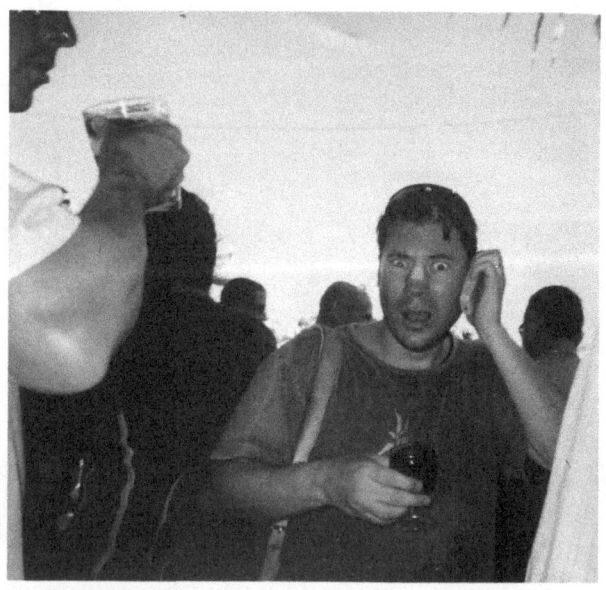

*Not a phone in sight - just ravers living in the moment.*

*Damian Gelle even makes Sangria look dangerous (Bora Bora 2009).*

*All hands on deck! The Voyage, 2005.*

*Exploring 'the other side' with Derek Acorah was never dull.*

*Bill the Robot stopping the traffic in downtown Innsbruck, April '93.*

*It's official: I'm certified!*

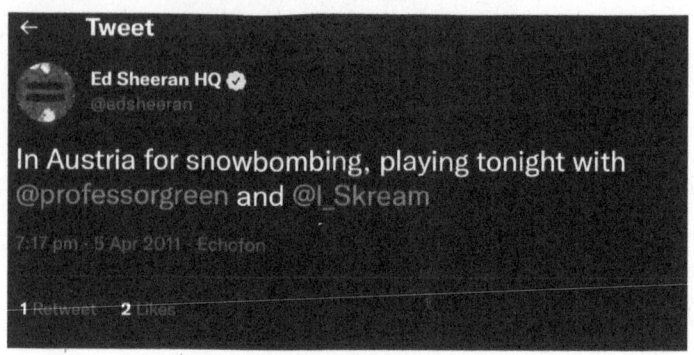

*It wasn't Ed's most popular post…*

*Our anti-war protest: Snowbombing makes a point.*

*There are worse offices.*

# 17

# PORN UNDER A BAD SIGN

A molten gold bar appears from the horizon, gradually growing into a crisp yellow disc which ascends, growing in intensity, lending radiance and an otherworldly glow to those who've danced until daylight in the World's Biggest Club™.

For a clubber in Privilege, watching the sun come up from the windows of the back room was a ritual as magical as any of Dawn's Greatest Hits; Machu Picchu, the Taj Mahal, Mount Kilimanjaro or Stonehenge at summer solstice. When the new day's virginal rays illuminated you, you not only saw, but *felt* the light; it filled you with an ecstasy which didn't come in a pill, but in electro-magnetic radiation which had travelled ninety-three million miles in the same time that it took Alfredo to play 'Love Story' by Layo & Bushwacka.

That particular dawn's ignition was being shared with DJ Magazine's in-house gonzo journalist, Simon A Morrison, who I'd invited to Ibiza to write about radical escape's Ibiza packages in his excellent column, 'Dispatches From The Far Side', to raise profile of my closing parties holiday package in September.

Having met him on a number of occasions, I was aware we shared a similar sense of humour and appreciation of the absurd. His previous review of the club cruise I did to Hamburg in the Force 9 storm had proved that not only was he worth giving a free holiday to, but would be good company also.

I drove him to Gatwick, leaving the car in the Long Stay car park prior to pre-flight pints. The highlight of the trip was Manumission at Privilege. At that time 10,000 people would attend each week, making it the largest single gathering *anywhere* on the planet every Monday.

After a trawl around the port and old town, we eventually bowled into Manumission around 3 a.m. in order to miss the first 'shift'; puking lads from Pontefract and fat Welsh girls with sunburnt legs who, having peaked too soon, would leave early after overindulging at the open bar before they boarded their Club 18–30 vomit comet to Privilege.

Manumission Promoter Andy McKay showed us around. He knew me from the Time Out Ibiza guides I'd done in the late '90s, and he was eager to show us that year's 'naughty nautical' theme; 'The Good Ship Manumission.' The main-stage was transformed into the huge bow of a cruise ship, with the dancers and PR girls wearing skimpy 'fantasy sailor' costumes. Andy's brother Mike Manumission grew his beard, so he looked like Brutus from Popeye, while his wife Claire opened the show with a live rendition of 'Anything Goes' – an appropriate title for Manumission in those days, 'cos anything did!

At one point I lost Simon. Everyone lost their friends in those days. It didn't matter, you'd just meet a new one. Eventually I found him chatting to Fatboy Slim. That was the night Norman played in every area; the mainstage, the Coco Loco room, and the toilets. Stuart from Manumission had the unenviable job of carrying Norman's heavy chrome record box through the packed crowd. I kept spotting him from my vantage point on the gantry, looking like one of those elegant African tribeswomen who balance a huge water jug on their heads.

'I wouldn't mind carrying his vinyl,' Stuart told me the next day in Bar M, 'but he ended up playing off DAT, as the monitors didn't work in the toilets, and the mixer in the Coco Loco room was sticky with Pina Colada.'

'Are you sure it was Pina Colada, Stuart?' I enquired; this *was* Manumission, remember...

'Well, it looked like Pina Colada, but I didn't taste it to find out.'

After the main room music stopped at 8 a.m. we moved to the CocoLoco room, where the bass kept throbbing for another good few hours. The crowd here were older, chic and more international than the gawping Brits with disposable cameras the sex show attracted. Smokin' Jo was playing, and it always felt special; the Balearic equivalent of a lock in at your favourite pub. Simon and I stayed until the end, and then spent another hour or so talking bollocks on the terrace to some randoms. Eventually, we were ushered out by the cleaners. It was at this point we discovered neither of us has any money for a cab. We didn't carry credit cards in those days, and the only cabs waiting were shady unlicensed cars who, despite our best efforts, weren't prepared to take a couple of wide-eyed wasters who didn't have a peseta between them.

I had the idea to blag a lift off some of the production crew to San An. But when we got to the car park, it was deserted. Everyone had left. Out of 10,000 people we were the last men standing. The sun had grown in height and strength, and we were starting to frazzle. We had half a small bottle of water left between us. My phone was dead, but Simon had one bar of battery life left, so there we had to move swiftly. Who did he know with a car who'd be awake, fit to drive and willing to pick us up at 10am on a Tuesday morning? He thought long and hard. I swallowed the last of the water, stamped on it and tossed the bottle into a nearby bin.

'I've got it! My mate James has just opened a bar on the main road between here and San An, and keeps hassling me to write about it.' He flicked open the phone like a mugger opens a flick knife and started scrolling through his contacts.

'Hello, mate, it's Simon from DJ Mag, me and a mate from Mixmag are stranded in the Privilege car park. We've got no cash or water. Is there any chance you can collect us? ... You can! Really? ...Yes, of course! I'm up for it and I'm sure Kirk'll be game too... Not at all, it's the least we can do... No, that doesn't matter, Kirk can hop in the boot. See you so...!'

And at that precise moment, his phone died.

'He's on his way in his Porsche. He's not usually awake at this time in the morning, but there's a film crew at his new bar and they need some extras. The ones he booked haven't shown up. In return for rescuing us, I said we'll help him out. We even get free drinks for the duration of the shoot!'

This was a dream; not only were we getting a lift in a Porsche, but we could continue partying.

'What are the crew shooting?'

Simon shrugged. 'Dunno, he didn't say. A music video probably.'

We searched for some shade and found it on the doorstep of a Privilege double-decker bus.

He looked ruefully at his flip top Ericsson T28s.

'One day, it'll be possible to pay for cabs with your phone,' declared Simon.

'How's that gonna work?'

'I was reading that in twenty years, phones will be connected to the internet. So, anything you can do on the internet now you'll be able to do on your phone in the future.'

There was a long pause, before we looked at one another, and said in unison, 'Porn?'

Simon continued. 'I'm serious, in fact you'll also be able to shoot it. Apple is working on a tiny camera which will be a feature of every desktop computer and can be used for video conferencing or chatting to friends.'

'You mean virtual business meetings?'

'Exactly! In 2020, we'll be able to call a cab, charge it up on the way, pay by credit card and even film ourselves having a laugh in the back, before posting it on our own webpage.'

This spun me out. 'I don't know if I want to live in a world in which everyone is filming themselves all the time and uploading it. It'd drive me crazy. Can you imagine the competition, one-upmanship and bullshit folk would share? It'd be enough to drive you insane.'

A white Porsche Carrera rumbled into view, tyres crackling over the stony car park, leaving a white cloud of dust in its slipstream. Thankfully I couldn't fit in the boot so we both piled into the front, me on Simon's knee. His mate James was clearly concerned that the lack of extras would result in the film crew not being able to do the shoot. Having bought the place only recently and not seeing any revenue from it as yet, the substantial location fee for the shoot was clearly much needed.

'We need at least eight extras to start filming,' he explained.

'Don't worry, you can count on us,' reassured Simon.

'Absolutely, it's the least we can do,' I added, not knowing what I was getting myself into.

## Status Quid Pro Quo

The bar in question was located on the main road between Privilege and San Antonio and was called Quid Pro Quo, which is Latin for a favour which is granted in return for something. With what was about to unfold, this couldn't have been more apt.

We walked in and after being handed a cool bottle of San Miguel were shown to an enclosed open-air terrace within a courtyard, which contained a dozen small tables. In one corner a bloke was fiddling with a camera, while another set up a tripod to which he affixed a light. Although it was light, the sun had still to rise above the stone walls which enclosed us.

Over the next hour, the courtyard gradually filled up until most tables were taken. At the next table a girl sat glumly, head in hands. As did another girl across the courtyard. Both looked thoroughly miserable. Their unspoken sullenness made us somewhat uncomfortable in our modified mood. There was a silent tension which became so palpable I felt compelled to 'break the ice' and approached one of the girls. I asked her if she was here for the filming. Her nodded confirmation oozed regret. She clearly didn't want to be here. I could see Simon talking to the other girl, whose grubby T-shirt, bikini bottoms and flip-flops suggested she'd just got out of bed; the look topped off with red eyes and a runny nose.

Then, pointing at the girl I was talking to, screamed, 'She's a dirty fucking whore.'

The girl in front of me jumped to her feet,

'Pot calling the kettle black! Slag!'

'You're the fackin' slag. Giving Jason a blowjob when I went to KFC! You think I don't know?'

The girl put her hand on her hips. 'Excuse me! It was me who he chatted up first. You wuz all over 'im, flashing yer fake tits in the toilet for a line of Charlie, and what about taking yer knickers off on the dancefloor and rubbing 'em over his face.'

'I didn't see Jason complaining. Get over it.'

Clearly, the girls knew each other and had fallen out.

The slanging match in the courtyard had taken everyone by surprise. Everyone that is, except the blokes who'd been fiddling with the camera and tripod, who stood nearby despairingly shaking their heads.

I looked at Simon. This was ruining our afterglow and poisoning the atmosphere. We each gently urged the girls to sit down. I sat down at her table and went into 'reconciliation holiday rep' mode. 'Hey, easy now. These things happen. People do things on holiday they wouldn't normally do at home. Best you two avoid one another until things calm down.'

She sat with crossed arms. 'Well, that's easier said than done, ain't it, Einstein?'

'Why's that?' I asked, somewhat taken aback at her venom.

'Well, I have to go down on her in twenty minutes, don't I?'

'I don't know, do you?'

She looked up at me defiantly. 'Just what do you think I'm doing here?'

My mind whirred but no words came out.

Her interrogation continued. 'Anyway, what are *you* doing here, sleazeball?'

'Well, I needed a lift from Manumission and—'

Unknown to me Simon was having the exact same conversation with her finger-lickin' friend, and had reached the same point of revelation.

'NOOOOOO!' Simon had his hands on his head. We met back at our table. No words were needed.

No sooner had the penny dropped that we were trapped on the set of a porn film, in the middle of nowhere, with no cash and no way out, when the director addressed the extras to explain what was required of them.

The plot – as is so often the case in porn – was implausible to the point of being absurd. Two female diners would start kissing before getting carried away and having wild sex on the table, whilst all around diners carried on regardless, not noticing what was taking place a few feet away. The road signs may have suggested we were in Ibiza, but we were in fact, in Pornville – where washing machine engineers aren't safe from nymphomaniac housewives, the hospitals are full of nurses queuing up to offer hand relief, and every school hockey match descends into a lesbian orgy. If I'd known where we were heading, I'd have called a fake taxi…

'I can't do it, Simon. What if my family find out?' I sat on my hands shaking my head.

'I think it's safe to assume it'll be on after the watershed, but I know what you mean. Maybe we can stay out of shot?'

'We're on the next sodding table!'

Framed in the doorway to the bar, James watched intently. Although out of earshot, he discerned the doubt from our body language and worried expressions.

He put up a thumb and mouthed, 'Okay?' We returned the gesture, smiling.

'We can't let him down. It was part of the deal, remember,' whispered Simon, pointing to the Quid Pro Quo sign which hung over the doorway to the finca.

'Bloody hell, Simon, what have we got ourselves into?'

James delivered another couple of beers, which only reinforced our debt as Simon went inside, returning with a pen and sheet of paper with which we weighed up the pros and cons of appearing in a porn film:

Pros:

Getting paid for getting your end away

Getting to wear a costume

Travelling to glamorous locations

Cons:

Embarrassing your family

Not knowing when it will surface, possibly discovered by a future partner

Risking a Sexually Transmitted Disease

Not being able to run for public office.

'Well, we're not gonna get our end away,' I reasoned.

'Or getting paid for it,' admitted Simon glumly.

'So that just leaves the dressing up.'

'What are the career options?' asked Simon, now hopeful.

'School headmaster, washing machine engineer or pizza delivery boy,' I replied.

Simon was unimpressed. 'Nah, what about something medical with a white coat and stethoscope, perhaps a doctor or consultant?'

'Maybe… though you're more likely to be cast as a bedbound patient covered in bandages.'

'Well, that'd solve the identification issues at least!' he mused.

'But the dialogue, the plot and character development…' I countered.

He nodded in agreement.

Putting my bottle down firmly I summed up the situation as I saw it, 'Look, the only reason to do it is to not let your mate down. But had we known it was a sex film we wouldn't have agreed in the first place, would we?'

'No,' agreed Simon. 'But how the hell do we escape?'

The girls were taking an eternity to get ready. After fifteen minutes, a couple of older blokes on one table got fed up and left. Another couple of saucer-eyed ravers who'd been hand jiving 'big box little box' to the silence followed, causing James to curse.

There were now only a handful of tables occupied. James paced around the courtyard, one hand on his forehead, saying, 'If anyone else leaves they can't do the shoot. How can they shoot a public sex scene without the public?'

Simon and I swapped glances. If we could persuade another table to leave, we'd be out of the skin flick slammer. A long-haired Italian hippy type in a waistcoat and purple yoga trousers at the adjacent table rose to go to the bar.

'Now's our chance,' urged Simon. I swiftly rose and followed him inside the finca. I asked him if he was gay, or just gay for pay.

'Che cosa?' he asked

I explained that the scene would develop into a bisexual group sex scene and held out my hand. As he took it, I said, 'I'm Troy, what's your name, handsome?'

Upon seeing this, the Italian's flat hand turned into a fist, which he stuck into his mouth before biting a knuckle. He spun around, a blur of long black hair and billowing trousers which disappeared out of the door. I picked up my drink and emerged just in time to hear a Vespa scooter start up and speed off into the distance, causing James to groan.

Returning to my seat I subtly chinked bottles with Simon to toast success. The fresh air of freedom was in sight! If we could keep the numbers low, we'd delay the filming until they gave up. It was getting hotter all the time and there was increasingly less shade in the courtyard.

At that moment, four middle-aged ladies entered the court-yard. One held a billowing piece of paper and a puzzled look, probably the result of driving around in circles following a rental car road map which was last updated in 1973.

James saw his chance. 'Ladies, please take a seat. I'll bring coffee and pastries. It's on the house.' They had no choice. He man-handled them to the recently vacated table and shouted for some breakfast pastries to be brought over while gesturing to the cameraman to get started.

The former friends were now sitting at the same table, arms folded, completely ignoring each other.

Goodness knows how they'd react when the action started. James was obviously desperate for his location fee; his behaviour increasingly erratic.

As there were the requisite minimum number of extras present, our escape was now impossible.

'Bugger!' Simon slammed his bottle down. 'We're doomed. We'll forever be associated with what's going to unfold in the next twenty minutes. Bang goes that career as an MP.'

Behind the lady, I saw one of the girls standing up and

walking around to the other, who automatically slid her hand up the unfeasibly short, pleated tartan skirt which she was now almost wearing.

Rather than moan, the recipient of the upskirt grope sneezed. 'CHOO! Sorry.'

'Again, from the top,' the director snapped

She sat back down to start the scene again. Evidently, none of the ladies had noticed, tucking into, and comparing the glazed pastries and stirring their complimentary coffees.

Then I saw them. Glinting in the late morning sun which had now climbed above the courtyard walls, defiant and dainty, was a small silver crucifix on a chain of rosary beads – they were nuns!

I rose, walked briskly over brushing past the cameraman and assertively led the girl in the mini skirt away into the bar, prompting the cameraman to protest.

James stormed after me.

'What's your fucking problem?'

When I told him about the nuns he was mortified, then got defensive. 'How was I to know? They don't look like nuns. Anyway, aren't they off duty?'

'They're still nuns, they don't knock off at 5 p.m. They may not be in all the clobber, but they're still nuns,' I countered.

'Shit! We'll have to wait for them to leave. What a waste of four pastries.'

Simon and I breathed a sigh of relief; this was another stay of execution – but for how long?

In an attempt to keep them there, we started chatting to the nuns. It transpired they were French. I asked them if they were on holiday. They replied they were on the island to raise deaf awareness and train social workers in sign language.

Simon found me in the toilets minutes later, I was staring in the mirror above a small sink. My face had been doused with water and my hair straggled across my forehead. I looked like a ghoul trapped on a porn set...which was exactly what I was.

'The nuns have left, they're about to start filming so James needs us on set.'

I said nothing and followed him out into the dazzling late morning sun, the air now fragrant with pine.

'AT-CHOO!'

'Bloody hell, Lucy. Okay, Jim, start the shot again,' spat the director.

'AT-CHOO!'

'Can we please continue?' the frustrated voice of the long-suffering director interrupted. 'Once again, from the top, places everyone. Aaand... action!'

Each time they tried to film, a loud sneeze would erupt, and they'd have to start again. Even when they cut straight to the cunnilingus scene, Lucy laying on the table as Sarah kneeled between her thighs, it was 'CHOOs!' rather than 'OOHs!' The only orifice oozing any moisture was Lucy's nose.

It all got so comical that those present started counting down from ten under their breath, so regular were the poor girl's sneezes.

The delayed start and constant restarts drained the battery on the camera, so a pause was called.

Simon searched his pockets for the hundredth time, checking his phone was still dead. He suddenly froze, stood up and pulled out a sweat-soaked, screwed-up piece of paper,

Taking great care, he spread it out on the table in the sun like it was a piece of the Turin Shroud or the Black Sea Scrolls. It was a 1,000 peseta note (equivalent to £4). We looked at one another and mimed in unison the word 'BUS!'.

After five minutes, expertly using a couple of cocktail sticks, he turned it over until it was baked crisp enough to pick up. We waited for James to go inside and slipped out unnoticed. At precisely that moment a bus appeared, shimmering through the midday heat wave over the brow of the hill. The nearest bus stop was a short sprint away, we hailed it as we sprinted along. Ten minutes later we were back to the relative sanity of San Antonio. That's probably the only time you'll ever see those words in close proximity.

On our last night we went to the mighty Cream at Amnesia, where promoter Mo Chaudry let us leave our bags in the dancer's area on the roof, before taking a cab to the airport for the red eye back to Gatwick.

After an hour of fruitlessly searching for my car in the searing heat, a couple of airport security guards appeared in a jeep and asked why we'd been wandering around the car park for the last hour, acting suspiciously.

'My car has been stolen! I swear I parked it in Row F, but it's not here. Look, this is my ticket.'

I handed them the creased, grubby, sweat-soaked car park ticket. He took one look and handed it back.

'This is a ticket for Car Park B, sir. This is Car Park A.'

### Aftersex

I believe they finally filmed the scene later that afternoon inside the bar earning James his location fee. I've never found the video we may be in... but I have seen one of its stars again. She's occasionally on television as she married someone famous. Wonder how her hay fever is?

After earning a Master's Degree in Novel Writing and

a PhD in the club scene, Simon Morrison is known as Dr Disco. Whether he wears a white coat and stethoscope remains unconfirmed at the time of going to press.

> **Top Tune: Porn Kings – Up to No Good (Original Mix) {Vendetta}**

## BEHIND THE BROCHURE

Huw (as we'll call him) was a soft-spoken charmer from the Welsh valleys and popular with the ladies. Together with his handsome roommate Owen, they made a deadly duo.

One morning in Ibiza he was dealing with the morning-after effects of mixing cocaine with Viagra, and had an erection which, no matter how hard he tried, he couldn't bring to a 'natural conclusion'.

Then he spied two girls sunning themselves on an adjacent balcony one floor below. A flirty cross-balcony conversation ensued which entailed him cheekily betting her €50 that she couldn't help him 'get over the line'. Amazingly, she agreed, and together with her friend was soon at the door, brandishing a bottle of baby oil and a lascivious smile before getting to grips with the situation.

I listened open-mouthed at the tale, which I believed one hundred per cent given the duo's success rate with women and the types of mad things that happen in Ibiza.

'Did you win the bet?'

'No, but it was the best €50 I've spent since I got here,' he replied in his sing-song Welsh accent.

# 18

## BEYOND THE GRAVE

Is there life after death? It's a question we've all asked at some point. I've always been interested in the supernatural. When I was a toddler my parents would hear me talking to entities at the end of my bed who introduced themselves as 'the blue voices'. My curiosity in the paranormal led to a group of us discovering a forgotten attic room where we'd hold Ouija board seances in the imposing Victorian detached house which served as a Sixth Form Centre. We stopped after three of our attendees lost their lives *in separate incidents* in as many months. Coincidence maybe, but scary enough for me to never do it again.

As the UK rushed to the end of the 1990s, the once in a thousand-year event had a subconscious whiff of end times about it. Fears of The Millennium Bug swirled, and just like the Victorian fascination for the occult a century before, the late twentieth century also witnessed a rise in popularity of spiritualism. Except this time around, instead of seances and Ouija boards, the masses turned to a former Blue Peter presenter and a camp scouse medium.

It was the Tuesday evening after *another* stormy weekend club cruise to a grim north German port. I was sat with my wife moaning about the logistical difficulties a rave on the waves is beset by; the eternally restless turntables which required copious amounts of bedding to absorb the motion of the ocean, the fragile stylus which needed weighing down with Blu-tack and coins, the lack of lasers and absence of smoke, which are forbidden by nautical regulations, and the diva-like behaviour by DJs who were increasingly demanding their own individual technical riders, bottles of expensive vodka and mood modification – as well as two flights back from Germany in order to get to their lucrative Saturday night gig.

I stared at the television watching *Most Haunted*, a dubious paranormal 'investigation' hosted by former Blue Peter presenter Yvette Fielding and featuring showbiz medium Derek Acorah and, I suspected, a production crew adept at making noises off camera in order to guarantee the next series was commissioned. At its height it was compulsive viewing. Weekly possessions and poltergeist presence in suitably spooky stately homes and draughty castles, which despite teasing the viewer with glimpses of ghostly goings on, never once during twenty-three series and Celebrity Halloween specials resulted in any tangible evidence of ghosts. Like a psychic striptease act, Most Haunted relied on the promise of what was to come without ever getting its kit off. Yvette's tendency to run away screaming when anything slightly scary happened meant nothing really scary ever did happen.

If there was a BAFTA for a television programme making a little go a long way, Yvette Fielding's mantlepiece would possess more masks than a pandemic.

Derek is halfway through a description of the spirit entities he believes are present at Bodmin jail. Yvette stares at him intently, hanging on his every word. Suddenly Derek grunts

'Yeugh!'

'Are you all right?' Yvette is getting ready to be scared.

Derek's eyes are now closed. Another guttural noise.

'Where's he going?' another man asks, sensing it wasn't back home to Southport.

The camera pans to Derek's face. He appears to be receiving a message. What ancient wisdom could it possibly be? What nugget of knowledge is he about to impart from another dimension? What eternal mystery is he about to solve? A new energy source, perhaps? The location of Atlantis? How they built the pyramids?

A pause. A nation holds its breath.

'Mary loves Dick! Mary loves Dick!' There's a pause. '… Mary loves Dick!'

Possessed Derek delivers a bravura performance. He never disappoints and is the reason I watch the show. I reaffirm to my wife my belief that the immaculately coiffed scouser is TV gold and has charisma by the bucketload.

'Why don't you put him on the boat instead?' she joked.

'What did you say?'

'Why don't you put him on the boat instead of DJs? He won't need turntables or a huge PA, and he certainly won't ask for a gram of cocaine before he goes on stage like that bloke did on Saturday.'

She had a point. Derek had now channelled his Ethiopian spirit guide, Sam. This was the clincher. 'You're right! Sam wouldn't demand an outside Commodore Cabin for himself, run up an astronomical bar tab I had to pick up or hassle me for Charlie,' I enthused.

'Really? How can you be so sure?'

'Because he'd been dead for 2000 years.'

That night I lay in bed being kept awake by the bloke gaming remotely in the flats opposite. My attempts at slumber were periodically pierced by cries of 'BASTARD!', 'YOU MOTHERFUCKER!' and 'OH, YOU TWAT!'. Then I had a thought, what if he wasn't gaming? What if instead he was engaging in S&M with a silent tormentor?

I tried not to picture the scene and thought about what Catherine had jokingly suggested and figured that not only did it make sense from a production perspective (no PA, turntables or lights to load in), involve no sound crew to feed and accommodate and no DJ agent politics, but it also presented an opportunity to watch one of the country's leading spiritual mediums up close and see if he really could commune with the dead.

Having seen ghosts and experienced some supernatural stuff, I know there's more to life than science can explain. But maybe by the end of the weekend with Derek I'd categorically know if there was life after death! The more I thought about it, the more excited I got, before drifting off to sleep to 'YOU CAN BLAST MY BOT, BUT I'M STILL STANDING, FUCKER!'

Radical Escapes was set up to cater for clubbers, but after a decade of decadence perhaps it was time to explore other avenues? When I set up in late 1999, no travel company catered exclusively for clubbers, and this was just as innovative. Life's too short to not do interesting things. At the very least it would be something to tell my mates about in the pub, or look back on when I'm old and grey... or when writing a book!

So, the next morning I emailed a proposal to Derek's management who called me straight back to check I could actually deliver it. It was then forwarded to Derek. They said it may appeal to him as he was a very 'forward looking' medium. I remember thinking that was a bit like saying a carpenter likes working with wood, or an F1 driver enjoys speed, but on reflection I guess they meant Derek welcomed new opportunities – which, I was to find out, was a curse as well as a blessing for me...

The next day Derek called me. He was in!

The ferry operators were happy to give it a go, probably relieved that it would avoid piquing the interest of the Harwich Customs and Immigration officers as my events usually did. The ship also reacted positively as the absence of all-night partying would allow the crew to go to bed before dawn for once.

The world's first psychic cruise set sail from Harwich in November 2005. After the ferry company rejected my working title 'Dead in the Water' for being 'too graphic', I settled on 'Spirit and the Sea' with the strapline, 'Cross over to the other side in style with a DFDS Seaways mini-cruise break'. (I know, I know, utterly shameless.)

Derek would appear on stage on both the outbound and inbound journeys, leaving me to suggest a suitable programme for the Saturday afternoon in Amsterdam. When I took clubbers on this route, the five-hour layover in Amsterdam would invariably be spent in the red light district and coffee shops. Despite the city's enviable array of world-class museums. It wasn't Van Gogh, Anne Frank or Rembrandt my guests flocked to see; it was the Sex Museum.

But as the clientele for this trip were mostly over sixties and female, I figured I had to lay on a more appropriate activity than a temple of Venus and penis, and found it in Gerd the Ghost Hunter: a mid-twenties history postgraduate with a penchant for black leather. After witnessing a ghost walk in London the previous summer, Gerd discovered some gruesome tales about the city in which he lived and, spotting a gap in the market, bought a medieval tailcoat in black leather and a black umbrella with a skull handle.

I offered his 'Haunted Amsterdam' tour as a bolt-on excursion, and it sold out within minutes. So, we added another which also sold out. In all, he ended up doing four fifty-five-minute tours and couldn't shake my hand long and enthusiastically enough as we bid goodbye. 'Let me know when you're next here,' he gushed as the buses departed from outside Hotel Victoria back to the port, waving us off with his black umbrella as his long vampire hunter coat billowed in the breeze as the wind appeared to be picking up...

As was usually the case, the journey back was made in a storm. Derek's show on the outbound leg had been well received, and with a successful and lucrative shore leave activity in the bag, all that stood between me and a new entertainment concept – *which I would own exclusively* – was the North Sea... in November.

The room we used for the performance was the ship's cinema, a dark internal room with steeply banked seating and an ineffective air-conditioning system. Derek's dressing room was the projection room in which he chain-smoked, and chain coughed. Smoking wasn't technically allowed, but Sven the Bursar turned a blind eye to it after Derek sent his mother's regards from the afterlife; a message whose authenticity was not in doubt as she congratulated her son on finally owning a Volvo, though it was 'a shame it was red as he knew it wasn't her favourite colour'.

A visibly shaken Sven accepted it as the real deal. 'She

always loved blue. How would he know such a thing?' he stuttered in awe.

Thick cigarette smoke snaked out whenever the door to the projection room was opened and hung spectre-like above the crowd, reinforcing the otherworldliness of the occasion. No one complained, not even the non-smokers, as it was Derek's smoke. I recall some may have even craned their necks to inhale it like they were receiving a sacrament.

Around half of the audience were comprised of his fan club who treated the trip as their annual convention. Many seemed to know him, and I couldn't help but wonder if he was aware of their social media profiles when he mentioned new homes, illnesses, holidays and family additions and losses during some readings.

It was clear some of the guests were not enjoying full health. Walking sticks were plentiful, which given the age group was to be expected, I guess. A lady called Rose took time to thank me for organising the trip. She explained that she had terminal cancer and had never left the UK before, buying a passport just for this trip.

'It's given me something to look forward to for months,' she explained.

'Wow! I hope you receive a message after going to all that trouble,' I replied.

'I hope I don't. It may be from my hubby, he was such a selfish man, I don't miss him at all!' She laughed guiltily before adding, 'To be honest I don't know if there's anything in it all, I just wanted to meet Derek and have one last weekend away with my cousin Eleanor and finally see Van Gogh's Sunflowers painting.'

It's 9 p.m. and the storm is making its presence felt. The

whole auditorium lurches from side to side like those Freedrop fairground rides. Ralph the support act, a part-time psychic investigator from Hartlepool has cut his act short to vomit into a duty-free carrier bag rather than a couple of septuagenarian sisters from Rochdale who are in the front row firing line.

Derek takes the stage doing that comedy side halt Norman Wisdom spent a career executing; three exaggerated hops before coming to a stop. His suit may be beige, but his face is green. Another wave hits and he shuffles across the stage and says, 'I'm... I'm getting the name... Mal... Whoa... who liked a flutter on the horses... oh-oh, here we go again...' Derek slides across the stage like a schoolkid on an iced-over playground puddle.

But there are no takers.

Now the vessel rises. Derek staggers back a few paces. As a veteran of the high seas, I know what's coming. Having reached its nadir on the huge crest, the ship starts to fall. Instinctively, the crowd grab their stomachs as they experience the humpback bridge effect. For a few seconds everyone is weightless. Derek is now in mid-air and automatically puts his arms out to steady himself. The sudden drop causes him to float a foot above the ground drawing gasps from the awestruck audience, before landing with a bump as the ship's bow meets the ocean with a huge BOOM!

Heroically, he perseveres for another forty-five minutes, delivering message after message in the midst of the tempest, psychically staggering around the stage, grabbing onto anything fastened to the floor. As playing under pain performances go, it was up there with Niki Lauder winning the Italian Grand Prix in blood-soaked bandages just six weeks after his horrific crash in 1976, and the limbless Knight in *Monty Python and the Holy Grail* who refuses to accept he's beaten, dismissing his amputations as flesh wounds. Derek was a trouper – a trouper on the soup.

After the show, whilst managing the queue for Derek's book signing in the Compass Club, Rose, the elderly lady with a walking stick I'd been talking to earlier, hovered nearby.

'Excuse me, dear, can I have a word?'

'Of course.'

She edged closer towards me, and beckoned for me to lower my head to her mouth and whispered, 'Did you see Derek levitate?'

She peered into my eyes. Her watery blue eyes were filled with childlike wonder. Derek didn't levitate, it was the ship's motion. But Rose saw it with her own eyes, and even if I'd explained he wasn't the messiah, she wouldn't have believed me. She had mere months to live and who could blame her for wanting to believe there was more to death than a hot fire followed by eternity trapped in an urn on a mantlepiece?

'I'll never forget it,' I truthfully confirmed.

Her eyes twinkled and she went to bed happy.

Books signed and selfies posed for, we retire to the bar. With a glass in one hand and a cigarette in the other, Derek is holding court. The storm has thankfully weakened. We talk about spirit, ancient Egypt, David Icke and Robbie Williams; both of whom Derek has spent time with recently. He tells me how Robbie sent a car to take him to his penthouse flat in Docklands, and how he had to take a private lift to the top floor which was guarded by a security fella who searched him on arrival.

'I told him, "I'm not carrying a knife or a gun, if that's what you're looking for".' He smiled but said nothing. Robbie told me it was him who was more concerned about hidden recording devices. See, he wanted to talk freely about some things which will remain between me and him. We spent the night talking and smoking cigarettes. No alcohol or anything else, just cigarettes. He was particularly keen on UFOs and aliens, which he's got some experiences of, actually.'

He said that David Icke contacted him after receiving a visit from some men in black. Icke had been posting accusations that President George W Bush was involved in a global paedophile ring. On his journey back from Gatwick to his house on the Isle of Wight following an overseas tour, he pulled into a petrol station on the M3 and was followed into the toilets, whereupon two smart-suited men with American accents read from a notebook. It was the precise timings of Icke's movements in the last twenty-four hours: where he'd been, what he'd done, who he'd spoken to and who he'd called. They told him his seat number on the plane, what he'd eaten on the flight, the bay he'd left his car in and the precise route he'd taken.

Derek said, David told him they knew where he was at all times, and that if he didn't cease slandering Mr President they knew where to find him. Understandably, Icke was shaken by this. Who wouldn't be?

Derek was fascinating company, surprisingly knowledgeable about the occult and a great gossip, whilst maintaining the confidence placed in him. By 5 a.m. everyone else had turned in, including the barman. I thanked Derek, we hugged and called it a night.

The following morning, as I walked across the car park to the cab which would take me to the airport, I noticed a photo pass in the window of a new blue Volvo. It read STAFF

PARKING, Chief Purser and had Sven's name.

A few days later, Derek's manager contacted me and told me Derek enjoyed the experience and would be interested in working with me again in the future – 'Only next time on dry land please.'

## Costa Del Acorah

A few months later The Derek Acorah Fan Club contacted me asking if I could put together an event for them. I was aware that Derek and his wife Gwen liked to spend time at their villa on the Costa Del Sol, and figured if we could find a location nearby it may work for everyone; Torremolinos wasn't far for Derek to travel, I'd save on accommodation costs and the fan club and I would get a weekend in the sun in November.

With the help of Nick at Vacation Club we secured a few hundred beds at a three- and four-star hotel complex in Torremolinos which was ideal: it had conference rooms which could be used for tarot and palm readings, and a large auditorium which was ideal for Derek's show.

'Spirit in the Sun' would feature two nightly shows headlined by Derek, and an imaginative bill which included an excellent mentalist who lived locally and another medium who offered private readings. All I needed was a ghost walk excursion for Sunday afternoon. I was sure I'd be able to find a haunted site somewhere close. But hours of fruitless searching confirmed that the most haunted spots in Spain were in Tenerife, Barcelona, Madrid – anywhere except the Costa Del Sol.

Then I saw a repeat of an award-winning documentary from 1988 called *Death on the Rock*. Although it was about a skirmish between the IRA and SAS, the title grabbed me. Further research revealed the Rock of Gibraltar possessed an abundance of apparitions, mostly the ghosts of British soldiers who died defending the rock in the thirty-four miles of tunnels which run through the rock connecting the cannon stations. Bingo!

'Ghost Hunting in Gibraltar' soon sold out.

On Sunday we took two coaches of ghost hunters an hour and a half down the A7 Cadiz–Malaga highway to the British enclave of Gibraltar.

Upon boarding, I was a little surprised to discover there were no toilets on the coach. The driver of my coach was called Ted, a smartly dressed expat from Fuengirola who reassured me we'd not be needing a 'latrine' as we'd be there by 'eleven hundred hours', but offered to facilitate a toilet stop halfway if we wanted.

When I took ravers and clubbers on coaches, I'd always insist on using coaches with toilets as there'd be constant drinking going on, but figured for the psychic oldies it wouldn't be an issue. A former sailor in the Royal Navy, Ted prided himself on timekeeping and discipline. His every utterance was imbued with a nautical air.

On drawing up to the hotel, he bellowed, 'All aboard!' before piping the old dears up the steps. As we set off, he grandly announced, 'Anchors away, setting a course south by southwest at a rate of eighty knots.'

Ted ran a tight ship – a tight ship without any toilets.

An hour later, the offer of a toilet stop still hadn't materialised. Discreet enquiries were placated by his finger pointing straight ahead at the imposing outline of 'The Rock' on the horizon, and the declaration 'port is within a couple of shakes,

ETA 1045 hours.' Our skipper was clearly reluctant to stop, which I put down to his military background and adherence to punctuality. To paraphrase Martin Sheen in *Apocalypse Now*, it may have been my excursion but sure as shit it was Ted's bus.

Sure enough, fifteen minutes later we arrived at the base of the iconic Rock of Gibraltar. And sure enough it was precisely 10.45. We were bang on time as Ted had predicted, which was just as well as many onboard were bursting for a wee.

Then we unexpectedly stopped at the side of what appeared to be a runway.

A number of ladies who had repeatedly indicated how much they were looking forward to spending a penny loudly groaned when the engine was turned off. After five minutes I asked Ted how much longer we'd be.

He peered down the runway into the late morning sun and sighed. 'Could be anything up to half an hour.'

I gulped hard. 'Half an hour? What's the problem?'

I then became aware of the sound of a distant drum. Through the heat haze I could see a wall of bright red shimmering and growing larger as the BOOM! BOOM! BOOM! was adjoined by the shrill metallic rasp of snare drums.

The driver unclipped his seatbelt and stood up, saying, 'Remembrance parade, they march along the runway to the War Memorial opposite City Hall remembering the fallen. Isn't it an honour to be here?'

I'd completely forgotten it was Remembrance Sunday! For a British military outpost, it's the most important day in the calendar. I was completely unaware the road into Gibraltar crossed the runway – which was now closed as it was on the parade route.

Over the microphone, I broke the news to my guests. A

mixture of protestations and panic. One lady was jigging in the central aisle. 'I need to go... now!' This prompted others to vocalise their struggle. Having been on the bus for nearly two hours, it was unreasonable to ask them to hold their straining bladders any longer.

I implored Ted, who was now standing to attention wearing a beret and proudly saluting as the massed ranks neared, telling him some ladies were in palpable discomfort.

But he ignored me and continued to stare straight ahead. 'The parade takes priority.'

'But they're in pain, they really need to get to a loo sharpish.'

Ted was unmoved,

'It's a small sacrifice to give for those who gave everything,' he replied stonily without averting his gaze.

Defeated, I slumped down in my seat, cursing my luck with coaches. Whenever I used them, something always seemed to go wrong. I thought about Nick and Rachel back at the hotel, lounging by the pool sipping cocktails.

Ten minutes later there was a shriek. 'I've just wet myself!'

'I bleedin' will too if I don't get to a loo sharpish!'

I had to act. I found myself shouting over the sound of the marching band which was now passing in front of us.

'Ted, there's going to be a mutiny if we don't do something.'

WEE-OO WEE-OO WEE-OO.

The sound of an alarm was followed by the angry hiss of the pneumatic doors opening. Someone had hit the emergency rear door opener. A group scuttled down the steps

'I gave no order to abandon ship!' bellowed Ted. But a full bladder doesn't seek permission.

Ted stared at the wing mirror and put his head in his hands. Through it, I could see a line of ladies squatting along the side of the bus... just as the open-topped car carrying dignitaries passed by.

As entrances go, it was a memorable one. Such was Ted's shame he never spoke another word to me or the guests. They found their time on the rock most productive; swapping video recordings of orbs and audio recordings of chains, and reports of ghostly apparitions all the way back to the hotel.

On arriving back, I walked into reception to find the hotel manager waiting for me wearing a concerned look.

'Mr Field, please go to the pool now. What is happening is... loco...' He walked away shaking his head. What the fuck was going on?

The sight which greeted me at the outdoor pool will be forever etched in my memory.

Along one side of the pool, my guests were kneeling in a line in front of Derek, who wore a thick white hotel towelling robe. His left hand held a tumbler of something with ice, while his right one – which held a cigarette – was placed on the forehead of the lady at the front of the line of genuflection, Derek uttered some words I couldn't quite catch, which caused the girl who was kneeling to hysterically writhe around screaming obscenities for a few seconds, before appearing to come to her senses and stand, calmy thanking Derek. Horrified hotel guests covered their children's ears and eyes. This process continued with the next girl in the queue.

Oh. My. Good. God. Derek Acorah was speaking in tongues and performing public exorcisms around a hotel pool in Torremolinos.

Ashamed as I am to admit it, my first thought was that I'd missed an opportunity; 'Throw your demons in the deep end with a Poolside Exorcism from the UK's leading Spirit

Medium!' would've made an eye-catching optional extra.

As a travel rep, I was used to being the party pooper. It was my job to tell the DJ to stop playing at the end of a party. If they didn't comply, I'd unplug the decks. Prematurely ending people's partying was one thing, but curtailing the casting out of demons was another level.

At that moment, Derek's wife Gwen appeared from the hotel with a face like thunder. Gwen was not to be messed with – even by Beelzebub – and swiftly brought things to a dignified close, saving me a job.

We celebrated that night with a paella, a couple of bottles of Ribera Del Duero and a midnight swim in the Med. Looking back it was a fantastic product, unique and innovative, and unlike my snow and Ibiza products, not limited by the seasons. Nick Vacation told me he thought it was the best event we'd done together. I had a solid working relationship with the most famous medium on the planet, the hotel group had forgiven the poolside possessions and the trip received a positive write-up in Spirit and Destiny magazine – the Mixmag of the psychic scene.

The following week I was contacted by an agent who wanted to take my 'Psychic Variety show' concept to the Benidorm Palace, the top cabaret venue in Europe with a capacity of 1,600.

Everything was looking up. What could possibly go wrong? As usual, it was something I had no control of whatsoever…

### Séancey

One Wednesday afternoon, I found a well-thumbed copy of the Daily Mirror on the train back to Enfield.

Derek had announced his biggest and most controversial

feat yet; to bring Michael Jackson back from the dead in a live séance. Sky TV said the show aimed 'to give fans a final chance to connect with The King of Pop' – who, they claimed, dabbled in the paranormal himself and once made contact with the ghost of Liberace via a Ouija board.

I felt this was an unnecessary risk, and more likely to awaken the critics rather than the spirits. I thought it was in bad taste and could backfire on any future events I did with Derek. I called his manager, who shared my doubts but told me Derek was insisting on going through with it after being approached by Sky.

As I feared, the channelling of Wacko Jacko was deemed a televisual low point. In an increasingly crowded market of TV mediums, Derek's possessions were his calling card. Not a week went by without a medieval Scottish monk, a cruel Cornish landowner or cockney serial killer using Derek's body to give messages from the grave (always in a gentle Liverpudlian accent, mind).

Sure enough, rather than the fragile high-pitched whisper he is remembered by, The King of Pop also spoke like a middle-aged scouse showman. The absence of any falsetto whoops or 'C'mon, girl!' only adding fuel to the critics' fire.

Like Jackson's 1987 album, it was bad – in fact, it could only have been worse had a possessed Derek declared 'Michael loves young Dick,' which thankfully he didn't.

*Michael Jackson: The Live Séance* was watched by over half a million people, yet a Yahoo poll voted it the worst programme of the year, The Guardian called it 'the worst single hour of television produced in 2009. Worse than Babestation, in fact.' (A station which no one has had cause to watch for an hour, incidentally.)

My heart sank. While I'd always regarded *Most Haunted* as entertaining melodrama rather than a spiritual experience, and had an open mind about mediumship, this gave the impression that Derek was more showman than shaman.

The negative reaction to the séance scuppered developing my Psychic Variety concept and I never worked with Derek again.

I needed a new medium and concept. I'd relocated to South Devon, over 300 miles from Harwich. I contacted Brittany Ferries, who sail from Poole and Plymouth, but they weren't interested as their routes were busy.

I worked with another household name in Torquay for a weekend I called 'Psychic Southwest'. Shortly before the show was due to start, his tour manager demanded a sea view suite. This wasn't in the contract, so we politely declined.

'Well then, the show doesn't go ahead,' was his reply.

With 400 people waiting for him to walk on, we had no choice, and forked out another £175, in addition to the perfectly decent four-star twin room we'd already booked and paid for. During the interval I followed the medium back to his dressing room. I think he was unaware I was behind him. If he was, perhaps he wouldn't have ripped down every poster of a popular female medium who was appearing at the same venue a few weeks later and wiped his feet on them as he made his way to the dressing room!

This was confirmation that the psychic world was very different behind the scenes and was filled with ego, jealousy, bitterness and greed. Everyone in the clubbing and music business knows it's full of sharks and snakes. I don't know anyone who hasn't been fucked over at least once, it's expected in a shady business. I naively believed the spiritual scene would be different. Looking back, it was worse.

## The Sexorcist

Around this time, I was asked by a local publican to organise Ghost Hunting weekends at his reputedly haunted sixteenth-century country pub in South Devon. A self-proclaimed exorcist offered to host the weekend; give a few talks and personal readings and lead the all-night vigil. I was somewhat surprised when he turned up with his girlfriend as he hadn't mentioned he was bringing someone else. This was a little naughty of him; it meant changing his room into a double and having to pay for another person's food. But as this was a new concept which I hoped would provide regular 'off-season' revenue, and as we were to be together for the weekend, in the interests of bonhomie, I swallowed it and said nothing.

His talks were interesting and the personal readings very popular (and at £20 for fifteen minutes, very lucrative for him, too) – so much so that he spent all day doing them!

But come 11 p.m., he was strangely absent from the vigil. People were understandably disappointed, so I knocked on his bedroom door, but received no reply other than pleasurable groans. I figured he'd be down soon afterwards and waited downstairs.

As it turned out, he wasn't needed; my guests filmed orbs floating around one room and captured footage of furniture moving of its own accord. They were so excited his lack of presence was forgiven.

The next morning, I asked the missing medium about his absence. He told me he was tired from the long drive to Devon and all the readings he'd delivered, and needed to conserve his psychic energy for the vigil later that night.

After another day of readings and his talk on a haunted

castle, we ate dinner and assembled around the fireplace and waited for the pub to close at 11 p.m. Everyone was there except our exorcist. We waited until midnight, when I went to his room, where once again I heard the grunts, groans and sighs of a couple having vigorous sex.

I returned half an hour later and they were still at it. An hour later I tried once more. This was the main event, what was he playing at? After repeatedly knocking, he opened the door a little, holding a towel around his waist, his sweat-soaked face etched with exhaustion.

'I'll be down in a bit,' he panted, before lowering his voice '…dealing with my own personal poltergeist at present,' and winking, closing the door on me.

Once again, he failed to show. Everyone could hear he was awake. The creaking bed and rhythmic knocking of the headboard on the wall made it impossible for me to cover for him.

The irony was it was easier to summon the spirits of eight-eenth-century sailors and a small girl who kept turning the lights on and off than my naughty necromancer.

The atmosphere at breakfast the next day was so tense you could've sliced it with a butter knife. People glared at the yawning medium, who acted like nothing was wrong.

I asked him for a word outside and demanded to know why he went to bed early again and hadn't come down as he'd promised. He replied that his girlfriend felt neglected as he'd spent all yesterday talking to other people, and felt she needed some 'TLC'.

I was speechless. He'd used my event as a dirty weekend, basically. He left with pockets full of cash from all the readings he did, and my concept was in tatters. The publican told me he'd had so many complaints from the guests that he didn't want to repeat the idea.

Having worked in this field, many ask if I believe in all that 'mumbo jumbo'. My answer is that having experienced things after people who were close to me have died, I feel there's definitely more to our existence than flesh and blood. I also believe that some people have access to another paradigm *some* of the time. But I don't believe that this can be turned on at will whenever a medium walks onto a stage. This is why they rely on cold reading and allegations of prior knowledge or information fed through hearing aids surface. As the star of the show – and the person whose performance *Most Haunted* relied on, Derek was undoubtedly under pressure from the production crew to come up with the goods week in, week out. He was in a Catch-22 situation: if he didn't find a connection, people may switch off, if he did, he risked being exposed as a fraud.

I feel there's a difference in pretending to be a dead highwayman for a TV show and misleading a vulnerable old lady that their deceased partner is sending them messages from beyond the grave to not trust someone whose name begins with B.

I hope my guests found comfort from any readings they received during my psychic events. If I believed any medium wasn't one hundred per cent genuine, I wouldn't work with them again – which probably explains why, like a T-shirt stall at a pop concert, I ran out of mediums.

At my 'Psychic Southwest' event I was invited to choose an angel card by one of the stall holders. I picked a card and turned it over. This prompted the following reading, which was printed out along with a photograph of my aura which was taken by a Kirlian camera.

'Angel Number one hundred and eighty-seven indicates both anxiety and stress, explore new ways to do business and trust in your intuition.'

At the very same time, deep below a thick layer of glacial ice, after sleeping peacefully for *precisely* one hundred and eighty-seven years, a volcanic eruption shook southern Iceland. Ash was ejected five miles into the sky, directly into the path of a southern jet stream. The plume reached mainland Europe causing the largest closure of international airspace since World War Two.

I had all my money tied up in over 500 flights and hotel beds for my Ibizan Heat package. While the airlines would've refunded the money, the hotels, being open, indicated they were not responsible for our transport and would not be issuing refunds, meaning I could be in a position where, through no fault of my own, I would not be able to deliver the holiday people had paid for – or be able to give them their money back. In short, I would be ruined financially and reputationally.

The eruption lasted for thirty-nine days, aviation disruptions continued into late May and eruptions lasted until June, finally ceasing a few days before my group holiday, Ibizan Heat, started. I got away with it. Again.

Upon reading this book back, prior to submission, I noticed the number one hundred and eighty-seven appears regularly; the Nostradamus quatrain relating to 9/11, the approximate distance in feet Eddie the Eagle twice jumped at the Calgary Olympics and the supposed year of my death when I was a sailor or pirate (1870). Coincidences, of course...

### Afterlife

Following allegations by another crew member that Derek's possessions were based on fake characters Derek left the show soon afterwards, taking all his possessions with him, and never speaking to, or of, Yvette again, citing a confidentiality clause in his contract. Yvette had no such qualms, spilling lurid accusations in her memoir – claims which Derek obviously can't respond to... Yvette hopes.

Derek passed away in early 2020. I have fond memories of him. I wish I could say the same for the other well-known mediums I worked with.

---

**Top Tune: Breather (Original Mix) – Afterlife {Topic}**

---

## BEHIND THE BROCHURE

To the holidaymaker it looks like the dream job – singing songs people love somewhere warm. But all jobs get boring, and the drudgery of playing the same songs six or seven nights a week over a five-month summer season is a challenge for all tourism troubadours.

Some change the chords to the songs. I know of one travelling minstrel who can play 'Hotel California' a different way each night, subtly substituting chords so it's always interesting for him.

Another friend does the same with the words; subtly sliding in seditious or obscene lyrics, the more shocking the better. His version of Bryan Adams' 'Summer of '69' opens with 'I got my first real sex dream', the bridge of 'Livin' On A Prayer' is 'It doesn't make a difference if we're naked or not'. But his favourite rewrite is to play the gentle Cuban folk song 'Guantanamero' to a room full of pensioners on a cruise ship, who sing and nod along, blissfully unaware he's actually singing, 'Wank on a mirror, why do you wank on a mirror?'

# 19

# TRIPPIN' ON SUNSHINE

*'People don't take trips. . . trips take people.'*
— John Steinbeck

*'Welcome aboard this Thomas Cook Boeing 737 to Ibiza...'* The calm and reassuring voice was one we would become very familiar with over the course of the most unforgettable flight I've ever taken.

Overhead lockers yawned and swallowed holdalls and jackets as people took their seats. Outside, a late September sun was still just visible over the flat roof of the terminal building, as the English autumn blew in on a gentle South Westerly breeze.

I walked down the central aisle and checked my boarding pass for the first time to see where I was sitting.

9... 10... 11... 12... 12A... 12B. Bugger! I was dismayed to find myself in a middle seat. No window to wonder from, nor fuselage on which to rest my head. No easy access to the toilet or opportunity to admire the uniforms working the central aisle.

The middle seat on a full plane is a dowdy housewife trapped in a loveless marriage, a cornered king on a chequered chessboard, a cabin-fever family on Bank Holiday Monday motionless on the M6. Whatever your age, when you're in the middle seat, you're back to being a hyperactive toddler strapped into a car seat. As the song nearly says, 'Clowns to the left of me, jokers to the right, here I am, stuck in the middle with me.'

Having bought eighty seats on the plane for my group, I was probably surrounded by my own guests. They were unaware I was the organiser of their package holiday which suited me, because if they were DJs, they'd be hassling me for slots.

Nearly two hours into the flight and all was well. People were chatting, conversations fuelled by the drinks trolley. Ibiza's eternal summer was only another thirty minutes away.

'BING!' A large sausage finger rose like a pink Saturn 5 rocket from the aisle seat next to me, scoring a direct hit on the button with the flight attendant figure on it. The digit belonged to the bloke next to me who'd been reading Mixmag for the duration of the flight and who I assumed was with the girl with short blonde hair in the aisle seat opposite. The flight attendant duly arrived, heard his request for a cup of water and returned a few minutes later holding a white plastic cup.

Then, after looking around to ensure he wasn't being observed, my neighbour, a moon-faced raver in his early thirties with close-cropped hair and crystal blue eyes, turned to face me to explain his request. 'Just a little something to help this go down.' In his hand he held a black speck. I was unsure what it was and examined it closely. His grin gave it away. It was a microdot – a dose of LSD.

Raising his hand to his mouth he licked the trip from his outstretched palm and took a swig of water. My expression was the facial equivalent of, 'Acid on a crowded plane – really?'

He read it and grinned. 'I'm playing at 4 a.m. in Judgement and like to be at the floaty part of the trip when I'm behind the decks. If I drop now, when we land I'll just be taking off!'

Further conversation revealed this was a routine he always followed when flying to Ibiza. If he was playing at Eden that night, he must be one of the DJs from my group. I hoped for both our sakes that he'd be able to hold it together and not make Judge Jules who'd given me the slots at his party regret it.

I made a mental note to be around the booth for the changeover with someone sane who could step in and play from 4 a.m. to 5 a.m. if needed. For the time being, it was best if he remained unaware of my identity.

'Enjoy this trip,' I said in my best 'Theme from S-Express' voice

He smiled and leaned over conspiratorially, mischievously confirming the next line, '...and it *is* a trip!'

He held out his hand and introduced himself, 'People call me Phil... Phil the Pill,' and winked. This was awkward. Even though he hadn't met me, he would've been aware someone called Kirk was running the event. So, rather than give a name, I merely replied, 'Nice to meet you, 'Phil'. I'm a federal undercover air marshal, and you're under arrest for possession of a Class A substance.'

He went white as a sheet, before my wink drew a relieved roar of laughter.

'Ha! You had me there!' He then turned to the blonde girl and said, 'Oi, babe, get this geezer!'

I sat back to listen to my Walkman.

All was quiet for the next ten minutes except for some excited 'oohs!' from a group of girls on the other side of the plane as we flew over Barcelona. The 'two hours in the air' queue for the toilet at the front grew halfway down the plane. Tanked-up and tattooed lads stood in line waiting to expel the three pints of Stella they'd drunk from the airside Wetherspoons earlier. Increasingly, the smooth ride became bumpy, causing periodic 'woah's!' as the line rose and fell like they were on one of my North Sea club cruises.

DING! The fasten seatbelt signs glowed amber.

'*Good evening ladies and gentlemen, this is Captain Chris Wills on the flightdeck. As you may have noticed the seatbelt signs are switched on as we're getting reports of a storm over Ibiza. Hopefully it'll have passed by the time we arrive, but in the meantime, please remain seated, return to your seats, and keep your seatbelts fastened. The toilets are now no longer in service.*'

'What?' shouted one person. The lads in the queue remonstrated with the flight attendant.

'I'm gunner piss moiself if oi downt 'av a slash sharpish,' one of them said.

The flight attendant was unmoved, putting her head on one side in a tokenistic display of sympathy. 'Sorry, Captain's orders, please return to your seat.'

Defeated, he turned on his heel. 'On your 'ed be it.'

This tickled Phil, who started giggling, drawing the attention of the cabin girl, who raised an eyebrow.

'Sorry, I'm just thinking about him weeing on your head.' He burst into a fit of laughter once more.

The flight attendant walked off, unimpressed.

The Pill kept giggling, occasionally emerging from his fit to assume a serious expression, before collapsing once again in laughter. His mirth was labelled 'microdot'.

BING BONG. '*Cabin crew dim lights for landing.*'

From my limited view out of the portside window, I could

see a huge cumulonimbus cloud rapidly growing. The rate at which it bubbled vertically upwards was striking. The next time I looked it had reached its nadir; the colder atmosphere air it couldn't penetrate causing it to spread horizontally forming a menacing mushroom cloud.

FLASH!

For a split second the inside of the plane was illuminated by a purple light.

FLASH!

Then another, this time also visible outside.

The plane shook as it entered a fresh bout of turbulence.

I could see from Phil the Pill's eyes that he was coming up, He gripped the armrests with both hands so tightly that his knuckles were white. His head was level and stared straight ahead. I wanted to tell him that his left hand wasn't clenching the armrest but my right hand, but he was miles, possibly universes away. His eyes protruded so far I wanted to pull out his tray to catch them before they dropped onto the floor.

BING BONG: '*As you may have seen, unfortunately the storm hasn't passed, so we're going into a holding pattern until it's safe to land. We do expect to encounter some turbulence, so please remain seated with seatbelts fastened.*'

'Oh, Christ,' muttered the Pill.

His girlfriend reached over and held his hand across the aisle. 'Hang on in there, babe, we'll be landing soon.'

Our holding circuit was effectively around the apocalyptic storm cloud; a towering, glowering vertical swirl of vicious water vapor which was now pulsing spectacularly with fork lightning.

'Wow! It's like something from a movie!' gushed the girl in the window seat.

'A bleedin' horror movie,' muttered the Pill.

The plane suddenly dropped, causing everyone's shoulders to rise in a synchronised shrug followed by the smell of multiple farts as half a dozen overhead lockers loudly sprang open, spewing forth its contents onto people's heads. Above the central aisle, lower jaws bounced on their hinges like giant monster mouths chewing.

'URGH!' The Pill's hand finally left mine as it was needed to catch his eyes. He leaned over and said something to his girlfriend, who pointed at the chattering open lockers slowly, caught my eye and exaggeratedly mouthed the words, 'Croc-o-diles, he thinks they're crocodiles,' to me.

This would explain why the Pill was pinned as far back in his seat as was physically possible, like a Red Arrows' pilot pulling 5G, his face was contorted like it was being yanked back by an invisible force. His mouth was stretched into an upside-down smile reminding me of a bar room Robert de Niro impression. The fella really was going through hell, trying to get as far away from the snapping monsters as his seatbelt would allow.

A flight attendant hurriedly appeared from the front, collected the jettisoned items, and slammed shut the gaping jaws.

''ere, I really need the loo...' the bladder-challenged vest shouted from further back.

'Remain seated,' she snapped back. You know it's time to worry when even the cabin crew are shitting themselves.

The plane continued its hellish circuit. Another three times around the fearsome thunderhead, each time progressively closer. The blue forked lightning was by now constant: a magnificent, malevolent skeletal strobe. When they have an electrical storm in the Mediterranean it's a light show worth sitting on your balcony with a glass of wine and watching. But when you're in a metal can flying around in it, it's no fun. The smell of farts was discernible. No one spoke. That's when you know people are really scared.

At this point I felt something I'd never felt before. With my stomach muscles clenched, my heart pumping far too fast for comfort, and my breathing shallower than a reality show contestant's ambition, I exhaled and completely relaxed. I found myself encased in a calm, peaceful state of Buddha-like serenity. It wasn't like I wasn't aware of the danger I was in, or thought it any less serious or life-threatening than I did previously, but that somehow, it was 'Okay.' A voice deep inside, deeper than my mind or conscience, more intimate than from my heart or soul told me – without using words – that my work was done and that I'd 'passed it on'. This gave rise to a subtle but comforting peace. It was the strangest sensation,

From that point on I enjoyed the ride. I marvelled at the atmospheric lightshow, absorbed each thunderclap, and stoically accepted my fate, whatever it was. I tried to soothe The Pill by offering him some water and focus on the end of my life, content, calm and in an accepting manner.

This wasn't an emotional reaction or governed by logic. My first child had been born earlier that year. At the age of forty I was finally a father. My wife had practically stopped working and I had no life insurance policy, so perishing in a plane crash would've been a problem financially and certainly not okay. Emotionally, I wanted to see him grow up, play football with him, be there when he wobbled through his teenage years. To miss this wasn't okay.

Looking back, the only way that this was acceptable was

from a genetic point of view. I believe it was my DNA talking. I'd finally got to enjoy the view rather than fear the impact.

The Pill stared at the ventilation nozzle in the overhead panel above. Despite blowing at its most forceful, his face remained masked in sweat and resembled a bloated red cabbage. I turned mine in his direction to increase the airflow, aligning it with his. He stared at the two gaping mouths and turned to the blonde girl. 'Babe, the chicks need feeding.'

'For fuck's sake...' the girl shook her head.

BING BONG: '*We're going to make an attempt to land, cabin crew, ten minutes to landing.*'

The Pill wiped his brow. 'Thank fuck for that.'

As we turned into the wind for our final approach, rain was audible as it was lashing at the windows, HISSS... HISSS... HISSS! before snaking down in trembling rivulets towards the rear of the window.

The Pill once again leant over to whisper something to his girlfriend. After getting him to repeat it, she resignedly shook her head and urged him to lean forward to create a direct eyeline to me. As the plane shook once more I carefully watched her lips form the word, 'Snakes,' whilst pointing at the window as it hissed once more.

My ears popped as we descended. Beneath my feet I heard the reassuring tummy rumble of the undercarriage being employed. The wings were wobbling alarmingly in the erratic wind outside, the horizon darting in and out of view through the rain-spattered window. Still, we continued our unsure descent, with the grace of a balsa wood plane's maiden flight when the weight at the front isn't in the right position and it plunges nose first into the ground.

When we were around fifty feet off the tarmac and anticipating a bump to signify the end of our nightmare, the engines instead emitted a huge roar, throwing us back into our seats as our speed sharply increased. The noise of the engines was deafening. Where there was silence, there was now a sustained scream as the pilot pulled back on the throttle. The plane started climbing sharply. I looked at the cabin crew who were sitting facing the passengers, seeking reassurance. Instead, my own expression stared back at me. They were as scared as we were.

As we soared back into the tempest the smell of dropped guts returned. Then things went to another level altogether: the oxygen masks dropped, bursting out like a mass of plastic tentacles into people's faces, prompting screams.

A calm recording – and it *must've* been a recording – struggled amongst the screams

'*Place the mask on your face first before helping your child.*'

'URGH! JELLYFISH!' The Pill turned away and reached out for his blonde partner who'd had enough.

'Crocodiles, snakes, hungry bloody birds, now jellyfish. It's a plane to bleedin' eye-beefa, Phil, not Noah's friggin' Ark.'

The captain explained over the intercom that due to the amount of surface water on the runway, he had to abort the landing, and the sudden change in gravity automatically released the oxygen masks, which were being worn by petrified passengers; clear plastic umbilical cords connecting them to the mothership.

Half an hour later we were attempting another landing, this time in Palma Mallorca. But as they'd also received a deluge, I could see the runway was still being cleared. So, we circled again. And again. An hour later it still wasn't safe to land. We'd been in a holding pattern for the duration, slowly but surely draining the fuel tanks. They had to allow people to use the toilet after a couple of lads insisted that if they weren't unlocked, they were going to do it in the aisle.

As it was now 3 a.m., my group realised they'd missed their first night out in Ibiza and decided to have the party on the plane. Pills were broken in half and swallowed, lines were chopped out on tray tables, and bottles of duty-free Vodka were liberated from overhead lockers and passed around in plastic bags. The flight attendants couldn't cope and gave up. The Pill appeared to have come through the worst and was rocking back and forth in his seat, sharing a set of Walkman earphones with his blonde partner. The cabin was filled with a triumphant sense of survival toasted by intoxication; it felt like a cross between VE Day and Dante's Inferno.

After another twenty minutes, the bonhomie was curtailed by Captain Wills.

'*Well, as you're aware, folks, it's taking them longer to clear the runway as there's some possible structural damage which needs to be examined before Air Traffic Control can give us permission to land. As we have finite fuel reserves, we have no alternative but to fly immediately to Menorca, where we'll refuel. Everyone will be removed from the aircraft and given breakfast, before we reboard you and take you on to your holiday in Ibiza.*'

By now, everyone was a tired and intoxicated emotional wreck. They could've said they were taking us to Siberia, and we wouldn't have minded. We just wanted to get out of this fart-filled tin can.

As far as the Pill was concerned, the Captain may as well have been speaking Cantonese. 'What's happening?' He pulled his earphone out and looked around.

'We're getting off, luv,' replied his long-suffering partner, '…thank God.' She glanced at me.

'Happy days!' The Pill pressed the attendant call button before standing up, recovered his small canvas rucksack from the overhead locker and strode to the front. It all happened so fast that no one could challenge him. Necks craned as the shambling figure walked past the cabin crew who were just belting themselves in having sat down for landing. I looked at the blonde girl. Her head was in her hands.

As the cabin crew rose as one to challenge him, the Pill patiently waited by the front door of the plane like he was expecting it to open. The cockpit door then opened and a concerned middle-aged male in a white shirt gently led the airborne acid casualty back to his seat.

'Who's with this passenger?' Reluctantly, the blonde girl slowly put her finger in the air.

Can you please explain to him that it may indeed be 'his stop', but he will remain in his seat until told otherwise? Sheepishly, she nodded. The Pill couldn't understand what all the fuss was about.

'You said it was time to get off?'

Thirty minutes later, we were sitting in the bright cafeteria in Menorca airport, drinking orange juice and struggling to digest a crusty complimentary croissant. The plane had been in the air for so long that the flight crew had to be changed which took another few hours. By the time this had been announced, one busload of passengers had already reboarded. I was on the second bus, which was mercifully held, allowing us more time to stretch our legs in the cafeteria. I couldn't see The Pill anywhere, meaning he was probably already back on the plane. I was relieved not to have to play co-pilot for anymore animal hallucinations and hoped his trip was now wearing off.

Whilst I was waiting I struck up conversation with a group

who I suspected were also on my trip. Beyond tired and loose tongued from the cheeky half they'd had on the plane to stay awake, they remarked they knew the bloke who was sitting next to me. He was called The Pill because he had access to a press which manufactured millions of a certain type of ecstasy tab in a lab in South London. Considering my position as a tour operator and given my previous run-ins with UK customs, The Pill was not the sort of person I should be sitting next to on a plane. As I've said previously, for the authorities, 'clubbing' plus 'travel' equates to a cover for drug trafficking.

I went to the toilet and splashed cold water on my face. So far, none of the cabin crew had seen me talking with him, and if he was detained for any reason there was no association between us other than that we had been seated together. I decided to maintain my distance from him for the last short hop to Ibiza. As we would only be in the air for less than an hour, it wouldn't be that hard – or so I thought.

At precisely this moment, The Pill was dismantling my Sony Walkman in the aircraft toilet. Twenty minutes later I returned to my seat and boy was he pleased to see me! Once I was sat down, much to my annoyance, he began conspiratorially whispering, 'Everything's okay, I've sorted it.'

I just humoured him. 'Good man,' I said, and began looking in the seat pocket for my Walkman. It wasn't there.

'They said thank you, and not to tell anyone about it, but you deserve to know 'cos it was in your seat.'

'What was?'

He looked around to ensure no one was watching, before conspiratorially whispering, 'The bomb.'

'Bomb?' I said out loud.

'Shhh!' He put his hand over my mouth. 'It's okay, I told

them I found it in the toilet, you're in the clear.'

I pulled his hand away. 'What are you talking about?

He leaned forward and beckoned me to do the same. 'We all had to leave the plane 'cos the pilot was told there was a bomb aboard, right? Well, they couldn't find it, so when I got on, I had a quick butchers and there it was in your seat pocket! So, I took it to the toilet and defused it. They kept knocking on the door, but when I handed them it, defused and all, they didn't mind at all and thanked me for the trouble I'd gone to.'

'What did the bomb look like?'

'The murderous bastards put it in a Sony Walkman, it looked exactly like a cassette. Clever, eh? But they didn't fool me.'

Over his shoulder I could see the blonde girl failing to stifle a giggle.

The cabin crew gave me my Walkman back but my mixtape of Paul Oakenfold immaculate set at Tribal Gathering in '95 now resembled a metallic brown mass of spaghetti tangled like the Pill's thought process in a black plastic bin liner.

We finally landed in Ibiza at 8.30 a.m. on Monday, ten hours after we took off from Gatwick. No one complained at having missed the first night of their holiday as they were just relieved to be alive. The euphoria of landing in Ibiza brought Phil up again. He stood goggle-eyed next to the luggage belt, hugging strangers and repeating the line, 'Oibeefa! I can't believe we're actually in Oibeefa.'

That year there was a poster in the arrivals' hall promoting different regions of Spain. This gave me an idea. I stood next to a large backlit illuminated poster of Galicia, a region in Northern Spain and called the Pill over.

'Mate, I think you're mistaken. We couldn't land in Ibiza. This is Galicia, look. We're taking buses to Valencia and getting on the ferry.'

'Wha-at? How long will that take?'

A few feet away a girl sat glumly behind the desk of a car rental company.

'Excuse me, how long does it take to drive to Valencia?' I asked her.

'Valenthee-a... Valenthee-a?'

She pulled a long face, forcefully exhaling through her mouth, causing her lips to make an equine farting noise. I expected her to start neighing. She clearly couldn't comprehend what I'd just said. It was like I'd asked her how many grains of sand there are on the beach, or what the weather was doing on the day I was born.

With her face frozen, mouth open showing her teeth, she began tapping at her keyboard, 'Valenthee-a... nine hours and sixteen minutes. You want a car?'

The Pill walked away shaking his head in disbelief.

I declined the offer and thanked her and caught up with the Pill reasoning, 'Spain's a big country, mate, we're on the other side. Nine hours is probably about right.'

'I don't doubt that,' the perspiring head replied, 'but when did horses learn how to use computers?'

The transfer bus to the hotels took twenty minutes to board as people were either smoking outside, still in the toilet, or had boarded the Thomson Holidays coach next to ours by mistake, scaring the life of the children and old people on it. On ours, the heat and arduous journey started taking its toll. Some people nodded off, including The Pill. When I woke him upon reaching his hotel half an hour later, I told him he'd slept all the way from Valencia, and we were finally in Ibiza. He was so happy he hugged me.

The following year, the Pill brought around a hundred people with him. I like to look after my promoters, so I upgraded him from a standard self-catering apartment to one of the deluxe twin rooms in another hotel, which also included breakfast and evening meal.

After checking in, he pulled me to one side and expressed regret that he didn't have self-catering facilities in his accommodation. This is unusual as the kitchens in self-catering units must be the most neglected gas hobs in the history of kitchen appliances. In twenty years of room visits, I've never once interrupted someone making a spaghetti bolognaise, beef stew or even heating up a tin of beans (they eat them cold from the tin, with a fork).

Only the South Africans would visit a butcher and get a 'braai' going on their terrace, controlling the heat by scientifically wafting with an empty cornflakes packet. The nearest to cooking most Ibiza holiday makers get is pouring boiling water into a Pot Noodle.

I reassured him. 'But, Phil, you don't need a kitchen! Simply go downstairs and order whatever you like. The cafe is open from 7 a.m. to midnight, it's all sorted!'

He walked back over to his wife and explained the situation. Despite my provision enabling them to eat for free whenever they liked, I could tell they still weren't satisfied – and sure enough ten minutes later she was at my table as I handed out wristbands to new arrivals.

'I really need an oven as I need to bake a cake for Phil's birthday on Monday,' she implored.

This was getting to be a pain. I'd upgraded them to a superior room, was offering to cover their food and here she was moaning because she didn't have a flaming oven.

I told him the self-catering apartments were all full now and that the owner of the hotel would be personally offended if they moved out after I'd specifically requested VIP treatment for them. I offered to ask the hotel if she could have access to the kitchen specifically to bake the cake on Monday morning. Once again, they discussed this with furrowed brows, and once again they appeared dissatisfied.

A few hours later I was at Itaca beach bar setting up the party and my phone rang.

It was Phil, asking if I knew of any camping shops.

'Camping shops? Why would you need a camping shop?'

'Erm, I need to buy some glow sticks for the party later.'

'You don't need a camping shop, Phil. There's a shop at the bottom of the west end which sells glow sticks. I can pick some up for you when I'm in there later if you want?'

I heard a female voice in the background say 'Walking boots'.

'Oh yes, I also need some walking boots, see?'

I thought I knew San Antonio like the back of my hand, but this request had me stumped. I didn't have him down as a hiker, but who was I to judge?

'I'll do some research and send you a text later.'

My phone rang again. It was a manager of one of the hotels we were using. Apparently one of my guests couldn't stop masturbating. He'd been walking around the hotel furiously power wanking, apparently unaware he was doing it. The police had been called, took one look and called for medical back up. I arrived at the accommodation on my scooter just as he was being removed from the building by two paramedics, strapped to an upright stretcher trolley as they couldn't fit a horizontal trolley in the small lift. Despite being restrained, he continued his rhythmic tugging as they loaded him into the ambulance, wild-eyed and shameless. Not a good look – but good timing; it was the pre-camera phone era, remember, so he got away with it... until now!

Understandably distracted, I completely forgot to ask anyone about the camping shop. As excuses go, it's a rock solid one which would stand up in court...

However, as I rode back to Itaca I passed a hardware shop and who should be emerging but Phil and his missus carrying a large box. I stopped to apologise for forgetting to contact them.

'It's okay, we're sorted,' he said, his moon face beaming.

'What've you got?'

'A stove.'

'A stove?' I still didn't get it. 'But you're half-board, Jonny will cook whatever you want from the menu.'

'What we want isn't on the menu, mate,' he said with a mischievous glint in his eye.

'I'm sure he could knock it up for you. All you've got to do is ask him. He does a great paella,' I said, but they had walked off.

A few days later at the end of the trip, he asked me if I knew anyone who wanted a camping stove for free. It was then I discovered the camping stove was to cook up the ketamine he'd brought over with him in liquid form.

**Top Tune: Josh Wink – Higher State of Consciousness (Tweekin Acid Funk Mix) {Strictly Rhythm}**

## BEHIND THE BROCHURE

In twenty-five years of evicting guests from their rooms at the behest of the hotels, no one has ever admitted guilt. It's always the room next door, an uninvited visitor (or in one case, stray cats) who caused the issue, never them. The introduction of security cameras made things easier… for a while…

I was called by the hotel at 9 a.m. one morning. When this happens it's always bad news. I arrived at a scene from a horror film: blood and broken glass covered the floor. The occupant, a Geordie lad in his early 20s was being interviewed by the local police and medics, all of whom wore latex gloves and resigned expressions on their faces who have experienced far too many of these scenes. The conversation went like this:

'What are yous doin' in me room?'

'We are here to help.'

'Okay, then give us sum coke or ket, or you can fuck off.'

He'd been hit over the head with a bottle of vodka after the brother of the girl he'd brought back to his hotel room – and allegedly wouldn't let leave – had arrived at his hotel room to 'rescue' her. After being hit, he chased him down the stairs and out into the car park bleeding profusely from the head wound and retaliated by lamping him with a bottle of rum. I know this because I watched it all on the hotel CCTV. The police strongly urged him to attend the hospital for treatment, but he was aware that unless they arrested him, he was under no obligation to seek medical treatment. They had just started their shift and were reluctant to take him into custody. I persuaded them to let me and the hotel deal with it, and told him to get his head down for a few hours.

When I returned late afternoon the place was spotless.

His roommates had cleaned the place from top to bottom as they didn't want to be thrown out. I calmly told him the hotel wanted him to leave. He refused, saying he'd done nothing wrong. I pointed to his gaping wound. He said he banged his head in the shower, and was in complete denial as to what had happened.

'It's my word against yours,' he kept repeating.

So, we showed him the hotel CCTV, which drew the response, 'AI! That's fucking AI. Why, I'm not buying this dodgy deep fake bullshit, it's a set-oop!'

# 20

## JUST ̵EAT

*Oh, we did like to e beside the seaside,*
*we did like to e beside the sea*
*Asking 'what's your name, where you from, what you on'?*
*as Spiderman danced to a tribal drum*
*Oh, we did like to e beside the seaside,*
*we did like to e beside the sea.*
*The sun, the sand, the beats the freaks*
*best of all – it was free!*
(*Bye Bye Bora Bora* – Kirk Field)

I sensed having done Ibiza, the promoters I'd launched my Ibiza packages, Fevah and Frantic, wanted to prioritise their London shows. So, I decided to go forward with Heat UK after being introduced to Damian 'Damo' Gelle at Retox in Covent Garden by the genial Justin Langton.

Straight away I could see Damo was a dynamo and potentially a strong partner, but his opening line threw me somewhat. After exchanging pleasantries, he sat back and folded his arms, saying, 'Look, I know you're the best at what you do, but your tours need to be even better if we're to work together.'

What the fuck? This could go one of two ways…

'What do you mean? I can get your DJs on at Manumission, Eden, Es Paradis and Kanya, can anyone else offer you that?'

'No, but I want to throw a party at Space. Deliver that and I'll bring you 500 people.'

This was a tall order. Space was being constantly awarded 'World's Best Club', and had a strict 'house music only' policy. Hard house was never heard there. It was programmed by a no-nonsense German called Fritz, who I was aware had turned away much bigger brands than us and went about his business with typical Teutonic efficiency – a rare commodity in Ibiza in those days.

Space had the pick of the promoters and every DJ on the planet wanted to play there. How could I get a bunch of hard house loving Aussies and their relatively unknown DJs into the most revered club on the planet?

By early May we had 387 booked for the first Ibiza Heat, so Damo and I flew out to try to secure the Space show which meant so much to him.

As many chancers and bullshit artists wash up on Ibiza's beaches as waves. I knew how every Tom Dick and Harry would promise venues the earth to get through the door, so I'd printed off the hotel reservations and flight list to prove we had the heads.

Additionally, Damo wore a T-shirt with the Ibizan Heat artwork on his back and walked around the island like a human flyer.

After a few days of trying, we finally got a meeting with the fearsome Fritz. We'd made the mistake of walking along the beach from Figuretas in the searing midday sun so we could say hi to Gee Moore at Bora Bora en route, and as a result arrived parched. Nervously, we went around the back of the club and pressed a small buzzer marked *oficina*. After giving our names, we were told Fritz was in a meeting, shown to a corridor and told to wait. This was the big time. We felt like two naughty schoolboys waiting to see the headmaster. We were relieved to see a water cooler next to us, and so we helped ourselves to a plastic cup of chilled water. It tasted good. So much so that we drank another. Ten minutes later we drank one more. It was at this point we remembered how much the water was in Space and worked out we'd just drank over €50s worth!

Another five minutes went by, we could still hear Fritz talking in his office, so we had another two complimentary cups of water. After another five minutes of waiting in silence, I was starting to feel we were wasting our time.

'I hope this bloody meeting is worth all the effort we've made to get here. It costs £110 each for the flights plus hotels and taxis, all to sit in a corridor and drink water.'

Damo jumped up and snatched my empty cup. 'Well, pardner, let's at least get our money's worth on the water!'

I loved it. During the thirty-five minutes we were kept waiting, we sank cup after cup of water which was sold in the club at this time for €8. We didn't stop until we'd each swallowed what we'd spent on the flights. We were literally throwing it down like it was a Guinness World Record attempt. After downing another cup, I stood up to go for a pee, but the frosted glass door suddenly opened and Fritz appeared, bidding goodbye to his previous guest and beckoning us in.

This was no time to go to the toilet.

We sat down and started our pitch. We'd rehearsed it thoroughly and traded lines in a choreographed presentation.

We were very clear about our areas of expertise. Damo was a promoter like no other who had the DJs and crowd, while I managed travel aspects and logistics, getting them to the club for opening in private buses and guaranteeing a minimum of 400 tickets in advance by pre-paying by bank transfer. We then showed him proof of our bookings, This impressed him, and showed we were confident we'd get the numbers.

'Is there a flyer for your event?' he asked.

Damo stood up, whipped off his jacket and spun around showing Fritz the Ibizan Heat artwork writ large across his shoulders. A bemused Fritz drew closer and traced the strapline with his forefinger. '500 people, fifty DJs, fifteen parties, seven days, one island...' He sat back down and checked his diary. 'What date do you say?'

'Sunday 26 June,' we chorused in unison.

He sat back down and checked his calendar once more. 'You can have the club from 8 a.m. opening until 4 p.m. and your DJs can play the opening sets on the terrace. But I need a favour.'

Damo folded his hands. 'Of course, fire away.'

Fritz grabbed his car keys from the desk and stood up.

'Come with me.'

The next thing we knew we were speeding towards Ibiza Town in a black BMW, giving me no opportunity to relieve my bulging bladder.

Where was he taking us? And what did he want in return? What could *we* possibly do for the guy who managed the World's Best Club?

After winding through a maze of narrow cobbled lanes, we arrived outside a building site at the back of a crumbling cul-de-sac beneath the old city walls. Surrounded by scaffold, it was a hive of activity; wooden boards rattled as work boots stomped across them. A bucket of cement clanged against the wall as it was being hoisted up to a second-storey window in a rope and pulley. Fritz signalled for the pneumatic drill which was inside the front door to cease its pummelling.

Fritz held out his hands like Christ the Redeemer. 'This is Angelo's, it was the first gay club to open in Ibiza in 1968.'

'Is there a toilet?' I interrupted, jiggling from one leg to the other. Fritz didn't notice, preferring to focus on the tanned shirtless builder in denim shorts who was working on the staircase.

'Sorry...?'

I repeated my question. 'There will be! It's been derelict for many years. I've bought it and will open late June, but I need a test event to see if it works and for my staff to have a dress rehearsal before our opening the night after your party.'

'Our party? I don't follow.'

'If you do a night here on Saturday, you can bring your group to Space afterwards.'

This wasn't ideal. For an all-day session at Space, we really wanted people to be fresh. Running an event here would mean they'd already be eight hours into oblivion before our all-important debut at the World's Best Club. But if we wanted the prize of hosting our own area at Space we didn't really have a choice, and any protracted discussion would've ended in me pissing my pants on the spot, so of course, we immediately accepted. We bade him goodbye and then excused ourselves to look for a loo. But couldn't find anywhere which was open, so we climbed some steep steps into a quiet alleyway and emptied our bulging bladders against a wall, our steaming stream of piss cascading down the steps, a rushing torrent of golden relief which pooled at the bottom where the alley was intersected by another lane. Then, through the rising steam a figure walked across the path at the bottom of the steps. Upon reaching the junction, he paused, gazed at the puddle, and followed the amber rivulet up the steps before his eyes came to rest on two street urchins, pissing in the street. It was Fritz.

We smiled and waved like nothing was happening. He acknowledged with a slight nod and walked on.

'Do you think we've blown it?' I asked?

'Nah, if he didn't charge so much for water in there, or keep us waiting, we wouldn't have drank so much of it. It's on him, mate.'

## Space: The Final Frontier

Our referral partners that year included Niall, an Irish as-they-come happy, go lucky Jack-the-lad with the same disarming face as the comedian Sean Hughes, sparkling blue eyes, and a charming lilting southern Irish brogue. Judging from the way Niall promoted the package he hadn't so much as kissed the Blarney Stone but snogged it to smithereens. In the pre-internet era of promoting, Niall was known for his 'imaginative' descriptions of the accommodation we used; the five-star suites with stunning sea views and hot tubs on the terrace which overlooked the sunset. This would've been all very well and good if we actually had any five-star suites with stunning sea views and hot tubs on the terrace which overlooked the sunset! We offered basic, but clean budget accommodation where people slept (or tried to), in between endless partying. His exaggerations were exacted to attain the best DJ slots for himself, which were allocated to the affiliate partner who brought the biggest numbers.

I remember dealing with a complaint from two of his guests, a couple who had sacrificed their first night partying in order to get up at the crack of dawn to sit on the rocks at Mambo for two hours, after Niall told them it was the most famous sunrise in the world.

'Where's the feckin' jacuzzi?' meetings were always my first appointment on the day after Niall's group arrived. He just couldn't help himself. To avoid the wrath of the group he'd misled, he'd avoid where they were staying and loiter around the Poniente (aka Ibizan Heat Hotel) bar until someone offered him the use of their sofa. On one memorable occasion no such invite arrived, and as the bar closed at 2 a.m. Niall was shunted into the tiny lift by the night manager... where he was found at 8 a.m. the following morning by the reception staff as they arrived for work. He'd spent all night going up and down like a teenage boy's right hand, reportedly snoring loudly in the foetus position, protectively hugging a bottle of Buckfast Tonic Wine.

Niall's figurative descriptions had earned him a covered slot at Space. He was to play the closing set in the Discotheque which closed at 4 p.m. In those days Space was open twenty-two hours a day, from 8 a.m. to 6 a.m.

At 7.55 a.m. we shepherded most of the group from Tantra a few minutes up the street to Space. Our first DJ went on and everyone was happy – everyone except Niall, who'd discovered there was no re-admission. He hadn't eaten anything for twenty-four hours and was starving.

Although he was starving, he knew that if he left, the door staff wouldn't let him back in. Any DJ reading this will appreciate how big a deal it was to play Space. It's the equivalent of a footballer playing at Wembley, a tennis player walking out on Centre Court or a cricketer scoring a century at Lords. His method of overcoming the hunger pangs he was feeling was to neck another cheeky half pill every few hours. But twelve hours is a long time to wait, and as morning turned into afternoon, Niall was struggling and tried another approach; drinking lots of water. But this being Space proved unsustainably expensive. Another hour went by, Niall stood at the side of the DJ stand, one hand on his stomach, bent double, 'My stomach's rumbling like a flamin' earthquake.'

The penultimate DJ went on. His set was within reach. If he could just hold out for just one more hour, all the pain and discomfort would be worthwhile. Another nibble would see him through, he thought. Someone asked him if he'd asked if they sell snacks at the bar.

A lightbulb went on. Why hadn't he thought of this? he admonished himself.

Dashing to the bar, shimmering and sweating, he finally caught the bar girl's attention.

'Do yous sell crisps?'

'Que? Creeps?'

'Crisps, Tayto crisps,' he mouthed, pulling out and biting a crisp.

The girl shook her head

'How about nuts, 'ere, fella, what the Spanish for nuts?'

The bloke next to him said something which Niall bellowed, growing ever more desperate, 'Noasis, noasis, have yous got any?'

Once again, the girl shook her head, but Niall's hunger was now over-riding logic. He just wouldn't take noasis for an answer.

'WHAT? YOU MUST HAVE SOMETHING TO EAT?!'

A tight black shirt with CONTROL across the shoulders appeared behind the increasingly shouty Irishman. The security at Space weren't hired for their diplomatic skills. They wielded batons, not reason, and could see Niall was the worse for wear, growing ever more agitated and remonstrating with the bar staff... so this was not the best time for him to plead with outstretched arms, 'MINI CHEDDARS? TWIGLETS? YOU MUST HAVE FECKIN' TWIGLETS, ROIGHT...?'

The bar girl just stared at him. Another CONTROL shirt appeared and together they dragged Niall backwards away from the bar, as he bellowed the words 'PORK SCRATCH-INGS?' whilst oinking like a pig.

They ejected him thinking he was having a fit. For the remainder of the party, he stood forlornly at the front entrance, discontentedly munching on slices of pizza from Tantra repeatedly telling the disinterested door staff, 'This is my set you know? I'm a DJ. Why don't you believe me?' as elasticated strings of mozzarella dangled from his chin.

Another one of my DJ/promoters also missed his set. No one could find him. Someone told me he was last seen looking somewhat sleepy, curled up in a corner as he'd over-indulged on ketamine, the silly sod. This was a growing problem at the time. I asked at the front door and clarified there'd been no recent medical issues. I had no other option than giving his set to someone else... only for him to turn up in the booth fifteen minutes later, absolutely soaking wet. It looked like he'd been swimming fully clothed.

As ketamine crept into clubbing in the early noughties, there were increasing incidences of the user taking too much leading to them falling into unconsciousness. Initially, venue security would alert the medical services for anyone in a 'ket coma', calling an ambulance to the front door, from which victims made a seemingly miraculous recovery as the animal tranquiliser wore off. Not only was this not a good look for the venue, but each medical emergency was also recorded, and would be taken into consideration at the licence renewal. So, it was rumoured the venue decided to take another approach. If anyone fainted or became drowsy, they'd be taken to an outside area somewhere at the back of the club where they'd be kept awake until the anaesthetic wore off. This was achieved by firing a high-pressure jet of water fire hose at them as they sat in the middle of the courtyard in a white plastic chair.

According to Josh the hose crew were kept busy; there were often a row of casualties being hosed down at any one time. If they responded well, and were polite and appreciative, they'd be allowed back into the club, emerging from a side door like a drowned rat.

## Recce Heads

The recce trip to Ibiza in May was my favourite trip of the calendar year. The season is new and filled with hope, venue owners were genuinely pleased to see us and looked after us accordingly, and best of all there were no guests to look after, so I was able to relax. One morning in early May, Damo and I would take the 6 a.m. easyJet red eye from Gatwick and spend a very enjoyable few days being wined and dined by our island partners.

The cab ride from the airport always gets the pulse quickening as the roadside billboards read like a Who's Who of DJs and world-famous parties. These are fought over by each promoter who demands a certain number in their contracts with the venues. They cost upwards from €2,000 each and reach over 100,000 people each day, which is appealing for any promoter. When I promoted Captured Festival, we were thrilled to feature on one – it shows you've arrived as a brand.

One year Es Paradis did the unthinkable and altered their artwork. For as long as anyone can remember, they would use the same Fiesta Del Agua logo to advertise their water party. No DJs were ever mentioned as it was all about the water. Then, one summer a circular image of a DJ no one had ever heard of appeared on all Es Paradis roadside hoardings. Who was this mystery DJ?

I did some digging and discovered that a Russian oligarch's son who was big in Uzbekistan had approached the club in the winter and offered to play for them for free. Having never heard of him, the club turned down his most generous offer, but being used to getting his own way, he blankly asked them what it would take for his photo to appear on the coveted roadside billboards. The club told him that if he wanted to cover the cost of the promotion for the season they'd add his photo in a small circle, but he could only play the last hour of the water party on a monthly basis and he had to buy a VIP table on the occasions he'd appear. To their utter astonishment, he accepted and forked out €20,000 to play three times to around eighty dripping wet ravers at 5 a.m. and point at his tiny face on the billboards to his sleazy entourage who filled the VIP section having been flown over for the night on his private jet

Whilst many saw them as a part of Ibiza's cultural heritage; a roadside reflection of the music on which Ibiza's reputation as the planet's party capital was built, the authorities felt they were a blot on the landscape and symbolic of the culture they were trying to eradicate.

During the Covid summers of 2020–22, the billboards gradually diminished in number. One morning a heavily photoshopped David Guetta would looking down at you in your car, whilst proclaiming 'F*** Me I'M Famous!' ( I could never work out whether he was genuinely surprised to have made it or it was a directive), and the next time you drove by, he'd disappeared. The Consell De Ibiza was waging war on the promo placards. Over fifty of them were removed after it was alleged they'd been erected illegally or sited on 'rustic' land. In retrospect, 'Fine Me, I'm Trespassing!' would've been more accurate.

It was rumoured that DC10 had eighteen of their billboards removed on the road to the airport, including my favourite: 'Miss your plane and go to DC10!'. The venue was known for its relaxed approach to licensing, when in 2008, it came to light that despite regularly packing in thousands of underground techno heads into the former hangar at the end of the airport runway, they only possessed a *Cafe Concerto* licence allowing them to serve coffee and toasties to a maximum of sixty-five people.

As the billboards disappeared, I felt downbeat. Yes, they were garish, spreading like Covid-19 and dominating the highways, but they were also proof that you were in the undisputed epicentre of clubbing. The sight of them looming out of the hard shoulder always made my heart race a little on first arriving and reinforced the regret of leaving.

We can't escape advertising. We're being marketed to from the moment we log into Facebook, to the minute we switch off the TV before bed. I'd rather look at a billboard for Supermarxte than a Supermarket, or a huge roadside banner for Cream as opposed to Lidl Mince Pies.

On one memorable recce trip we hooked up with a wild Spanish guy called Wamma who looked like a cross between a Latin music heartthrob, D'Artagnan the musketeer, and Johnny Depp's wicked cousin. His long jet-black hair framed green piercing eyes which oozed mischief and naughtiness. Just being in his presence felt illegal. So naturally, he'd be the first person we'd call after landing. Wamma knew *everyone*. He was once enjoying a three-day party with an Iraqi friend who'd flown in 'under the radar' on a private jet on a false passport. The noise from the house they were partying in caused the neighbours to call the police. They were met by a wide-eyed Wamma, who placated them with a bundle of cash. The party continued until the shift changed and another local police car pulled up. Wamma once again opened the door and tried to bribe the police but instead the officer was not cooperative and insisted on entering and searching the villa.

Solemnly, Wamma explained that if they did this it would cause a big problem for the officer in question, as there was a very important person in the villa who was in 'a state of relaxation.'

The officer was insistent, until Wamma explained to the motorsport-loving cop that his hero – a legend of his sport – was inside the villa.

'If you can ask him to sign an autograph for my son, I'll walk away,' the officer offered.

Wamma disappeared inside for a few minutes before reappearing, triumphantly brandishing a signed photo of the superstar. The officer cursorily examined it, nodded his satisfaction and left, leaving the party to continue for another night.

'Blimey, that was close,' I said.

'You're telling me,' grinned Wamma. 'The VIP I needed to protect wasn't the sportsman, it was my other guest.'

I leaned closer. 'And who was your other guest?'

'Uday, Saddam Hussein's eldest son. His dad didn't know he was here.'

He ended the tale by telling me that after seventy hours of wild partying, Uday left, leaving Wamma and his sportsman mate to finally crash out and get some sleep. Wamma awoke late afternoon and, remembering with horror that his friend had to be in Spain as it was the qualifying session for a very important race, leapt to his feet and ran through to the front room where his friend was sleeping on the sofa. But he wasn't there. Instead, a scribbled note which read 'Gracias, amigo' lay on the sofa.

Wamma showered, squeezed some fresh orange juice, and turned on the television to watch the qualifying session on Eurosport... just in time to see his recently departed sofa surfer set a new lap record.

> **Top Tune: Love Story (Original Mix) – Layo &
> Bushwacka {XL Recordings}**

## BEHIND THE BROCHURE

Ibiza and naughtiness go together like strawberries and cream. When Luke and Lisa, a newly married couple, failed to show for both the boat party *and* Cream at Amnesia, I grew concerned. In the pre-mobile phone era, there was no option other than to knock on their door. From inside I heard a muffled voice, yet no one answered the door. I returned with a hotel porter who had a master key and opened the door. There in front of me, tied spread-eagled to the bed, naked except for a ballgag, was Lisa. When released, she furiously divulged her husband had gone out the day before to buy some cigarettes and not returned.

After checking no one had seen him, we alerted the police.

He turned up the following day after returning from a villa party he'd been invited to by a jeep full of Italian girls outside the supermarket whilst buying cigarettes. He'd completely forgotten about tying his wife up, and upon walking through the door, received a black eye from the suitcase which was hurled at him, already packed with his clothes. She flew home the next day. I figured it would be a short marriage.

# 21

# WHEN SHIT GETS SERIOUS

I gazed into the hole on my guest's head. The pink, shiny membrane glistened beneath the casualty department's harsh fluorescent strip lights. It shouldn't have been visible, but it was. Instead of looking at bone and hair, I now realise I was looking at the periosteal layer of *dura mata*: the outer layer of the human brain.

Taut black lines criss-crossed the two-inch diameter cranial crater revealing a mass of soft, moist flesh. These were woefully inadequate, ineptly applied stitches attempting to pull together the surrounding skin – which wasn't cooperating. I was lost for words.

I'm the squeamish type, see. I can't watch those fly-on-the-hospital-wall TV shows featuring operations and do my best to avoid any scenes of mammals giving birth (including my own, according to my mother).

Giving birth may be a miracle, and I get that miracles are usually pretty spectacular; walking on water, and turning water into wine for example, but that doesn't mean they automatically qualify as spectator sports. Don't get me wrong, I love the human form and have spent hours studying various aspects of it down the years since reaching puberty, but only the exterior. They say 'beauty is skin deep' for a reason.

I shot a part-incredulous, part-concerned expression to the young doctor who was solely responsible for the San Antonio casualty department that night. It was 2 a.m. and he had the look of someone who'd been awake since the previous 2 a.m., unshaven with a pasty complexion and dark rings beneath his eyes. He looked like he was straight out of medical school. He clearly didn't share my worry, insisting my guest didn't require any further treatment.

'Really, she can go?' I asked, hoping my doubt would prompt a rethink.

'Si, but wake her every hour.'

I called a cab for her and waited until it arrived before getting on my scooter for the short ride back to my hotel which was situated close by to theirs.

Sandra (as we'll call her) had come straight to the airport from her place of work in the City of London. She'd met up with her husband Lance (as we'll call him) and a group of friends to catch the late-night flight from Gatwick. She only drank one glass of wine on the plane yet appeared noticeably drowsy on arrival in Ibiza. I remember her being helped to the transfer bus by her friends. I naturally thought she'd been over-indulging, especially when I heard her slurring her words as we shared a welcome hug. Sandra and Lance were regular customers, this must've been their fourth or fifth time on Ibizan Heat. They were a joy to look after, always polite, and well behaved, and had never caused me any trouble. I regarded them as part of the Ibizan Heat family, so my concern was not merely professional.

Sandra had only been on the island an hour before she was taken to hospital. She had been on my airport transfer. Upon arrival at the Ibizan Heat Hotel where they were staying, the double decker drew to a halt. Inbound transfers were always lively. New arrivals are naturally excited about finally starting their holiday, and the inevitable early morning or late night anti-social flight slots the low-cost carriers use in Ibiza only make things worse, resulting in lack of sleep or copious alcohol consumption prior – and after – take off.

On disembarkation, it's procedure for the rep who's managing the transfer to stand by the door the passengers exit, allowing them to direct them to the right hotels. The units we used were often situated close to one another and served by the same transfer bus and all look the same, so this is necessary. As I was doing this I became aware of a group of my guests standing outside the bus further down the coach. I was unaware the driver had also opened the middle door. This was unusual as there was no one to manage this exit. Instinctively, I walked towards the group to assist them. As I got to the bottom of the door I saw Sandra inside the bus on the top deck at the top of the stairs about to descend. She then turned around as though she'd forgotten something and appeared to faint, falling backwards in slow motion some four metres down the steps, landing on the back of her head with a sickening CRACK on the tarmac at my feet. Screams rose from the surrounding hotel balconies, where earlier arrivals were eagerly waiting for their friends who were on later flights. I bent down. She was unconscious and a pool of blood was forming, oozing from where her short, cropped blonde hair met the asphalt.

Another guest who identified himself as a qualified first responder, told me an ambulance was on its way and not to move her, as she may have a spinal injury. My mind was racing.

Was she still alive? Her continued motionlessness drew more screams from the balconies on either side of the road above us; the hysteria made worse by the intoxication. Everyone wanted to help but were crowding around her. If she was still alive, she needed air, I tried in vain to move people back but fuelled by first night fever, they ignored me. A particularly drunk girl who was wearing a pink sash which read HEN pushed her way to the front and declared, 'Oh, my God! She's dead, she's dead!' before running back to her fat friends. This drew more screams and wailing from the balconies.

Within minutes, the deep crimson pool around her motionless head reflected the blue lights of an ambulance. Lance accompanied her stretchered body and they both departed.

I wanted to join them, but only one other person was allowed, besides which I still had seventy people to check in. I told Lance I'd be there as soon as I could. He asked me to bring him a packet of cigarettes which I did, arriving at Centro De Salud, San Antonio hospital around forty-five minutes later.

It was deserted, I soon located Lance who told me Sandra was not only alive, but fully conscious and was currently receiving stitches. My initial huge relief receded into suspicion. I couldn't believe what he was saying. Sure enough, ten minutes later a smiling Sandra appeared.

'We can go! I really need to sleep.'

I asked if I could see the wound. She bent down and presented her crown. I was aghast at what I saw and queried her statement when moments later a young doctor emerged, yawning. He answered my question confidently, so I had no choice other than calling them a cab.

Sandra waited inside while Lance had a cigarette outside.

I joined him and told him I wasn't convinced, urging him to keep a close eye on her, and asking him to call me should her condition change.

Around three-thirty, my head finally hit the pillow and, utterly exhausted from a day of airport ruins and the last few hours, fell straight asleep, making sure I left my Nokia on while it was charging.

An hour or so later I found myself wide awake staring at the ceiling. I was alert to the degree of being annoyed. I needed to sleep, why was my adrenaline still pumping? I figured as I was awake I may as well have a piss. At the precise moment I walked back into my bedroom from my ensuite toilet, my phone came to life, vibrating and glowing yellow. I grabbed it and the display pulsed LANCE.

'Sandra's vomiting blood,' he said.

'Stay with her, I'll call an ambulance. What's your room number?'

I called my hotel reception. The night porter answered. I explained that one of my guests in the Poniente needed an ambulance immediately.

'She is not our guest, tell the Poniente reception,' he replied.

It would take me five minutes to get dressed and over to the Poniente reception, who may well not be there if they were managing a noise complaint – and with five floors and long winding corridors it could've taken another fifteen minutes to locate him and convince him of the urgency, while ensuring he called a 'proper' public ambulance rather than a Galeno private clinic, who would just take her back to San Antonio. I felt she needed to get to Can Misses, the main hospital in Ibiza Town rather than an A & E dept with exhausted skeleton staff. I tried to remain calm, but the stress in my voice was palpable.

'There's no time, this is urgent. She's MY guest, and I'm asking you to please call an ambulance, senor.'

A minute later, I spilled down the stairs into reception, confirmed the night porter had done as I'd asked, thanked him, and sprinted out into the dawn, dodging a dustbin lorry on its rounds. A black cat flowed across the road in front of me. I couldn't remember whether this was a portent of good or bad luck.

As I arrived at the Poniente an ambulance appeared. I guided them to Sandra's apartment which looked like Charles Manson had been partying there. Lance was cradling Sandra as she convulsed on the blood-stained sofa.

I'm always impressed by the calmness and unflustered vibe of paramedics. Nothing seems to faze them. But as I watched them go about their work, tight-lipped and muttering to each other in Spanish, their concern was evident.

After strapping her into a stretcher they told me they were taking her to hospital.

'Can Misses?' I asked, just to make sure.

'Si, to begin with...' Grant grabbed an overnight bag as requested and climbed into the ambulance, I watched its blue lights reflect from the whitewashed buildings as it disappeared.

I walked back to my hotel, my head spinning and mind whirring. 'To begin with?' What did he mean by that?

Back in my room I collapsed on the bed. A gap in the curtains framed a new moon like a cat's claw piercing the pitch black; hope amidst the darkness? Thoughts bounced around my skull like animated atoms as I went over the procedure I prayed I'd never have to employ.

If a guest dies in a resort their next of kin must be notified as soon as possible. This wasn't just the decent thing to do, it would avoid them reading or hearing about it in a newspaper first. The British press love nothing more than printing bad news about Ibiza, gleefully lapping up every balcony fall, drug overdose or road accident.

If the worst happened, my name would be given to the press who would ask for a statement. Should I give them one? Offering no comment may be interpreted as me trying to hide something.

The Spanish-based consul of the guest's country would also have to be notified. There would then be a coroner's inquest into the cause of death. This could lead to charges of corporate negligence being brought against any party who had contributed to the death.

I recalled watching Sandra emerge from the airport stumbling towards the bus in her friend's arms. Was it remiss of me to allow her to sit upstairs, knowing she was wobbly?

It was too early to call Nick, so to break the spell I stood in the shower, a high-pressure water jet pummelled my shoulders as I stood with my head bowed. Amidst the white noise I replayed her fall from the upper deck over and over again. Could I have caught her?

Up to this point I'd taken around 5,000 people away on holiday – 4,999 of them returning safe and sound (although I use that term loosely!). The fella who went missing was a loner who had gone to the north of the island a few days in. He was a solo traveller, not known to anyone on the trip and had behaved bizarrely from the moment he arrived, trance dancing in the middle of Kanya... before the warm up DJ started playing

But this was different. Sandra was part of the Ibizan Heat family. Her loss would deeply affect everyone else on the trip.

We would probably offer them an early flight home as they wouldn't want to continue their holiday in these circumstances. Buying hundreds of flights at short notice would have serious financial implications. I was a small operator and always treated my guests as I'd want to be treated on holiday. I resigned myself to the fact that I'd be ruined by this, and vowed to leave travel and get another job without risks.

I turned off the shower. The sound of water was replaced by a phone ringing.

It was Nick from Vacation Club.

'Just letting you know that one of our guests, Sandra, who's staying in the Poniente is currently undergoing surgery in Palma to remove a blood clot in her brain. An air ambulance took her from Can Misses. Apparently she fell off the transfer bus?'

My tinnitus went up a notch to the level marked 'Dentist's drill'.

Palma? That was in Mallorca.

'Correct, she was taken by helicopter to Palma, where they do the serious operations. Lance just called me. They X-rayed her in Can Misses and put her straight on a helicopter. It's a race against time to relieve the pressure. She's not out of the woods yet. Let's meet for a coffee and discuss how we take things from here.'

The welcome meeting at Kanya that day was naturally subdued. Everyone was asking me what the situation was. The rumour that the fall had killed her had gathered momentum and needed addressing. I told the group over the mic what the situation was and asked them to pray to whatever god or goddess they believed in and to send light.

From the wristband collection at Kanya, usually everyone

would board buses to take them to our private party at the zoo, but no one was really up for it. But it was too late to cancel the buses, and they duly appeared at the appointed hour. Around my neck, on my lanyard, like millstone around my neck, my phone started dancing, vibrating an incoming call alert:

I walked outside and sat on the coast path wall beneath the open-air swimming pool where it was quieter. I gazed out at the calm ocean, knowing I'd remember this call for the rest of my life.

'Sandra's awake, but groggy. The doctors say they caught it in time – but only just. Another hour or two more and she wouldn't still be with us. Thanks for your help last night, mate. We won't be needing our wristbands.'

'How are you doing?'

'Well, missing the zoo and Space is a pisser, but I'll settle for how it turned out.'

I stood up and exhaled, engulfed with relief. I was unaware that I was being watched until I turned around. People were hanging over the perimeter fence of Kanya. I put my thumb up. A cheer went up. This was the news everyone was praying for. Everyone boarded the buses to the zoo. Smiles returned. As you'll hear later, it was some party.

Sandra spent six weeks recovering in hospital in Palma and had to avoid flying for a further three months, finally returning to London via ferry and train in September. The medical bill was over €150,000 (€50,000 for the helicopter alone). Luckily Lance had a Gold American Express card which offered free comprehensive travel insurance.

As I recall, Lance and Sandra returned to Ibizan Heat the following year.

Looking back, after experiencing friends who've suffered aneurysms, Sandra's symptoms tick all the boxes. This would explain her slurred speech and loss of balance. She wasn't intoxicated, and her friends were confused why she acted like she did.

I count myself lucky that I've never had to deal with the death of one of my guests. Each summer sees body bags repatriated, Road accidents, balcony falls and cardiac arrests; almost all of them drink/drug related.

## Aftercare

I know of at least one hotel pool which has been repositioned to deter guests from jumping into it from upper floors. Deaths are ranked according to floors fallen by the Federació Balear de Balconing (Balearic Balconing Federation), which also sells merchandise, and has 55,000 followers on its X account. Its dark, devoid of compassion league table a symptom of the increasing anti-tourist movement caused by endless growth and Brits behaving badly. The Balearic Government recently unveiled plans to fine holidaymakers €36,000 (£31,000) if they were found guilty of balconing.

'Sandra' sadly passed away in 2023 of an unrelated health issue. This was her favourite tune at the time she partied in Ibiza:

---

**Top Tune: I Got A Feeling (Extended Mix) – Black Eyed Peas {Interscope}**

---

## BEHIND THE BROCHURE

My knack at eking out a meagre living from niche travel inspired a mate to set up his own travel company. After identifying a gap in the market, he proudly told me his aim was to own the hunting and shooting weekend break for the UK's 150,000 certified firearm owners.

He found a remote mountain hut in the middle of a large forest in Slovenia which was stocked with ample Wild Boar and advertised in The Shooting Times, soon filling all eight places and booking up a further three trips. He'd done a great job, but overlooked one thing...

November in Central Europe is often dominated by thick fog, and indeed this was the case, meaning no hunting was allowed on the first day. The hours were spent drinking, swapping hunting tales, and playing cards.

The same occurred on day two. More alcohol, alpha male boasting and gambling. They awoke on day three to find the fog still hadn't lifted. More of the same behaviour ensued. By sundown all eight were at each other's throats; irritable, inebriated and suffering from cabin fever. Throw the proximity of loaded guns into the mix and you can imagine what unfolded. The local police arrested two of my friend's guests, took one to hospital and one to the morgue.

I asked him if it had put him off travel,

'Nah,' he breezily replied, 'I'm moving into angling breaks, there's over a million of 'em out there... AND they can fish in fog.'

# 22

# WHITE ISLAND WHISPERS

They say that if you're an Ibiza person, the island will find a way to keep you, call you back, and support you in your journey along the way. That's always been the case with me (and with many others reading this, I'm sure). My personal relationship with Ibiza has enriched me both spiritually and materially; in return I always endeavour to honour and respect the island's protector Goddess Tanit's values; sensual expression, fertility and acceptance... something to bear in mind as you read about the wildest party I've ever thrown there...

The opening day of my Ibizan Heat package was a baptism of fire; commencing with wristband collection around the pool at Kanya, before moving onto an abandoned zoo in the hills a few kilometres away from San Antonio. From here, some would go onto Space in the evening, where they'd stay until 8 a.m. the next morning.

On one occasion there must have been a batch of particularly erotic pills, as everyone was sex mad. I was standing at the small circular bar when a buxom blonde girl with surgically enhanced breasts appeared next to me, accompanied by Danny Gilligan, one of our DJs. She told me she worked as a telephone model on Babestation, one of the late-night adult digital television stations which sprang up around that time to relieve lonely men of their cash as they relieved themselves into Kleenex; simultaneously spunking £1.99 a minute to hear the fake moans of glamour girls wearing nothing except tattoos and tiny gussets. On this occasion she was relatively overdressed. A pair of faded denim shorts and a tight white blouse unbuttoned to reveal a generous cleavage. She ordered a vodka limon and asked the elderly Spanish barman for a cup of ice... which she proceeded to rub over her now exposed nipples, one by one, until the ice cubes had all melted. At which point the old Spanish barman darted to the freezer, pulled out a large plastic bag bearing the word 'hielo', and eagerly plonked it on the bar for her to get busy with!

I was asked to go to the front door. A minibus had arrived whose cargo, seven glamorous females, were asking to enter. This was most unusual as this was an unadvertised private party, and in those days no one knew the zoo existed other than the locals who used it as a wedding venue. I arrived at the front entrance where Angelo, the head of security was engaging the ladies. They claimed they had received an invite from someone on the trip. As they appeared polite, well dressed and sober, I figured they'd be an asset to my party and welcomed them. 'Are you on holiday?' I enquired as I walked them from the front door to the pool area.

The pale and pouty posse wore beauty like it was a curse, their strides driven by ambition and purpose.

'N'yet...' they sultrily replied, executing a pout and walk more suited to the catwalk than an abandoned zoo

'Ahhh, you're from Russia, enjoy the party, ladies.'

Fifteen minutes later, in full view of all who sat around it, two of them were in the swimming pool engaging in semi-submerged aquasex. Another was spotted in the BBQ area with another couple of my guests enjoying the type of spit roast which doesn't involve any food. I've thrown countless parties in Ibiza, but this was the wildest, most sensuous, and closest to raw libertarian hedonism by far. Everywhere I looked people were dancing, embracing, or humping in the fragrant afternoon air; a pine aroma-infused bacchanalian gathering worthy of depiction on any Grecian urn or the search results for 'open-air', 'public' and 'orgy'.

At one point I sat on a small wall talking with Stevie Sideburns and owner Bartolo, when Angelo, the head of security approached wearing a strange expression.

'Que pasa?' asked Barty.

Angelo replied in Spanish, causing Barty to roar with laughter. 'Tell him,' he urged, pointing at me.

In broken English Angelo explained, 'We listen to noise in the trees and here is one of your guests.'

'What was he doing?'

'He was having sex.'

'Who with?' I asked, as you do.

Angelo looked at Barty and hesitated. It was clear he didn't want to tell me. Why could this be? Once more Barty provided the impetus. 'Tell him!'

But Angelo just shook his head, clearly reluctant to divulge more details and merely muttered, 'Eet's okay now, no problem.'

What on earth had gone on? Why wouldn't he tell me? I could only think it involved another guy, or perhaps one of my staff. If this was the case I needed to know. There was a rule for my staff that they didn't fuck the guests. It's tawdry and what Club 18–30 reps would do (mind you, what they got up to on the last night, when they'd technically finished work, was up to them).

'Angelo, I need to know who he was having sex with. Was it a girl?'

Angelo shook his head.

'Okay, a guy?'

Another shake of the head.

My mind was racing now. There are cats everywhere in Ibiza, and the zoo was sandwiched between a residential area and farmland and possessed a kitchen which would attract feral felines. It was me who was now hesitating, 'Not a cat, surely?'

'A cat? Ay dios mío!' They looked at me in disbelief.

'Tell him, before he moves onto dogs,' urged Barty.

Angelo fixed me with an 'okay, you asked for it' look, and spoke slowly,

'He was fucking a tree.'

'A tree?'

'They are very nice trees, I brought them from Galicia,' offered Barty as way of a possible explanation.

Angelo mimed someone shagging a tree, mimicking what he'd heard, 'Oh baby, oh baby... he was really enjoying it,' before bursting out laughing, incredulously.

'He was actually fucking a tree,' he repeated over and over again, shaking his head in disbelief.

Stevie turned to me. 'Where *did* they get these pills... and are there any left?'

## The Magic Roundabout

As numbers grew to in excess of 600 people, 'Aussie week' started to attract the attention of dealers. Whilst this was inevitable, it became blatant and started to get out of order.

One year I'd only been in my hotel room a matter of minutes and was in the process of unpacking, when there was a knock on the door. I opened it to find a skinny girl in a Space vest with a notebook and pen. 'Hi, welcome to Ibizan Heat! We offer a room service.' She handed me a card. It was a price list of drugs.

'Just order what you want, I'll pick it up and bring it back to your room within the hour. You don't have to pay anything other than a €50 deposit. We can sort out the balance when I bring you the goodies. Also, as you are on Ibizan Heat, you get a ten per cent discount on any orders over €100.'

I was incredulous and couldn't conceal my anger. I told her who I was, and that I didn't recall hiring her to deliver drugs to my guest's hotel rooms and told her to leave the hotel immediately, accompanying her downstairs and alerting the reception staff so they could clock her face if she returned.

I put the word out a few crews who I knew worked San Antonio, who respected me (or thought I was a fool!) for not asking for kickbacks for access to my guests. They all swore they didn't employ the girl, but told me she was a cokehead who owed them both money.

As I suspected, she had no access to the goods she was offering. It was a scam to get €50 from each room before disappearing to the north of the island, where she would lay low and get high until my group left a week later.

The few rooms who'd fallen for it were naturally embarrassed but trusted her as she told them she worked for Ibizan Heat. From this point on, the Aussies took care of this side of things themselves. I was unaware of this at the time. In fact, I made a point of being unaware of this. If people wanted to break the law and risk their freedom that was their choice. I wanted no part in it, and neither asked for or was ever offered any financial reward. All I knew was that the pills were clean, not too strong, and from a trusted source. This translated into considerably fewer medical issues than there would've been if people were scoring from random and unscrupulous sources.

This approach of managing the issue, rather than ignoring it and pretending it didn't exist, can also be seen as condoning people taking drugs at my events. I'd be a hypocrite if I tried to do otherwise. Ecstasy transformed my life in a positive way in the 1989 'summer of love', and there's an evangelical aspect to people who have experienced positive results from taking MDMA. But I decided when I launched Radical Escapes that I wouldn't get involved in distribution. I chose to make my money the hard way. If I'd run the drugs on all the trips I've done, I'd either own Tesla (the company, not a car), be serving time at Her Majesty's pleasure, or be buried in a shallow grave. It wasn't the life for me. Dealing is not sustainable without one of the above outcomes. It nearly always ends in tears. I knew that in order to be able to do the crime, you need to be prepared to do the time, and so I took the decision to be poor and free and be able to sleep soundly at night, rather than rich, behind bars and looking over my shoulder all the time.

At the end of the week there would invariably be some stock left unsold. Unlike Ibiza there are customs checks when entering the UK and as they returned every year, it made sense for those entrepreneurs to secrete the remaining stock in a place it could be easily retrieved the following year.

On the northern fringes of San Antonio there's a round-about. In the middle of the roundabout there was as scruffy Mediterranean scrubland; a few withered trees, some scattered rocks and dusty earth maybe littered with a squashed plastic water bottle.

At dawn on the day they flew home, a certain member of the group would set off with a small spade and bury the unsold pills in the exact centre of the roundabout. The following year, a few hours after landing, rather than go out, he'd patiently wait until dawn, in the hour nighttime dissolves into pale daylight, he'd make the same solitary stroll and dig up the 'treasure' for distribution amongst the new arrivals.

Each June, whilst bringing the buses in, I'd get on the mic and point out all the iconic landmarks, 'On the right up ahead, you may be able to make out what looks like a spaceship in the trees – that's the World's Biggest club, Privilege, where we'll spend Monday night at Manumission. The gold dome and glass pyramid up ahead by the bungee tower are Eden and Es Paradis, where we'll be hosting room two tomorrow at Judgment Sunday...'

These commentaries became an annual ritual, causing my business partner Damo to request to always ride on my coach, specifically to hear the spiel. He said it never failed to give him butterflies as it was effectively the curtain opening speech for the week of adventures ahead. With this in mind, and the bus hanging onto my every word, I couldn't resist adding another landmark to the list. 'Coming up on the left is perhaps the most sacred site in San Antonio. Although it isn't much to look at, its significance to Ibizan Heat cannot be understated. Here it is, ladies and gentlemen, the Ibizan Heat Roundabout!' People would crane their necks as we swung around the junction. Occasionally a camera would flash; white hot halogen momentarily lighting up the expectant faces. This became a feature of the commentary every June.

Until one memorable midsummer night...

Damo and some regulars sat on the backseat as usual. I was doing my tour guide schtick, 'We're just approaching the Ibizan Heat Hotel, but before we get there there's one landmark left to point out. Coming up on the left is perhaps the most sacred site in San Antonio. Although it isn't much to look at, its significance to Ibizan Heat cannot be... Oh...'

The roundabout was unrecognisable! Following an EU grant to the municipality of San Antonio, it had undergone a considerable makeover, and now boasted mature palm trees, a manicured rockery and signpost with directions to Ibiza Rocks Hotel and The Sunset.

An anguished chorus of 'Noooooo!' rose from the back of the bus. I was speechless. The newly landscaped burial site appeared to take an age to navigate, drawing out the torture for those whose eyes were glued to it in horror.

Five minutes later, panicked expressions poured off the bus. I heard that after checking in, they made a pilgrimage to the site and stood silently coming to terms with their loss, aimlessly rooting in the shrubbery, like a bereaved dog still nosing sadly around his departed master's armchair and abandoned slippers.

During Ibizan Heat in 2009 the island was crawling with reporters on the trail of Kate Moss and Pete Doherty who were hanging out in Ibiza. Kate, having lived there for many years, had a tight circle of friends so the tabloids never got anywhere near them, and were instead reduced to mundane eye-witness reports by random members of the public who claimed to have spotted them: 'They looked very much in love,' a holidaymaker told The Sun. 'They were just the same as me and my girlfriend on holiday – only they wouldn't take off their drainpipe jeans.'

Denied any scoops, tabloid reporters will justify their time on the island at their papers expense by finding other things to write about. And if nothing turns up, they'll make something happen to write about.

So, when, one morning I received a call from a formidable local character at the ungodly hour of 10am asking me the whereabouts of one of my group leaders – we'll call him Vaughn – I immediately knew something wasn't right. This was followed by him knocking on my hotel room. He wanted to know the bloke's hotel room number. Now this bloke was not to be messed around with, a former Hell's Angel, he was built like a mountain and had a reputation for not taking any nonsense, but divulging this information was not ethical, and I could be condemning the fella to certain death... at the very least.

This was a dilemma. Luckily I remembered that Vaughn had changed rooms after the first night, and I hadn't updated the rooming list. I explained this and to prove it, accompanied the gentleman to the room in question, to show him the person of interest wasn't there. Luckily, the hotel also hadn't updated their rooming list.

Try as I might, he wouldn't tell me why he was looking for him, but I knew it must've been really serious. Nothing stays a secret in Ibiza for long, and after he left I started making enquiries to find out what had gone down.

After the party finished in the Superclub, one of the DJs invited some friends and VIPs back to his villa for an after-party.

Being an Olympic standard blag artist, Vaughn had wangled an invite. He arrived at the party with a glamorous twenty-something blonde on his arm. Not the best-looking bloke on the island, this raised a few eyebrows. Apparently he'd only met her that night, when she latched onto him in the VIP area asking him if he knew a certain DJ.

'Know him? We're tight as anything!' Vaughan replied, untruthfully, offering to introduce her at the after party at his villa.

Unfortunately for her, the star DJ in question had an early flight the next morning and went straight to bed – but this didn't stop her from making the most of her time there.

She asked Vaughn to score some coke, which he did. It must've been strong stuff, as they were soon copulating in the villa pool in full view of everyone. Strangely, with the party in full swing, she abruptly left, jumping into a cab which had just deposited another girl who recognised the departing blonde as a... *News of The World* reporter.

This was bad news. Although the DJ in question – a household name – was in bed at the time I could already imagine the front-page headline: IBIZA SEX AND DRUG PARTY AT R1 DJ's VILLA. This would mean the sack for the DJ in question. This was unfair, as he was completely unaware of any illegal activity. His weekly residency would probably be pulled due to the adverse publicity and his career finished.

The reporter *had* to be found, and Vaughn was the best bet. Over the next few days, a manhunt took place. Throughout the day beach bars and hotel pools were scoured and known haunts searched. Airport contacts were alerted to provide notification if Vaughn or the tabloid traitor's name appeared on any flight lists. Hotel night porters received surreptitious envelopes in return for rooming lists, and I understand a well-known PR agency was engaged in the interests of damage limitation. But it was all to no avail. It was suspected the reporter had got back to London via a ferry to Valencia, and Vaughn had vanished into thin air.

We all braced for the News of The World to hit the news-stands on Sunday morning. I felt somehow responsible as Vaughan was my associate and it was because of me he was on the island.

On Thursday night, shortly after midnight I walked into the toilets at Cream in Amnesia and the conversation I heard changed everything. Michael Jackson had been rushed to hospital and was in a coma. Then someone else rushed in, shock etched across his young face, 'Michael Jackson's dead!' Cream that night was strangely subdued, Paul Van Dyk's last tune was Billie Jean. *Everyone* danced, including the security team.

For the following days the world could talk about nothing else, was it murder? Suicide? Why did the King of Pop die?

More importantly, for the household name DJ, his head of security, and Vaughn, that Sunday, the *News of The World* could also talk of nothing else, devoting six pages to Jacko's passing, which together with Peter Andre splitting up with Katie Price, left no column inches for the Ibiza story.

The next day Vaughn broke cover, claiming he knew nothing about anything and was completely unaware of any potential scandal he had almost caused. But he was overheard describing himself as 'Michael Jackson's biggest fan' on a clubbing forum a few days later.

As you've read, Jacko's spirit would return to even the score some years later!

Up until 2010 my Ibiza packages would include a flight and airport transfer. I'd buy a number of seats which sometimes led to having eighty or one hundred seats on the plane. This gave my guests a shared experience from the off and exuded a presence which I think reinforced the brand.

When I set up Radical Escapes, I harboured no grand ambitions to grow the company, float on the stock exchange and retire as a millionaire. I just wanted to

fill a gap in the market, show my guests the very best a destination offered, and make enough money to avoid getting a 'proper job'.

There was one aspiration; however, I thought it would be very cool to charter a plane exclusively for Radical Escapes; *Ibizan Heat* emblazoned on the fuselage and in-flight entertainment from DJs playing on portable decks.

Within a few years I was confident I'd fill all 230 seats on the Boeing 73 and made an inquiry. When I was told the cost was £12,000 each leg, I worked out a cost element of £105 each return, which was around what I was bulk buying the seats in for at the time. So, I indicated I wanted to proceed and reserved the aircraft. Imagine my surprise when the proforma invoice arrived asking for £48,000! Naturally, I queried this, pointing out.

They were charging me for 4 x £12,000 legs when I only needed two; the journey out to Ibiza, and the inbound leg back to Gatwick a week later.

'Sir, it's your guests who are spending a week on holiday in Ibiza, not the aircraft. It needs to fly home again the same day, as the crew have other flights to operate, as does the aircraft.'

Effectively, I was paying for an empty plane to fly back and then out to Ibiza again the following week to bring us home. If I had a rolling weekly programme, or was flying people out and back the same day (e.g. a football match) it would work out okay, but for the one-off packages I was putting together, it just didn't make any sense, which is why I never achieved my dream.

---

**Top Tune: Billie Jean (Long version) – Michael Jackson {Epic}**

---

## BEHIND THE BROCHURE

San Antonio, Ibiza: a sundowner beach bar party was in full swing; everyone was dancing and laughing except one female guest who was sitting in a corner being comforted by her friend. She was bawling loudly and clearly in some anguish, so I discreetly asked her friend if I could help.

'Her granny died recently, and she feels really guilty about her partying,' came the reply.

I offered to have a word, which was accepted.

I suggested we go outside somewhere quieter and watch the sunset, which, sobbing, she agreed to. We found a nearby bench on the coast path, where she confirmed she couldn't stop thinking about her dear departed gran.

I sympathised with her and gently explained that death is a part of life and although sad, we should hold onto the good times we shared with the departed and give thanks for them being a part of our lives, concluding that her gran wouldn't want her to mope around and be sad – especially on her holiday, and that she really shouldn't feel guilty about having a good time.

With her head bowed and in her hands she mumbled, 'It's

not as simple as that…'

Still sobbing, she explained how the family had divided the ashes between her and her siblings. Unable to afford an urn, she'd taken her share in an envelope to bring out to Ibiza and scatter at her gran's favourite beach in Es Cana, but, in the haze of a three-day bender which had started at the airport, completely forgot she had the ashes, which she mistook for something else.

She turned and glared at me with blazing red ringed eyes, and tightly grabbing my wrists wailed in anguish, something to which I had no answer.

'I snorted my gran.'

## Holiday Horror

There was one issue I couldn't sort out with a phone call to a parent, and which leaves me cold whenever I recall it. I'll do so here in order to illustrate how vulnerable young people are when they go overseas on holiday and the dangers which lurk.

It happened on a student Ibiza holiday package for which I was consultant/resort manager. The operator and resort staff were all diligent and professional, yet one night this happened…

3.12 a.m.: One of the students, we'll call her Emma to preserve anonymity, left the west end club night early. She hadn't been feeling too well, and perhaps should have eaten before the shots started appearing for her friend's birthday celebration. Her friends tried to persuade her to stay, but she was tired and there was a boat party tomorrow which she was really looking forward to and didn't want to miss, so she left the club alone. She walked into her hotel's reception, shyly acknowledged the night porter's smile, took the lift to the third floor, whereupon she remembered her roommate had the key card.

She returned to reception and explained the situation to the night porter. Although sympathetic, he explained that he couldn't simply issue a key card for the room without knowing it really was her room, but would let her into the room with his master key,

He ushered her to the lift, and noted she was a little unsteady, tottering on her high-heeled shoes. At one point she stumbled slightly, and he supported her, a muscular hairy around her slim waist.

They emerged from the lift and turned left, prompting Emma to question this.

'My room's down there,' she said, pointing behind her. But with a muscular hairy arm around her tiny waist, she was powerless to resist.

They stopped at a door. 'Your room,' he declared, presenting the key card, opening the door and gently edging her inside.

Emma took one look at the black suitcase on the floor and cigarettes in the ashtray.

She froze with fear. 'This isn't my room. I don't smoke and neither does my...'

Before she could finish her sentence she was firmly ushered into the empty room, together with the night porter, who then locked the door and pushed her onto a sofa.

Nine minutes later, they left the room and Emma was shown to the correct room, where she sobbed, still fully clothed on her bed until her friend arrived some hours later.

11.30 p.m.: I'm sitting in silence in the offices of the Guardia Civil with a hollow, haunted eighteen-year-old girl. We've been here over an hour. Emma wears the same pastel blue dress that she wore last night. She stares at the floor like she's ashamed. As couples of officers arrive and depart, they exchange a word about the English girl with red eyes, shrug in a 'here we go again' manner before walking away.

Another fifteen minutes elapse. I check with an officer at a desk if the form we filled in earlier has been processed. It will provide us with a crime reference number and prove Emma reported the assault which can't be investigated without one

The officer tells me he doesn't speak English. Coincidentally, no Guardia Civil officer I've spoken to since arriving speaks a word of English. What are the chances of that? My limited Spanish stretches to asking where the form is.

He shrugs and gives me another form. Then I see the form on the chair next to his desk and reach for it. He gets there first, screws it up and throws it in the bin.

He thrusts another form into my chest. I return to Emma and fill it in again, a process which causes her to burst into tears. We continue waiting. At one point I leave on my Vespa to buy sandwiches and water from the petrol station down the road. I don't miss anything. As I hand Emma the tuna sandwich, she avoids eye contact. She's like a vacant building; the shell is physically sound, but no one's at home. I believed her statement completely. From her demeanour it was evident she'd been assaulted and wasn't putting in a performance worthy of an Oscar, up there with Shelley Duval's in *The Shining*.

Another hour passes. I check once more on the progress of the second form. It lies untouched on the desk where I dropped it over an hour earlier.

'This girl has been raped, she needs to speak to a female officer and see a doctor now,' I remonstrate.

Reluctantly, he rises and calls in a female officer who had just arrived. She was the first female I'd seen since I arrived nearly three hours ago[7]. They spoke briefly in Spanish.

The female officer turned to me and said in perfect English, 'The English-speaking officer is here on Tuesday and Thursday from 9 a.m. to 1 p.m.'

It was Wednesday.

'I have a guest outside who's been raped. We need a crime number and a medical examination. Waiting until tomorrow is not an option, evidence may be lost.'

She nodded before repeating robotically, 'The English-speaking officer is here on Tuesday and Thursday from 9 a.m. to 1 p.m.'

The bloke behind the desk sat back folding his arms as if to say, 'Take it or leave it, but that's all you're getting.'

I'd accompanied my guests to the Guardia Civil office on previous occasions in order to get a crime reference number for insurance purposes; lost cameras, stolen wallets or room theft and had received similar treatment. By refusing to cooperate they have less paperwork and there's less crime reported, which makes them look good. I mistakenly thought they'd operate a triage system and recognise that this was an altogether more serious allegation and one which warranted acknowledging. I was wrong.

Emma had had enough and wanted to leave. No amount of persuading on my part could get her to stay. She was tired and wanted to shower. I told her that she should see a doctor

---

7. Female officers account for only seven per cent of Guardia Civil staff. Many of whom are administration roles. The gender imbalance coupled with a series of controversial rape cases involving Guardia Civil officers led to the appointment of the services first woman chief in 2020.

first. Reluctantly, she agreed, and I ordered a cab to take her to the Accident and Emergency unit in San Antonio, where I met her five minutes later. The doctor examined her and called the local police. Who took her to the Guardia Civil offices... who told her to come back the following day when the English-speaking officer was present.

I spoke to the owner of the hotel, who confirmed they were in the throes of recruiting personnel, and as a result were still using some staff from the hotel's former regime. One of these was the night porter, who'd done the job for many years. This sent cold shivers down my spine. How many girls had been taken advantage of during his predatory tenure? Although the CCTV wasn't operational throughout the hotel, the key card leaves a record of when a room is occupied each time it is inserted into the wall. The DNA evidence led to a forty-seven-year-old Spanish man being charged with rape some months later.

## Aftercrime

Three years later, Emma bravely returned to Ibiza to testify, and endure allegations that the sex was not only consensual, but she actively seduced the monster who raped her and was dressed in a manner which invited men to take an interest in her.

It's highly unlikely this was the first time he'd executed this plan. His position behind the reception desk enabled him to know which rooms were unoccupied. This was essential as he would carry out his assault in a room which wouldn't be subject to forensic examination should his victim go to the police. Emma received support from a woman's rights group in Ibiza who helped her to send him to prison for six years.

# 23

# IBIZA GOES TO HOLLYWOOD

*I holiday in Ibiza, 'cos I'm a trendsetter*
*I've just made a hefty transfer payment*
*to the Bank of David Guetta.*
(stAN AntOniO – *Sardines in Pacha*)

As Ibiza gradually morphed from a destination into a brand, it was inevitable that Hollywood A-listers would discover and descend and want to be seen living their best life (urgh!) in the World's 'premier party island' TM.

I recall one night when my Ibiza Trance Event brand hosted the main room at Cream @ Amnesia. My co-promoters and I were unusually kept waiting at the front door as Cream Ibiza promoter Nick Ferguson and his team were preoccupied with managing the imminent arrival of movie star Will Smith. What he made of Eddie Halliwell playing house that night I'd love to know. Perhaps he thought it was Paris Hilton's party, 'Foam and Diamonds' and was there by mistake.

Foam and Diamonds? This is a coupling second only to small children and matches in the What Could Possibly Go Wrong? Olympics. This new low took place on four Saturdays at Amnesia in 2014 for which she received a cool €2 million.

'Half a million euros a week and she can't even mix,' scoffed many on the island. But Paris proved her critics wrong when she appeared to execute an immaculate series of mixes whilst wearing sunglasses (her own brand, naturally). For many seasoned observers, this wasn't a foam cannon as much as a smoking gun which suggested that her set – just like her dirty weekend in Paris – was recorded.

Following a few hours of frivolous EDM involving Paris pouting, waving, and periodically shaking her trillion-dollar trust-fund tush, the party built up to a messy, shuddering climax which involved a diamante bikini clad Paris firing a huge phallic-shaped foam cannon over the crowd. Clearly not adverse to receiving facials, she would regularly get covered in sticky white stuff too.

When a billionaire heiress who found fame through a leaked sex tape is offered a weekly residency at Amnesia, it's an indication that things have changed. Ibiza didn't so much as embrace the concept of Celebrity, but hitched up her skirt, dropped her knickers and spread her legs wide. Before you could say 'paparazzi', Cristiano Ronaldo's yacht was moored off Formentera, Shakira was sunbathing in the Marina complex, the Clooney's were struggling with seafood at Es Torrent, Orlando Bloom was struggling with Justin Bieber at Cipriani and the Kardashian's were struggling with reality.

San Antonio police would arrive at noisy villa parties and instead of finding coked up city boys would be met by Kate Moss, Naomi Campbell, Paris Hilton, Kim Kardashian, Kanye West, Pedro Almodóvar and Puff Daddy.

In 2001 Sean Combs, who'd become Puff Daddy now became 'P Diddy. As I write this he's facing serious allegations. The following stories are perhaps an indication that sooner or later his behaviour would catch up with him – like it does for us all.

The Diddyman arrived in Ibiza to record an album in seven days at the height of the summer season. After dropping his stuff off and freshening up, Diddy went out for dinner, then started clubbing. He finally returned to the villa, where Stuart Price and Nellee Hooper had been patiently waiting, to start recording his vocals some *seven days* later.

On another visit he had a necklace worth six million pounds stolen from his villa. From that point he would prefer to arrive and leave in a luxury yacht, out of reach of the thieves.

One night, after a rooftop *hierbas* in the Old Town I took a boat across the harbour to Miss Moneypennies at El Divino, and immediately spotted Mr Combs surrounded by silver buckets and long legs in the VIP area wearing what appeared to be a white fur coat and a black trilby.

At one point he erupted animatedly, hugging his entourage and high fiving anyone within the vicinity of his booth. Even over the music their whoops could be heard. Next thing I know, he was in the DJ's ear... who, in the middle of a mix at the time, shook his head, prompting a look of disbelief on the celebrity's face. This went on for a few minutes until the venue manager appeared. Following more pleading, shrugging and nodding, Puff the Magic Blagger appeared alongside the DJ, who handed him one side of a set of headphones. This meant only one thing: Puffy was going to address the crowd. As any rave MC knows, headphones can be used as a basic microphone if plugged into the input instead of the output socket. The effect is basic and not easy on the ear, but for essential announcements it does the job... whilst turning the authority-craving orator into a rasping Dalek.

'People, I've just heard my new record has gone straight in at Number 1 in the States.' He paused for cheering, which didn't happen, except for a few 'Whoops!' from the VIP section.

'So, to celebrate I'd like to buy everyone a drink!' This prompted a huge cheer.

People rushed to the bars, and sure enough, they were offering complimentary drinks. Clubbers aren't daft, so groups of friends each went to a different bar and ordered a round. Very little beer or water was requested. But a lot of Vodka Limon and Jack Daniels and Coke crossed the bar in the next half an hour. Diddy remained in the DJ stand, chinking glasses, high-fiving and revelling in being the centre of attention.

Over the following days, Diddy's round was the talk of the island. Just like the Beatles playing the Cavern club or the Sex Pistol's 100 Club shows, everyone claimed to have been there. To this day it's debated and argued about like a Virgin Mary apparition, with some steadfastly refusing to believe it happened.

I can assure you it did. What people don't know is what legend has it happened next...

After the tills were reset, the receipts were collected, and the total presented to Puffy, who rather grandly slapped his card onto the plate upon which the receipt was presented. The story goes that the card was refused and so the venue manager returned to speak to Diddy. As the sum was substantial, the venue was naturally keen to settle it that night. Diddy is said to have written them a cheque and left some time later.

The next morning, the venue manager sat ashen faced in the bank manager's office. His worst fears had just been confirmed; the cheque had bounced.

They called the few hotels where celebs always stayed. No

one had a Mr S. Combs, Puff Daddy, P Diddy or anyone matching his description.

It was then the brother of the venue manager who happened to be the harbour master, called him upon hearing of the act of generosity which had occurred in El Divino the previous night to ask him if it was true.

When he heard there was an unpaid bill and that Puffy's whereabouts were unknown, he said he could help.

Fifteen minutes later a small rib chugged its way across the harbour of Ibiza town in the direction of a large sleek six-storey superyacht, moored in Marina Botafoch. It carried three men; the harbour master, the venue manager, and their cousin – who happened to be the chief of police.

After showing their ID, they boarded to find the party still in full swing.

After a quick shower, a small rib chugged its way back across Ibiza Town harbour. Only this time, it carried four men; the harbour master, the venue manager, their cousin who happened to be the chief of police and a freshly showered, party-loving popstar who had accepted an invitation for lunch at the best restaurant in the Old Town, to thank him for his business after he personally requested an immediate international bank transfer of €72,000.

## Never Mind the Bollinger

The fall of the Soviet Union gave rise to a new wave of Ibiza visitors; oligarchs whose fortunes were derived from the sale of state assets. While Ibiza has always attracted extravagance and excess, this was another level. Their arrival coincided with the rise of social media, enabling them to show *in real time* how much they were worth. From footballers with Lamborghinis, to ghetto drug dealers with gold chains; 'new money' always likes to show off.

My mate Seb provides high-end concierge service for owners of private jets. He collects his clients from the private terminal at Ibiza airport, takes them to their villas, and then spends the week ferrying them to the most sought-after tables at the best places on the island, he's good at his job. However, on this occasion he was nervous. He pointed to the elevated table in the VIP area where his guests, a group of middle-aged Russians dripping in Gucci were sitting, surrounded by long-legged model types who pranced around them, smiling and sipping from Magnums of champagne.

The roped-off raised platform on which they partied was only overlooked by one nearby table. A few feet higher, this was the most expensive table in the venue.

Seb explained that he couldn't get them onto this table as it had been reserved by a Chinese party; middle-aged Chinese men accompanied by more long-legged, micro-skirted model types. Instead of drinking from a magnum of champagne. Ivan, the Russian group leader called Seb over and asked him to arrange a Jeroboam. A waiter was dispatched and soon returned with a bigger bottle than the Chinese men were enjoying. Upon seeing this, the Chinese called their own waiter, who returned carrying an even bigger bottle of champagne. Seb smiled knowingly, 'They've ordered a Jeroboam.' This didn't go unnoticed by the Russian's who, after another hour called their waiter over.

'They've upped the game to a Methuselah, this costs €5,000 a bottle. They don't want the Chinese to make them look cheap,' Seb explained, before adding, 'what we have here is an intercontinental pissing contest.'

Another hour went by until I saw a trolley snaking its way through the crowd, a path being cleared in advance by two CONTROL staff as it approached the Chinese platform.

Seb put his hand over his mouth and leaning over to my ear confirmed the cargo, 'Fuck me, they've ordered a Salmanazar! That'll set 'em back €8,000. Ivan ain't going to like it.'

But having sunk more bubbles than an Aero factory, the Chinese had no intention of drinking more. They instructed their two private security men to vigorously shake it before popping the cork, which shot high above the crowd towards the stage, narrowly missing David Guetta. Champagne sprayed everywhere, soaking the Chinese who fought for control of the ejaculating green bottle, but also resulting in the Russians being completely soaked. This caused much mirth amongst the Chinese, who then started spraying each other with the various oversized half-empty bottles of bubbly from the ice buckets on their table.

Seb froze. 'Now we've got a problem.'

The Russian security automatically reached inside their jackets. The Chinese security did the same. Insults were hurled across the red rope separating the two levels as each sides' muscle stood off looking like Napoleon Bonaparte's.

'Are they really wearing guns?' I asked

'They're not supposed to, but these people are a law to themselves,' Seb replied, ashen-faced.

Seb called a manager over and explained what had happened.

'We need another Salmanazar for my group to spray.'

'We have no more Salmanazar I'm sorry. Only one Balthazar, the cost is €10,000.'

'My group has already spent €50,000 in here and I have

others from the same organisation booked through the summer. If you don't act quickly, we'll have an international incident on our hands. People are watching this, and if I was you, I'd sort it out sharpish.'

The manager looked around. Seb wasn't wrong. More people were watching the Russo-Chinese stand-off than were watching David Guetta's exaggerated tweaking of a mid-range button (which judging from his strained expression, appeared to be made of granite. Or he was taking a shit behind the decks. He was certainly taking the piss behind there, being paid €1,000 a minute for playing what was basically a wedding DJ's set with pyrotechnics and more drops than a wayward golfer.

The manager nodded and spoke into his radio.

Seb told a dripping, incandescent Oleg what was happening. He in turn briefed his security. The Chinese continued to roar with laughter, all completely sozzled

Like a cruise missile on Mayday in Moscow, the Balthazar arrived on wheels; a symbol of Russian might and intent. The Chinese, pissed beyond the point of caring, frantically egged the Russians on.

The huge bottle was shaken by three burly men, while a fourth twisted the ginormous cork. Whether by accident or design, a build began, kick drum shuddering as a siren-like loop slowed to a halt. Five thousand people got ready for the drop, raising phones in readiness for the pyrotechnic flames which accompanied the designer drops in Ushuaia.

First, you see them; fiery fingers extending upwards... then a fierce roar, as the compressed $CO_2$ hits the warm air, instantly invigorating the front rows of the crowd who experience a sudden drop in temperature to -4 degrees. Dry Ice Cannons are the superclub equivalent of a cold shower, provoking a huge roar as the drop hit. The smoke from the pyro plumes drifted towards us, a wispy spectre momentarily obscuring the scene.

A single gunshot rang out. Girls screamed. Who'd fired first? Instinctively, I crouched down. A shooting in Ushuaia! The UK press would lap this up. I could see the headlines now: MURDER ON THE DANCEFLOOR. They just love a bad news story from Ibiza, be it a balcony jumper, overdose or just the fact it's warmer in the UK. 'Skegness Hotter Than Ibiza!' (Believe me, if you go to the right places with the right people, nowhere is hotter than Ibiza.)

The smoke cleared to reveal a fine wall of champagne covering the Chinese delegation, beautiful girls stood, soaked mini dresses clinging to them, as they smoothed their hair back with their hands as they gleefully received the barrage of bubbles being discharged by the Russians. It wasn't a gun exploding; it was a cork!

Their honour reclaimed, the Russians and Chinese shook hands over the rope. It was then unclipped, allowing them to mingle. Smiles and hugs; kisses for the girls. Each sides' henchmen reluctantly shook hands with their opposite numbers.

Seb shook the hand of the manager, 'Good call, amigo; World War Three averted.'

## Aftersun

In October 2024, the Washington Post reported that Combs would be facing 120 charges for assaults, sex trafficking and racketeering that took place between 2000 and 2020. The police revealed they'd uncovered firearms, ammunition and more than 1,000 bottles of lube during raids on Combs' homes in Miami and Los Angeles in what was obviously a slick operation. Whenever the indictment refers to Diddy, it does so as 'SEAN COMBS', aka 'Puff Daddy', aka 'P Diddy', aka 'Diddy', aka 'PD', aka 'Love'.

> **Top Tune: Lady (Modjo's Dyrt Remix) – Modjo {Nightlite}**

## BEHIND THE BROCHURE

There was a time when no one would eat anything in Ibiza. Beach bars then gradually evolved into eateries; the former Kanya started serving sushi, booking a table at Sunset Ashram now involves compulsory curry and Mambo charges €35 for a salad.

These days all people seem to do in Ibiza is eat – which makes waiting tables at large beach bars in Ibiza physically demanding; the hours are long, the sun is hot and the customers impatient

I was stood just inside the kitchen entrance discussing a group takeover of one newly opened venue with the owner, congratulated him on the industry of his waiting staff, who were constantly walking past us with empty plates and full glasses at a truly impressive pace and intensity, pausing in their endeavours only to dip a licked finger into a small wooden bowl on a shelf just inside the entrance. They would then pop the finger in their mouth and continue.

The owner noticed my interest.

'Salt?' I asked, assuming they were replenishing essential

minerals lost as they sweated their way through their shift in the sweltering midsummer heat.

He nodded. 'Special salt.'

'Really? Himalayan?' I ventured.

'Peruvian, actually,' he corrected, handing me the bowl, 'try some.'

'Naively, I did so, licking my forefinger and putting it on my tongue.'

Within a minute I couldn't feel my tongue and was gibbering like a Flowerpot Man.

# 24

# SUMMIT FUNNY GOING ON

A bold claim maybe, but one which I believe is true; Radical Escapes created the first alpine clubbing holiday package. It was called 'Kiss in the Snow' and ran from 1997 to 2002. The concept was to replace the cheesy après ski music with house and garage played by the station's presenters (in this case Alex P, Brandon Block and Chris Phillips), who would play to a few hundred listeners who'd bought the package advertised on the radio. This gave the resort exposure and profile to a cool demographic, in addition to a new type of guest, and provided the station in question with some advertising revenue, along with some interesting content with which they could attract sponsors. Well, that was the theory. In the event the only sponsor they ever secured was Pop Tarts. On arrival, everyone was given a few packets of Pop Tarts as a welcome gift. The palatability of Pop Tarts is reliant on the presence of a toaster or microwave. The hotel rooms had neither. What's more, as there was no late-night takeaway option in those days, resulting in hungry clubbers returning to their rooms in the early hours having no option other than breaking open the silver foil and disconsolately chewing their way through the cold, plasticky pastry envelopes – which, after being stored in sub-zero temperatures on the balcony, would be either brittle and shatter, or simply turn to a jammy mush.

The other problem these trips had was one common to all alpine resorts – gender imbalance. More blokes like to go skiing and snowboarding than girls. Millions of euros are spent trying to tempt female visitors to fall over in the snow, something lots of ladies don't enjoy doing (as opposed to males, whose fondest memories often involve wrestling, fighting or falling).

I looked around the welcome meeting and grimaced. There were 176 guests, 160 of which were male. Ten of the girls were with their boyfriends and one looked like she could be gay (which it turned out she was, and by the end of the week was 'one of the lads', holding her own both on the slopes and in the bars). This left two girls from Chingford, who looked around the room like they had just died and gone to hunk heaven.

After many requests, I found myself organising the type of excursion which focussed not on snow, schnapps or schnitzels, but sex. Each evening after dinner, a minibus of frustrated blokes would depart for a welcoming establishment in Innsbruck.

I started hearing stories of how the only two single girls were being very active indeed. An increasing number of reports filtered back about brief encounters in the cable car, the hotel sauna and their room, which may as well have had a revolving door, such was the frequency of visitors.

I saw how they'd emerge from the lift and walk into the lobby bar, be offered a drink and then disappear with one, two or even three lads for half an hour, before returning, slightly flushed.

The tales grew ever more salacious. Rumours circulated of a video shot on the hotel balcony starring one of the girls and a €10 sausage from my friend Hans the Butcher's shop. It was being shared by the girls themselves, who were clearly having the time of their lives.

They were so popular that I think my underwear was the only pair of boxers they hadn't got into. So, I was waiting for the approach, and had prepared my defence.

After a backcountry party which involved me MCing a cow milking competition (yes, really) and after tobogganing down a remote, steep, snow-covered, mountain road, I was walking the group back down to the waiting bus, crunching through the snow when one of the girls sidled up to me and began to flirt.

I explained that I was happily married and was not available, but thanks for the offer.

'That's what they all say, I won't tell a soul, darlin'.'

We reached the bus, and as she was about to get onboard, I repeated what I'd told her and told her friendly but firmly, that I really wasn't up for anything, period, and had a three-month-old baby son waiting for me back in Enfield.

'Oh, that's really nice. Not many men would act like that, I really respect your decision. Your wife's lucky having a man like you. I'll leave you alone in that case.'

She began to board the bus, then paused as she climbed the stairs, turned round and said with a mischievous glint in her eye, 'But if you want a wank, I'm in room 219.'

Looking back, I witnessed much more naughtiness in the snow than under the Ibizan sun. Maybe it's the romantic setting; us Brits just love the snow, it makes us feel like kids again pulling back the curtain first thing one winter's morning and seeing everything covered in white) and throw in an avalanche of alcohol which fuel Austrian resorts in particular, and it perhaps explains some of the stories I'm about to tell...

After I'd written a piece in Ministry Magazine about how rave culture was starting to permeate the alps, I was asked to present an idea how the Ministry of Sound could get involved. They had a very successful label called Clubbers Guide... and so, with the vision and energy of their Head of Marketing, Adam Lockhart, we put together the Ministry of Sound's first ski plus snowboard holiday, Clubbers Guide to... Snow.

None other than the Godfather of Balearic Beat Alfredo Florito was signed up to play an exclusive private party in an amazing mountain-top pyramid-shaped restaurant, in which twenty of our Clubbers Guide guests were waiting as a blizzard raged outside. This was something really special. Sadly, it didn't happen after Alfredo fell and broke his leg as we skied over to the venue and was airlifted to hospital in a helicopter.

I can still hear Adam's reaction when I walked in from the blizzard without him. 'You had one job...'

We conceived a competition to give away two holidays on a national radio station. To enter, listeners had to send in a picture of themselves in winter sports gear which acknowledged club culture. As we expected, pics of fluorescent ski jackets, baseball caps and ski gloves holding glow sticks began arriving. Then the producer's eye was caught by a photo of two pretty girls engaged in a passionate kiss, whilst wearing Russian fur hats, one woollen scarf between them and very little else.

He showed it to the presenter, who thought they'd be perfect winners, who needed to be extroverted and pen a blog on their return for the new website. These were the very early dial up days, and the media were starting to prepare for the future; establishing an online presence and creating content to promote engagement to their demographic.

So, after calling them up to see if they had sent it them-selves, and it wasn't some sort of revenge porn situation, they were invited into the studio to talk on air about how thrilled they were to win and what they were most looking forward to.

They were interviewed in a small vocal booth with the producer and presenter in the adjacent studio. The interview finished, the girls were thanked and told they could leave. But there was no reply. Probably because they were snogging. As it was outside office hours, there was no one around but the producer and presenter... who continued to enjoy a fifteen-minute session of sapphic desire. According to my producer mate, the girls tore each other's clothes off and in a move which showed it was a premeditated exhibitionist fantasy which would feature in one of those 'Where's the most unusual place you've had sex?' after-dinner conversations, produced a double-ended flesh-coloured dildo to help them 'bond'.

It was at this point the producer saw a little red light on the newly installed studio webcam. He glanced at the website and was utterly horrified to see a grainy image of two naked girls writhing around as Pulp's 'Disco 2000' played. The show was going out live across the nation. Whether anyone witnessed the sapphic show will never be known.

Although *The Clubbers Guide...* trip was blighted by Alfredo breaking his leg, the tourist board liked what they saw, and asked me to run more clubbing-orientated holidays, which, with the passion of Pam Withington, I did with Vibe FM (a dance music type station for East Anglia). I also worked with Essex FM, Classic FM, Power FM and Classic Gold amongst others.

## Border Fun

The airport transfer to Salzburg airport at the end of a very long week was always a great opportunity to execute a favourite wind-up. The twisting alpine road to Salzburg strays into Germany for a short while before re-entering Austria. The border guards were aware that every Saturday afternoon a never-ending stream of the same tour operator coaches would go back and forth all day ferrying British holiday guests between the ski resorts in the Tyrol and Salzburg airport, without stopping in Germany at all. This resulted in a tokenistic checking of documents at the border; the buses would slow down to a crawl and open the door preparing to stop, prior to being waved on. Very rarely, a customs officer would board and take a cursory walk down the coach checking a few random passports, but this was highly unusual.

The driver knew this. I knew this. But the guests didn't...

Half an hour away from the border, I'd announce over the mic that we were approaching the German border at which the guards were very officious and diligent in checking passports, and that anyone removed from the coach would be held in a cold cell until their passport details could be checked with a central database, before being released after a few hours to find themselves standing alone with their suitcase at a desolate mountain pass... as darkness was falling. This was met with a stony silence.

Fifteen minutes later, I repeated the warning, telling everyone to get their passports ready for inspection, and that if they held them up to the window next to their faces, we may be waved through and save enough time to stop for the toilet and smoking break. As people rummaged through their bags to locate their passports, I added, 'And if anyone's appearance has altered significantly and they no longer look like their passport photo, come to the front of the coach now, please.'

This led to a motley queue of people whose appearance had altered significantly since the photo was taken. Some had lost their hair or grown a beard. There was always one bloke whose mates had shaved his eyebrows off on the first night of the holiday. The driver would be smirking by this point, knowing what was coming.

At this point I'd take the microphone. 'The driver's just heard from a colleague up ahead that today's guards are being particularly strict as they have an inspection. Can everyone please attempt to look as close to their passport photo as possible. We have no time to be stopped, and cannot wait for anyone who is taken off the coach, so please cooperate. Recreate the hairstyle, wear the same colour top and, most importantly of all, practice the expression with the person in the seat next to you and correct each other until you all look *exactly* like your passport photos.'

This was not an option for the people who'd come to the front, obviously, who received solemn shakes of the head from both me and the driver when they presented their passport photo.

'Sorry, pal. There's no way they'll accept that this is you. We'll have to hide you and hope they don't board.'

Any girls whose appearance had changed (usually different coloured hair) were told to lock themselves in the small toilet, while the blokes were instructed to go to the back and lay down on the floor in front of the back seat.

An announcement was made for people to donate ski jackets to cover the unfortunate ones laying on the floor. At this point the driver would turn the heating up to full at the rear of the coach for good measure.

As they left, I shook each of their hands and issued them with final instructions. 'Stay absolutely still, don't make a noise, and most importantly of all, whatever you do, do *not* come out until I make the announcement that all is clear and we've left Germany again, as sometimes the customs officer stays on the bus until we get to the next border.'

Now I had their attention, I'd periodically countdown each kilometre until the border was in sight. My voice growing ever more serious as I repeated the necessity to present an identical facial image through the windows. At the rear of the coach, I could see a big pile of jackets on the floor behind the legs of those sat on the backseat. As we approached the border, I'd make a plea for even more jackets to be donated to cover the poor sweltering souls on the floor.

We then arrived at the border itself; a bleak, windswept outpost in the middle of nowhere which looked like something out of The Great Escape; uniformed officers stood around staring at every approaching vehicle like it was a terrorist cell, some with semi-automatic rifles slung over their shoulders. In the middle of two lanes was a small wooden kiosk nestling between two raised barriers, pointing at the towering cloud-concealed mountains which surrounded us. We slowed to join the queue of vehicles edging towards the metallic sign, saying, 'Bundesrepublik Deutschland'.

My voice now changed to concern, I spoke slower and with reverence, 'All right, everyone, here we are. What happens next determines whether we make the flight home or not. Please hold your passport open at the photo page to the window and assume the same expression.' The driver couldn't resist glancing up into the large convex mirror which showed a compliant coach gawping out of the windows with expressionless faces next to their open passports.

The driver applied the brakes and with a loud HISS edged the coach to a brief halt. After a few seconds, the guards, as expected, waved us on.

This was acknowledged by me giving everyone the thumbs up, before pointing to the toilet and backseat and making a 'Shhh' gesture with my finger to my lips.

I'd then walk loudly down the central aisle occasionally muttering, 'Reisepass... danke,' in the deepest voice I could muster like I was inspecting passports whilst at the same time, winking and repeating the 'Shhh' gesture. Row by row, they gradually realised the joke was on the poor buggers beneath the mountain of coats. Any suspicion over the passport charade was replaced with the glee of conspiracy.

We kept this up until those suffocating beneath a dozen heavy jackets could stand the heat no longer. A cloud of Nylon and Gore Tex would explode into the air from the back as a ruddy, sweat-soaked face appeared, gasping for air and begging for water. This prompted much laughter, which was the cue for the toilet door slowly opening followed by inquisitive faces.

After they'd rehydrated with a complimentary beer from the driver's fridge, they'd see the funny side. Finally, upon arriving at the airport, after making the customary announcement about not leaving anything on the coach and wishing everyone a safe flight, I'd add, 'Oh, and thanks for your cooperation at the border earlier, passport checks were done away with when Austria joined the EU, but it made the driver's day!'

## Let Me Ski Your Fantasy

Introducing people to skiing and snowboarding was a main objective, and so we included lessons in the price of the holiday package. This fostered a sense of shared experience whilst also reducing the likelihood of injuries. A bad injury would involve the helicopter airlifting them straight to the hospital and a three-hour round trip to the hospital by one of my reps to take the person's belongings and check on them. I feel a sense of responsibility for all my guests and so it also made sense logistically to do my best to ensure they were taught by the best: SMT Ski School.

A feature of the trips was the live broadcast back to Grey Britain from the Austrian Alps during the Breakfast Show. The idea being the listener would be listening to poetic descriptions of clear blue skies pierced by toothpaste box peaks, as they drove through the drizzle to work.

So, fifteen lucky listeners joined the breakfast show presenters in the spectacular Schneekarte mountain top pyramid where we spent the night in order to be in position at 8 a.m. the next day when the live broadcast would take place. The venue consists of a ground floor restaurant complete with open fire, well-stocked bar and kitchen, with the second floor being the location for a number of bedrooms for staff and VIPs. The top floor is a dormitory which sleeps around fifteen people on a number of single or double beds.

After watching the sun set over the surrounding peaks and enjoying a three-course traditional dinner, the entertainment would consist of snow running, star gazing, or playing the Who Am I? game, before retiring for a good nights' sleep at 11 p.m. As the bar stock was accessible, and security cameras hadn't been fitted, someone had to guard the bar throughout the night. In this instance, as the live broadcast kit was already set up and similarly unsecured, I decided to sleep under the table on a mattress myself.

By midnight, the giggles and laughter from upstairs had given way to silence, but then I heard footsteps on the wooden staircase. From my position on the floor, I could see halfway up the stairs to the first landing, which via a large full-length window, offered panoramic views across the summits. A full moon illuminated a glowing luminescent landscape, against which the bottom half of two silhouetted figures could be seen. One knelt before the other, her head held by the standing figure's hands, nodding backwards and forward. As they weren't in the bar, or threatening to interfere with the radio kit, I decided to leave them to it. Eventually, the shadow puppet porn show came to fruition. Boxer shorts were pulled up from ankles, and after a few giggles and whispers, the couple disappeared back upstairs. After another ten minutes of silence, I allowed myself to drift off to sleep.

I was woken sometime later by the rhythmic movement of the table. I opened my eyes and could see four feet pointing towards me, one of which was partially covered in a black lace thong wrapped around the ankle. Two pairs of bare legs, one without hairs behind which another, hairier pair shook with ever-increasing vigour. From above I could hear heavy breathing, and occasional guttural groans, and a hastily whispered, 'Harder... yeeesss!' I froze. A couple were shagging inches away from me. I couldn't interrupt now... could I?

I decided to remain hidden and breathed shallowly, trying not to think about sneezing. But it was too late. The more I thought about not sneezing, the more I wanted to sneeze. I scrunched up my eyes, clamped my mouth firmly closed and held my nose in an attempt to stifle it. On the other side of the table, I could see a woman's shocking pink polished fingernails dig into the underside as her hands gripped both sides of the table. One finger however, her largest, also featured a black *Playboy* bunny symbol. The poor table was now rolling galleon-like around the Cape of Good Hope; rocking two and fro.

I could hold it no longer, the inside of my nostrils bristled and the pressure in my throat became unmanageable...

'Oh, my God, I'm coming!' she hissed. At the same time, a lower voice emitted a prolonged low growl. I could see the hairy legs tremble as they jerked forward one last time. As they did the woman shuddered and emitted a high-pitched 'OHH, GOD!'.

At precisely the same time, the sneeze I'd been stifling also came. 'MMMP-TSCH!'

A sharp pain shot across my throat, like I'd swallowed a razor blade.

'Bless you,' she panted. Shit! I'd been heard. The game was up. This was so embarrassing. I was just about to crawl out from beneath the table when I heard a gruff Essex voice say under his breath, 'Thanks, treacle, 'ope you enjoyed it as mach as oi did.'

They uncoupled. I watched a hand retrieve the thong and hold it open for the other foot to step into before it was slid up the limbs, out of sight.

After sharing one more kiss, they crept upstairs leaving me alone once again. My first thought was the tech kit on the table. If it was damaged the live broadcast would be just as screwed as the shocking pink and *Playboy* nail polish girl. To my relief it was untouched. I looked at the time on my phone.

It was half past one in the morning. Climbing back under my Austrian duvet, I once again fell asleep... only to be woken up around an hour later by the sound of the table moving. Again, I opened an eye, and could see someone kneeling next to the table. What was he doing? I turned my head up to the table and there were two familiar hands gripping the underside. The nail polish was shocking pink with one finger featuring a *Playboy* bunny symbol. But where was the rest of her? No limbs dangled down, meaning she must've been laying on her back on the table, with her legs in the air. I could hear slurping sounds, with occasional, muffled, 'MHMM,' as he buried his head further, eliciting semi-controlled gasps. My head was spinning. The West Ham tattoo on the ankle told me that this happy eater was a different bloke. I remained stock still in my duvet under that table for the best part of fifteen minutes as the hungry Hammer chomped, lapped and licked his midnight snack to the point of explosion. This time her orgasm, shuddered the whole table, rattling the technical equipment and causing the central chrome stand to vibrate and alarmingly inch across the wooden floor for about a foot.

I just hoped he didn't want dessert. I was exhausted from breathing so shallowly in order to avoid being discovered, and only exhaled deeply when I watched the tattooed ankle disappear from view as it ascended the wooden stairs back to the dorm above.

The next morning, I awoke at half past six to check the sky was clear, and roused every guest to ask them if they wanted to witness the alpine sunrise.

Most of them did, pulling their salopettes on and emerging bleary eyed into the crisp spring morning. Sunrise in the mountains is one of the most beautiful sights, the moment the golden orb appears through the jagged horizon is stunning – but what follows is every bit as special, as the changing shadows create an animation across the mountains. I've seen tough roofers from Romford shed tears and cynical gangsta types reduced to awestruck silence. The best thing about taking clubbers to the alps is that they leave with an awareness or connection with nature, they'd perhaps lost sight of living in an urban environment.

It was almost time for the live broadcast, and I went back inside to find the two presenters already chatting off air to the studio back in the UK, the link was working loud and clear and the weather at the mountain top was stunning; this would be a great advert for the resort, the mountains and my holiday company.

I listened to the first few links and then went for a ski down Red 7 which was my favourite piste. But I'd forgotten my sunglasses, and the cold air made my eyes water, leaving me looking like a bad case of conjunctivitis.

After one run, I rode the chairlift back up and returned for some breakfast, but as I kicked off my skis I was approached by one of the presenters. They told me they wanted to interview me live on air after the next song, and get me to describe the wonderful sunrise we'd just experienced.

So, I put on some headphones and waited for the track to finish, and after being introduced as the host and organiser, the presenter passed me the microphone. As I took it from her, I noticed her fingernails were decorated in shocking pink nail varnish... with a *Playboy* bunny on one finger.

I was dumbstruck. There she was, nonchalantly talking to around a hundred thousand listeners back home... sat at the very table on which she'd had sex with three different men in the previous few hours.

'That was "It's in his Kiss" by Cher. It certainly is, ladies. Next I want to introduce you to the lovely Kirk Field from Radical Escapes. Thanks ever so much for bringing us to the amazing place. I've never slept in a pyramid before. I should explain to the listeners that we all slept in a dormitory at the top of the pyramid, which was a lot of fun as you might imagine. I noticed you weren't in the dormitory with us, Kirk, do you have your own private room?'

This was too good to be true. I couldn't resist.

'No, sadly I missed the fun because I had to sleep downstairs, guarding the bar and equipment.'

She grew pale. 'Really? There's a bedroom down here also?'

'Oh, no. I just put a mattress under a table. It's a great place to get your head down...'

She stared at me in stony silence before weakly enquiring. 'W-which table?'

I smiled at her and, grasping both sides of the table like she did, said with a smile, 'This one.'

Silence. She was dumbstruck.

I turned the screw.

'How did you sleep? Did you enjoy the traditional sausage I saw you eating for supper?'

She was trapped. Squirming live on air, with no escape. Glowering at me through gritted teeth she had nowhere to run.

'Err, yes, it was delicious.'

'I never thought you'd manage it all, you must've been ravenous.'

'Yes. Here's Byron Stingily with "Get Up".' The song began. Slowly removing her headphones, she leaned towards me and hissed in my ear, 'You fucking bastard!'

After swearing me to secrecy, she could see the funny side. I loved the fact she was unrepentant and unashamed, making the valid point that if she was a man her conquests would be lauded as heroic. Her secret remained exactly that… until now!

The radio presenters I worked with were always good fun, in particular Chris Philips, Paul Thomas, Trevor Nelson and Alex P, Baz Jones, Big Kev Harden, Glen White, Mike Porter and Busta Brooka.

But none generated as much entertainment as a certain presenter who didn't like to spend his money…

---

**Top Tune: RIP Groove – Double 99 {Satellite}**

---

## BEHIND THE BROCHURE

'Kirk, come in here – quick or you'll miss it.' My wife rarely raises her voice but sounded particularly excited.

'What is it? I'm busy.'

'There's a guy on Dragon's Den who's doing exactly the same as you!'

Sure enough, there in front of Duncan, Deborah Peter and Theo was the guy who'd asked to meet me at the World Travel Market some months earlier.

I sat open-mouthed as he outlined his proposal – my business model, basically – to offer the Dragons a share of his burgeoning clubbing travel business, outlining his genius practice of bulk buying of club tickets in Ibiza and offering referral promoters and DJs opening slots.

Some of the phrases he used were so recognisable as mine

that it felt like I was listening to myself.

'He obviously paid attention,' my wife said, almost in admiration.

'Or recorded me!' I added, incredulous at what I was watching.

Perhaps this explained why he was so keen to meet me at the World Travel Market a few months earlier. After the forty-five-minute meeting he left, prompting my colleague Nick Cade to remark, 'He asks an awful lot of questions. I hope you haven't given him too many ideas.' Nick was right, my tongue was too loose, probably from the complimentary schnapps the Tyrol tourist board were handing out all afternoon. I thought it odd he hadn't been in touch since I met him to follow up the things we'd discussed, and now here he was in my front room. The Dragons were impressed – so impressed that they offered him £150,000 investment! They say imitation is the sincerest form of flattery.

I wish him all the best – even though I'm still waiting for my consultancy commission for his Dragon's Den presentation!

# 25

# WHITE LIES & BLACK RUNS

The dance music radio station's listener trips were a success, so I approached *Classic Gold FM*. It was quite a departure from working with dance music orientated station, but with a baby bulge growing bigger each day inside my wife, and a monthly mortgage to pay on our first house, I decided to substitute all night clubs for sixties and seventies disco and party-loving twenty-somethings for over sixties pensioners.

The trip nearly never happened. On launch day I'd driven up the A10 to Herford through near horizontal sleet in the dark winter pre-dawn.

I turned on the car radio to catch the 7 a.m. news. '*Beatle George Harrison has died of cancer. The Beatle died during the night aged 58...*'

WHAT?! My mind raced. Another Beatle. We measure our lives by such moments.

A stationary lorry with no lights on suddenly appeared through the wiper blades. I jerked the wheel to the right and felt the car shudder at the sudden change of direction. How I missed it, to this day I still don't know. It couldn't have been any closer. I was still shaken when I arrived at the studio. It was late November and the last chance to put a product on sale before folk's attention turned to Christmas. With the trip taking place in March and balances needing to be paid six weeks before departure (and January notoriously quiet, sales-wise), this was my last chance to launch the trip, or face cancelling it. I badly needed the money, as my wife wasn't working, due to being heavily pregnant, so I was super keen to announce it and get some deposits in before those little cardboard doors on Advent calendars began opening.

I rang the buzzer and announced my arrival. The door clicked open, and I walked into the empty reception to be met by a flustered producer.

'Hi, Kirk, sorry, you'll have to bear with us – please take a seat.'

Ten minutes went by. The switchboard, still unattended, started flashing as phones rang.

In the event of a national disaster like a terrorist attack or a death of a senior Royal, UK radio stations have a coordinated plan to transition the public to bad news. When a special blue light flashes in the office, producers know it's time to switch the music to something sombre and inoffensive before the big announcement is made.

The death of a Beatle surely counts as musical royalty, particularly for a station playing hits from the very era they ruled, and I was growing increasingly concerned that they would shelve my interview and launch, and simply play non-stop Beatles records as a tribute.

I needed this trip to happen and to launch it this morning. I needed to think fast...

Sure enough, another ten minutes later, my fears were confirmed. The frazzled breakfast show producer emerged to tell me the bad news; due to George's passing, it was considered inappropriate to talk about a ski holiday and only Beatles-related content was to be broadcast.

I was prepared…

'That's such a shame, as George just loved to ski…'

'He did?'

'Yes, he was passionate. Went every year.'

'Really? I was unaware.'

Warming to my theme, I regaled my white lie. 'Yes, remember the Beatles' 1965 movie *Help!* which featured them all fooling around on skis for 'Ticket To Ride?' Well, they all became keen skiers after that, none more so than George.'

The penny dropped; he had a scoop. 'Yes, I remember now, they were messing about in the snow. Where was that filmed?'

I knew it was shot in Obertauern, not Mayrhofen, where I worked, but these were the days before google, so there was no way of verifying this without calling up a Beatles expert, which would've taken hours.

'In the Austrian alps… in the very same resort we are taking the listeners! His face lit up. 'And what's more, the instructor who taught George to ski, Max is. a friend of mine who now runs the ski-school we'll be using.'

'Fantastic! The station controller just called and said cancel all guests, but this is appropriate, so let's get you on air straight away.'

The trip was launched, and I spent a very memorable week looking after a couple of hundred music loving listeners whose average age was sixty-eight!

As I mentioned earlier, the station sent out a presenter we'll call Gary, as Tony Blackburn had a nasty virus and Dave Lee Travis wanted too much money. Gary was a pleasant, inoffensive, professional regional radio presenter in the mould of Alan Partridge. He was polite, good company, diligent and had loads of experience – mainly of avoiding spending his own money.

When I worked on Snowbombing I was given a budget to grease the media's tongues with schnapps and sausages in order to get a good write up, but in these early days, I relied on a sense of decency when socialising with the radio presenters, and expected them to buy a round every now and then. But Gary's was tighter than a Yorkshireman saving up to be Scottish. He was doing everyone's heads in. He always had an excuse for not having any cash, and the last straw came when he borrowed my phone to make an 'important call to the station', as his battery had run out. Again.

So, a plan was hatched. Chris Philips from Kiss FM and my reps Pabs and Elliot Cox were all in on it, and we set it up by talking up a day's skiing at the Tux glacier.

Simon was a little unsure about joining us as his standard of skiing wasn't great, and it can be challenging up there, especially in bad weather. It's Austria's highest lifted point, 10,000 feet above sea level with 360-degree views of endless mountain peaks.

But when I told him that we were only really going to take advantage of the free phone calls his interest perked up immediately. We explained that due to the potential of danger on the glacier, it was a little-known fact that a special network had been set up called 'TuxerTel', which meant you would never run out of credit whilst stranded, or be unable to call for help because your account was barred, or you'd exceeded your spending limit. We told Gary they'd failed to limit the calls to the local area, meaning you could call anywhere on the planet and talk for up to fifteen minutes at a time without it costing a bean!

As we sat in the cable car ascending above the treeline, we entered the routine we'd rehearsed the previous night over dinner.

Pabs: 'Hello, Shaggy, it's me, I'm calling from Austria, how are things in Ibiza?'

As he pretended to chat to his mate in the Balearics, Gary inquisitively looked on. Then Elliot punched some numbers into his phone, 'Sis, are you still awake? What time is it in Sydney?'

This was Chris's cue to 'dial up 'David Rodigan, who was in Jamaica (naturally).

Then I struck up an imaginary conversation with an old friend in Hong Kong. That was it!

He spent the next 15 minutes calling friends across the UK and in Malta where he had mates in the Army.

He was so keen to catch up, that when we paused for lunch, he didn't eat, but instead spent the hour making a succession of fourteen minute and thirty second calls ( having set an alarm on his watch to alert him when the allotted 'free' time period would elapse) to friends and family around the World.

'Hiii! It's Nige, yes, I'm skiing in Austria...'

Then after a few minutes we'd hear

'There's no hurry, we can keep chatting as it's free... it's a secret rescue network on the glacier called TuxerTel... sure, put her on...' Simon spent the whole hour gabbing. And the longer he talked, the more we struggled to contain our mirth.

While we chose to ski back down to the bus, Gary preferred to ride the succession of cable cars back to the valley in order to make the most of his complimentary airtime.

The boys wanted to tell him it was a wind up, but I thought

it may affect his output, as we still had two more live breakfast broadcasts to do. So, we weren't able to enjoy the 'reveal' on this. But as he continued to keep his wallet close to his chest, we were able to pull one last wind up. It was the last night, and Nige had still not bought a round for the lads. So, we hatched a plan which involved a local bar owner, glasses of water and the strongest schnapps in the valley...

The bar owner prepared tray after tray of shot glasses filled with the new 'alcohol free' schnapps which we told Gary was being trialled at the time.

We proceeded to order the trays, which of course held four glasses of tap water and one containing Didi's own home distilled *Meisterwurz* schnapps, which was around sixty per cent.

For the third time, five glasses hit the table simultaneously, as five faces grimaced and exhaled.

'Jeez, are you sure this stuff is alcohol free?' Gart asked. 'It tastes lethal.'

I stared at the empty glass through a wizened expression with one eye closed. 'Yup, it certainly tastes like the real deal. But after three my head is crystal clear, how about you, Chris?'

Chis nodded in agreement. 'Sober as a judge, it's amazing.'

As more rounds were sunk, Gary began to slur his words, and visibly relaxed; telling us unrepeatable tales about how he'd got his leg over with two sisters from Paisley at The National Sandwich Awards, which he'd recently hosted.

'You could say I was the meat in that particular sandwich!'

By midnight, he was legless, literally. Chris and I had to carry him back to his hotel room, where we took his boots off, put a waste bin by his bed, poured him a glass of water, and left him fully dressed on his bed, in the coma position.

I checked on him the next morning, but he'd already left for the airport to fly home.

A few months later, I was walking in an Enfield park on a sunny May morning, pushing a buggy with a three-month-old baby boy when my phone rang.

I glanced at the throbbing screen which read 'NIGEL C'. GOLD. I paused, then pressed the green button.

'Hi, Ni—'

'YOU BASTARD! YOU ABSOLUTE BASTARD! I've just got a £300 phone bill! I called the lift company telling them their network was faulty and they told me THERE'S NO SUCH THING AS TUXERTAL. If I ever catch up with you, you're for it.'

Click.

I smiled. Revenge is a dish best eaten cold.

The Ziller valley was alive with bass: Kiss in the Snow was now well both established and successful for everyone involved; the resort, the radio station and importantly myself, accounting for about twenty-five per cent of my annual income.

So, when I heard the new boss of Emap wasn't a skier, I wasn't too concerned. The previous trip had made a healthy profit of £25,000, and the Mayrhofen Tourist Board had agreed financial support for the following March.

Then came the bombshell in early October that 25k profit wasn't sufficient to justify continuing. Before I could approach the resort to explore if there was a possibility of raising the support, it was cancelled.

I had a budget from the resort to allocate for music-driven group holidays. I also had a mortgage to pay (and a house to lose if it wasn't paid). What was I going to do? I had a resort which was conductive to clubbers which I'd been finely tuning for seven winters, but here I was without a marketing client.

My first idea was to approach my contacts in the London gay club scene with the concept of a gay skiing holiday who I worked with on The Famous Five parties at Bagleys , for whom I penned innuendo-laden flyer copy.

They loved my title 'Man Mountain': skiing's just the half of it, which offered its guests a chance to 'bend ze knees and prepare to pleasurably plant your pole...'. The resort who welcomed the concept was Solden (or 'Sodom' as a priest in a rival resort was overheard to call it). Other resorts were approached to host but declined on religious reasons. Staunchly Roman Catholic, they obviously chose to believe in a God who creates souls but forbids them to express their love. Jesus may have said, 'I am the light and love,' but they added a caveat, '...but only if you're straight.'

> **Top Tune: My Sweet Lord (2014 Remaster)**
> **– George Harrison {Apple}**

## BEHIND THE BROCHURE

'Welcome back!' I suffer from prosopagnosia (face blindness) which, in my role as group holiday host, is about as useful as a taxi driver without a sense of direction, or a roofer afraid of heights. Yet, as I stood in the airport holding the IBIZAN HEAT clipboard, I instantly recognised the familiar couple who'd just emerged from the baggage hall. The previous summer Luke and Lisa were on their honeymoon – which Luke had ruined after going missing for two days with a group of Italian girls, leaving her tied to the bed.

'You've forgiven him, then?' I joked.

'Yes, he's agreed to make it up to me. This year he's agreed to do *exactly* what I want to do; girly things like a yoga day, the Hippy Market, flamenco demonstration and a cookery class.'

Luke nodded ruefully, clearly regretting his undertaking; 'What have I let myself in for?'

I mumbled something about it being good to sometimes step out of your comfort zone, wished them happy anniversary and wished them a great holiday.

One week later, I was waiting at the bus to take them back to the airport and watched them approach, Luke walking awkwardly towards me with two suitcases behind a beaming, sprightly Lisa.

'Well, was it as bad as you thought?' I light-heartedly enquired as he put the suitcases in the hold.

But before he could answer, Lisa jumped in. 'You were right about trying new things; Luke's learned something about himself, haven't you, luv?'

Luke nodded bashfully.

'That's great to hear, what did you enjoy the most? Don't tell me, the cookery class?'

Luke's reticence to reply was punctured by his gleeful partner,

'No, I'd definitely say the pegging, wouldn't you, luv?'

Luke gingerly climbed the bus in some discomfort. Lisa leaned over and whispered, 'That'll serve the fucker right for ruining our honeymoon,' winked, and climbed aboard.

# 26

# THE GREATEST SHOW ON SNOW

Man Mountain wasn't my event, and Solden wasn't my resort. I needed to develop something in Mayrhofen, where the rivers from four valleys meet and the energy swirls. I believe in 'spirit of place'; the unique personality or 'feel' of a location, and Mayrhofen is in the same bracket as Ibiza and London.

That November I was having dinner in Soho with my good friend and Mayrhofen hotelier Erich Roscher. I told him about an event I'd heard about called Snowbombing. It was at this point the waiter, who introduced himself as Jonny Bain from Sombrero Sound System confessed to have been eavesdropping and having heard the gist of the conversation, interrupted and told me he was also a DJ and played at Snowbombing, and offered to introduce me to Gareth Cooper who ran it.

A few days later, one misty Saturday morning in November I found myself sitting in a riverside pub in Richmond, where Erich Roscher and myself talked him into relocating Snowbombing to Mayrhofen. So began a twenty-year love affair with what I christened the 'World's Greatest Show on Snow'.

Since 2005, I've worked on Snowbombing in some capacity; from copywriting the website, establishing the self-deprecative brand tone and coming up with concepts and themes to managing igloo parties and challenging Fatboy Slim to play all our mountain venues in one afternoon.

There are so many tales from this amazing event, which I saw grow and develop from a ski and snowboard holiday for a few hundred clubbers to a multi-arena festival attended by over 6,000 people (which sounds small by festival standards but in a small alpine village, it's an invasion). But it nearly started in disaster due to the climax of the week; Mylo's show which was to take place on Friday falling on Easter Weekend. Alpine parishes are staunchly catholic and regard Good Friday as a 'silent holiday'. As in neighbouring Bavaria sporting events and 'musical performances of any kind in rooms with bars' are prohibited. Holiday peace and quiet should not be disturbed – especially near churches. Breaking the rule can result in a fine of up to €10,000. All week this hung over the event like a dark cloud. Eventually wily owner of the Strass Hotel and Arena club Erich Roscher came up with a solution. The club would open at 11 p.m. and be seated with chill out music playing. The bars downstairs would not be open... *initially*. People would be served drinks at their table from the hotel bar upstairs. Then, at the stroke of midnight, the opening DJ would start up, the bars would open, and the party would start. As I recall, the priest who was there to observe the by law was upheld, was afforded the best seat and wine in the house!

Occasionally, the remote Alpine location gave rise to misunderstandings. After I introduced Snowbombing to the resort in 2005, things moved up another level altogether, with huge festival production, five thousand clubbers and big names such as The Prodigy, Fatboy Slim, Grandmaster Flash and 2 Many DJs/Radio Soulwax. The latter of which caused considerable intrigue when their personal rider section of the contract contained the following request:

*Hummus – enough for 4 people.*

As I returned from a day's skiing, I clunked past the Ice Bar in clumsy ski boots with my skis over my shoulder when I heard my name being called. Through the window I could see Stocky the Arena's excellent resident DJ and Christof the venue manager, both of whom were pouring over the contract. They beckoned me inside and said, 'Look at this.' The contract was thrust into my hand.

It was the standard festival rider, asking for towels, fresh fruit, copious amounts of premier brand alcohol and snacks.

'Why do they want hummus?' asked a clearly bewildered Stocky, scratching his head.

'Well, it's very popular these days,' I explained.

'For sure, but what will they do with it?' added Christof

'Dip breadsticks in it, probably.'

'WHAAAAT???'

They looked at each other in disgust, before concurring, 'Typisch Belgisch.' *Typical Belgians.*

Aware as I was that Tyrolean cuisine was itself basic, I was taken aback that my mates weren't aware of the Greek dip.

They continued quizzically studying the rider.

'And how much is enough for four people?' implored Cristoph.

'Four or five containers should be adequate,' I replied. Having never seen hummus in the supermarkets, I asked them if they'd be able to get their hands on any.

They looked at one another and laughed. 'Oh, we have

plenty of hummus in the valley! They can have a container each – and one for the tour manager – no problem. One thing we do have plenty of is hummus!'

'Great, thanks guys.' So what was the problem? I asked myself as I walked away.

A few hours later, I was sitting in Erich's office enjoying a beer. There was a knock at the door. There were 2 Many DJs tour managers looking uncomfortable.

'Everything okay?' I asked.

'The dressing room is... not so big... can you maybe do something to help?'

'Yes, it's not huge, sorry, but that's all there is... what do you suggest we can do to make it bigger, knock a wall down maybe?' asked Erich, by now well aware of ever-demanding tour managers and growing weary of their demands

'Well, if you removed the sacks of fertilizer, we would at least be able to get in.'

We looked at each other, then raced down to the dressing room to find five large forty-litre sacks labelled 'Worm Humus'.

That was the day that myself, David, and his brother Stephen Dewaele discovered that humus is the German word for compost.

Despite Snowbombing being known as an electronic music festival, in 2011 I took a call from a record label I'd never heard of offering us a singer songwriter who played love songs on an acoustic guitar, who was destined for great thing; 'major push', 'priority artist', 'biggest breakthrough act of the year', 'stadiums within three years' – all the usual lingo. I politely told them the line-up was complete and we had no budget left. An hour later he called back offering his artist for no fee, just travel expenses and accommodation. I told him we had no flight allocation left, and the resort was like Bethlehem in late December. Then he offered to cover all travel and accommodation expenses, 'Whatever it takes to get hm on the show.'

I explained that Snowbombers liked their bass and beats, and we didn't feature balladeers with acoustic guitars. But then we had an artist cancel who was due to play the Snowbombing Roadtrip; an overland car rally in pimped-up, liveried vehicles. I called the guy back and told him that the only way we could make this happen was to give his boy a slot at the overnight 'pit-stop' in Frankfurt, but they would need to provide the car and a driver. He leapt at it, and his guy drove out with everyone else and played to around fifty people in a budget motel bar in Frankfurt.

The Roadtrip arrival heralds the start of Snowbombing; folk line the high-street as the participating petrolheads receive a hero's reception. I was stood at the finish line outside Hotel Strass when a small lad with a guitar tapped me on the shoulder. He introduced himself and thanked me for letting him play the Roadtrip. He asked me if there was anywhere else he could play. I told him programming wasn't my area and that I managed the Arctic Disco; the mountain top igloo parties. His eyes widened, could he play there, he asked. I told him it was a DJ thing and we had Fatboy Slim, Example and James Zabiela already confirmed. He nodded and glumly walked away.

Ten minutes later he returned. 'I believe there's a queue whilst people wait at the bottom for the cable car?' he ventured.

'That's right, but the crowd turn up very lively from an afternoon's partying – and in all manner of fancy dress.'

'Could I busk there while they wait?'

While I admired his eagerness, it was overshadowed by

pragmatism.

'Mate, they would shout over you and probably take the piss, and I wouldn't want to put you in that situation.'

He told me he was used to being ignored and told me he was still willing to give it a try.

As much as he pleaded, I stood firm. I couldn't see how it would work. I had visions of the poor lad being tormented by a group of leary Munchkins or schnapps-fuelled Smurfs.

Reluctantly, he accepted with grace, resignedly walking off with his guitar slung over his shoulder.

And that's how I turned down three free Ed Sheeran shows.

Snowbombing headliners have included The Prodigy, Liam Gallagher, Fatboy Slim, Dizzee Rascal, Madness, De La Soul and Grandmaster Flash, although Snoop Dogg and Stormzy were also billed to appear but cancelled for very different reasons.

In 2012, we'd lined up Snoop Dog to headline the Forest party, and as usual, being a relatively small festival, we needed to renegotiate the artists festival contract as it was drawn up for huge events the size of Coachella or Glastonbury, rather than an intimate 5,000 gathering in an alpine forest clearing in an Austrian village surrounded by snow-covered peaks (which, although stunning visually, was limiting in terms of capacity and production potential).

The contract arrived for signature, and my job was to manage and renegotiate the artist hospitality rider to reflect the size of the festival.

While the specific brand of vodka and rum he demanded wasn't a problem, and the black Mercedes reserved (*'please note: dark brown is not acceptable!'*) to drive him from his hotel to the venue (a two-minute walk away), there was one item on the rider which was causing issues; the provision of three portacabins.

In the forest clearing there was barely room for any portacabins. We used the existing log cabins for dressing rooms which the artists spent minimal time in, prior to and post-performance, before heading back to their five-star hotel a few streets away.

It was left to me to persuade Snoop to do the same. As there was no budget – or room – for three extra portacabins on site it was essential they complied, or it would mean cutting capacity… meaning not everyone would be able to get in to see the festival headliner having paid for a wristband in their package.

His management were based in LA, who are eight hours behind UK time, so I had to wait until early evening before making the call.

'So, you got the contract and rider, when can we expect it to be signed and returned?' he asked.

'Yes, thanks for sending, mostly all good, just need to go through something with you re. the provision of portacabins,' I replied

'Sure, go ahead.'

'It says, "Three portacabins for private use of artist" – is that right?'

'Yes, sirree, that's correct.'

'Can I just check why there's three required?'

'Sure thing, one for Snoop and one for the band.'

'That's two, what about the third?'

There was a pause. 'The third is the most important one of all; that's the lurve room.'

In the event, Snoop cancelled on us as he had a better offer;

he had to rehearse a ground-breaking holographic show with Tupak and Dr Dre for Coachella, and as it was classed as a 'major TV appearance', his contract allowed him to reschedule. So, Dizzee Rascal stepped in as a replacement and did a great job – and made no Bonkers demands, either!

In 2018 both Liam Gallagher and Idris Elba appeared at Snowbombing. My role was to oversee the mountain venues we use including managing the Arctic Disco – an igloo village on top of a mountain which is only accessible by cable car. Idris was a regular there and was a dream to work with; polite, professional and down to earth. Always happy to chat to the clubbers, but reluctant to pose for endless selfies, which is reasonable.

I thought it would be a nice idea to give Liam a skidoo tour of the ski area while his lads were in snowboard lessons; the snowpark, the steepest black run in Austria, and our mountain stage where Idris was playing.

The sound of a skidoo roaring up and down the huge kickers grew ever near. Out of respect, I told Idris who was playing that Liam Gallagher's arrival was imminent and he'd be in the VIP room immediately behind the balcony where the decks were set up.

Idris just shrugged, 'No problem, man,' and went back to his mixing.

I grabbed a couple of beers and ran outside – to see banks of photographer's waiting for Liam's arrival. I was unsure this was an official photo opportunity and asked them to hold fire until I'd checked with Liam.

The skidoo juddered to a halt. I shook hands with Liam, who wasn't wearing any gloves. He was freezing. I've shaken warmer fish fingers.

'What the fook are *they* waitin' for?' he asked nodding towards the photographers.

'You! Is it okay to get a few shots on the skidoo?'

'No, I look like fookin' shit. Me 'airs all over the place and I haven't shaved, man.'

Behind my shoulder, the crowd cheered at the opening bars of the Frankie Knuckles anthem 'Your Love'. Idris was hitting the spot

I offered Liam a bottle of beer, which he accepted.

'Who's playin' anyway?'

'Idris Elba, he's smashing it as usual.'

Liam handed back the bottle. 'I've got to be getting back to my sons. Their lessons just finished, and I said I'd meet 'em for a drink.'

I gave the nod for the driver to open the throttle and they sped away, Liam holding his hood over his face so the photographers couldn't get their shots. To add to their disappointment, he didn't look back in anger, either...

I went over and told them what had happened, and they all smiled knowingly.

'Well, it was either that, or the celebrity fight of the century,' one said.

I asked him what he meant. I must've been the only person on the mountain who was unaware that Idris and Liam weren't the best of friends.

Their feud began at the 2013 NME Awards when Liam tried to knock Idris's red bobble hat off, leading Idris to ruffle Liam's hair. It nearly kicked off at the after-show party at the Ivy, too, with them going toe-to-toe like boxers at a weigh-in. When asked about the almost altercation, Liam told Absolute Radio, 'I don't give a fuck who he is, you don't touch a man's haircut, especially if you've got a red bobbly hat on.'

Which is a reasonable call I think, but a point of view not shared by Idris who retorted,

'Fuck off. Next time walk with a fucking hairdresser, then.'

Liam took to the Forest Stage that night and questioned the absence of snow in the valley.

'Not much fucking snow is there?'

A wag shouted something inaudible but also inevitable.

'Well, yeah, plenty of *that* snow, there's always plenty of that,' Liam retorted.

At another Arctic Disco, Carl Cox had just arrived by skidoo and I wanted to check he was okay for drinks. Walking around the back of the igloo I could see a furry figure crouched in the doorway. It looked like a Yeti taking a crap, but it turned out to be the daughter of a World-famous rock star in a fur coat having a pee. This was bad form; not only would her golden gift freeze and create a trip hazard, but some of it would also be trickle into the DJ booth. Without thinking, I reached under her arms, and scooping her up, walked off with her shrieking – leaving a thin yellow line behind like a plane's vapour trail. After realising I wasn't accosting her, she apologised and told me it was 'Our secret, right?'

'Of course,' I replied. 'Until I write my memoir.'

She laughed. She's not laughing now!

Success always spawns replicas, and Snowbombing's year-on-year growth inevitably led to inferior copycat events springing up. As there are only a finite number of artists, there was increasing comparisons between line ups. The geographical exclusivity clause forbidding the artist from accepting any other dates 14 days either side of the show you were booking them for in the same territory was no help – as the rival events took place in France or Andorra.

So, Gareth Cooper was keen to keep Snowbombing different and one step ahead, and bestowed on me the title, 'Director of Daft'. My remit was to bring bonkers stuff into the festival, which was getting increasingly serious with po-faced techno DJs in black T-shirts and endless grime acts. It was all too cool for school – and certainly too cool for a holiday at the end of a long, grey, wet winter in the UK. Pop-up oompah bands were promptly booked and fancy-dress themes devised. Pat Sharp was rescued from a P&O cruise ship and resuscitated. Mr Motivator was flown in from the Caribbean and we were stoked to see his leotard still fit him, and he was still in great shape. 'Say, "yeah"!'

## Where Eagles Dare

With his *Mr Magoo* glasses and prominent jawline, Michael 'Eddie The Eagle' Edwards was won the hearts of a nation – mine included – with his plucky courage at the 1988 Olympics. I thought he'd be a natural fit for Snowbombing; to host the press and hang out with our guests. Festival Director Gareth Cooper agreed and gave me the responsibility of looking after him the whole week.

'The whole week? What if he's a twat?' I asked Gareth.

'That's tough shit, Kirk, he was your idea.'

So, I chaperoned Eddie, spending the days skiing with press and artists, and each evening checking out the acts around the resort. You may be surprised to learn that Eddie's a fantastic skier; the best British skier I've shared a chairlift with in fact. He only took up ski jumping because they wouldn't let him in the GB downhill team of six – even though he was fourth fastest in qualifying. He explained to me how he didn't fit in with the posh lot being a plasterer from Stroud. This resonated with me, as I also suffered class discrimination at my RAF pilot selection in Biggin Hill, where I found myself outnumbered and outmanoeuvred by the groups of public-school snobs who were on the course and wouldn't allow me any input into the leadership and aptitude exercises. The RAF rejected me – but not before asking what my father did. What the fuck did that have to do with flying a Phantom?

So, I saw in Eddie a kindred spirit, and I got to hear some great stories about the Olympics over lunches in my friend Mara's mountaintop restaurant. But being Eddie, he'd forget it the next day, when we were hosting the press, so I usually ended up telling it for him!

My favourite described his arrival in the UK, which is very different to how the film portrayed it![8] Eddie turned up at Calgary without any gear, support or even accommodation. Initially he was staying in a camper van belonging to Canadian TV who'd already given him his nickname. There was a huge banner in the car park that read: WELCOME TO CALGARY, EDDIE THE EAGLE!

'Who's he?' Eddie asked.

Canadian TV was aware of him from previous ski jumping competitions and began to feature him in their coverage. Then American TV did the same. This, totally unbeknown to Eddie, led to him becoming a cult figure, and his performance on the seventy-metre ski jumping event only added to his appeal, finishing second to last, but displaying sheer determination to

---

8. The 'Eddie the Eagle' movie concludes with Eddie receiving a hero's reception at Heathrow. This is not accurate and was probably used to provide a happy ending to the movie.

fulfil his dream and represent his country in the Olympic Games.

There were no mobiles or internet, and as the BBC (another establishment run by ex-public-school boys), saw him as a national embarrassment rather than a national treasure, they ignored him, focussing instead on the Women's Curling team... as they do at every Winter Olympics.

Eddie told me how he was eating breakfast alone one morning in the Olympic village, and a portly guy with slicked back hair in a sharp suit asked if he could sit down opposite. Eddie, halfway through a mouthful of hash brown, beans, and sausage, nodded. The stranger slid a business card towards Eddie, sat back in his chair and slowly surveyed the munching Eddie like he was a thoroughbred with potential in the parade ring.

'Eddie the Eagle!... Eddie the Eagle,' he kept repeating. He then leaned forward to conceal his conversation. 'Eddie, I have a question. How much would it cost to put your face on a T-shirt?' Pausing the next fork full of food, which was about to enter his mouth, he thought for a while...

Eddie told him there's a shop in the mall who would do it for $10.

The man laughed. 'Oh Eddie, you're such a card. How much would it cost to put your face on lots of shirts, say... (he glanced in both directions as if he was about to cross a road) ... thousands of T-shirts?'

Enthusiastically chewing, Eddie appeared to be doing mental arithmetic and gestured for the stranger to wait until his mouth was empty. The stranger leaned further forward, the smell of tobacco and cheap after shave now discernible.

Eddie swallowed, washed it down with a gulp of coffee and suggested they'd maybe give discount for a multiple order.

The stranger stared at Eddie and smiled. Producing a

chequebook from his pocket, he wrote out a cheque for $10,000 for the rights to print official Eddie the Eagle T-shirts.

Eddie looked at it, shook his head in disbelief. And handed it back, apologising.

'You want more? Jeez, you drive a hard bargain.'

Eddie told him the issue was he didn't have a bank account, but could he do cash.

The next morning at breakfast, the stranger returned with a bulging envelope of cash and a colleague, 'This is my cousin Hymie. He's in the ballpoint pen game and has an offer for you...'

This was repeated for the next few days, until Eddie had a suitcase containing $54,000 under his bed (equivalent worth today would be $118,897.68).

Back in those days the Olympics were for strictly amateur sportsmen/women only. Professional participants weren't allowed. But as this was image rights, he felt he wasn't being paid to compete, though harboured an ever-increasing nagging doubt he was breaking the rules. But he had to balance his precarious financial situation, and the money would enable him to continue competing and buy his own pair of boots, which wasn't going happen if he was to rely on the British Olympic Association (BOA) to fund him. Since the ninety-metre hill, they had done their best to eschew him; treating him like an unwelcome gatecrasher and failing to pass on interview requests from the British press. As a result, secure in his Olympic village, shielded from the outside world, Eddie was completely unaware that he was the star of the Winter Olympics and the man of the moment.

Michael Edwards boarded a plane back to the UK with a suitcase full of used dollar bills.

As the Boeing 747 crossed the Atlantic, his stress grew. He was no criminal, and by the time he arrived at Heathrow he was beside himself with worry. As he waited at the baggage carousel for the incriminating suitcase he was a nervous wreck, half hoping the case had gone missing. But there it was rumbling along the conveyor belt towards him. He reached out and grabbed the handle.

'I'll help you with that, sir.' A dark blue sleeve appeared and took the suitcase. A Metropolitan Policeman stood either side of him. One carried the case and the other beckoned with his arm, saying, 'This way, sir.' Eddie's heart stopped. His head span. Walking through the baggage hall flanked by Policemen, Eddie was aware of the other athletes casting unapproving glances. They walked past the green 'Nothing to Declare' and red 'Goods to Declare' corridors, instead exiting the baggage hall through an unmarked door, down along a long corridor with several corners before finally emerging into the open air – where a police range rover awaited in a quiet road at the back of Terminal 4, engine running. After the police checked there was no one waiting around the inconspicuous backdoor, Eddie was told to get in and was joined on the backseat by the two policemen, one on either side.

The vehicle pulled away with the suitcase resting on his lap. As they drove past the front of the arrival's hall, Eddie could see banks of camera flash bulbs popping as Team GB emerged.

The police exchanged glances. 'Job done.'

He could take it no more and explained he was going to declare the money, which he explained was payment for T-shirts and pens and all legal.

'Sorry, sir?'

Eddie explained the cash money in his case was received

for letting people put his face on things.

'We're not interested in that, sir. We're here to take you home and avoid the media circus waiting for you.'

Eddie was startled and informed them he lived in Cheltenham.

'That's correct sir, St Paul's Street North. Would you mind signing this for my wife, she loves you.' The policeman in the passenger seat passed back a copy of a newspaper to sign. It was a review of the games, one paragraph stood out:

'No Olympian won more attention, had more fun or gave more joy to fans than Eddie 'The Eagle' Edwards, the overweight, under-trained plasterer from Cheltenham with Mr Magoo glasses and indefatigable grin – who reminded everyone that these games are more about trying than winning.'

Shocked beyond words, Eddie was most shocked by the weight jibe. Insisting to the officers he wasn't overweight.

'But you *are* a national treasure, sir.'

During the drive, the four coppers explained how he'd captured the hearts of the nation, and the authorities were keen to 'protect' him from the huge media and public interest awaiting at Heathrow1 On arrival at his house in Cheltenham, he pushed the front door past the mountains of mail which had built up during his time away and rushed upstairs to the loo as he was busting for a pee, ignoring a ringing phone. A minute later it rang again and bladder now empty, he picked up the receiver.

'Hi, Eddie, my names Peter Estall, I produce the Wogan show for the BBC and would like to invite you on tonight's show.'

Eddie told them he'd just got in and needed a shower.

'It's just turned three forty-five in the afternoon. If you jump in the shower now, and grab a bite to eat, we'll get a car to you in thirty minutes. The show airs at 7 p.m., so there's ample time.'

Eddie had no clean clothes, so wore his Team GB tracksuit, further embarrassing the suits at the BOA. After the show, there was still no respite; ITV tracked him down and booked him for 'Celebrity Squares' the next evening... and so it went on and on – a rollercoaster ride he never dreamed of, making a little (jump) go a very long way.

## Afterjump

Idris and Liam made their peace later that year on The Graham Norton Show.

Sadly, that's not the case with Eddie. I developed an 'In Conversation With' spoken word show with him which went down really well at some big festivals, and which I believed we could develop for theatre. After considerable effort, I finally found a promoter to take us on.

Then my Dad became seriously ill. I spent most weekends driving from Devon to Cumbria to visit him. I didn't hear from Eddie or the promoter for three months. In October, the week my Dad died, I opened a booklet for the Northcott Theatre in Exeter to see my words being used to promote Eddie The Eagle's 'one-man' UK theatre tour. One-man show? I called and messaged Eddie but received no reply. So I called the promoter, who said Eddie had decided to do it without me. I told him it wouldn't work as Eddie wouldn't talk about the class discrimination, bankruptcy, facial reconstruction and his marital breakup and only focus on the Olympics and that a two-hour theatre show needs more gravitas than a twenty-minute after dinner talk. But it was to no avail; my concept was executed as Eddie wanted. As I predicted, ticket sales weren't what they hoped for and it never happened again.

I invoiced both the promoter and Eddie for the expenses I'd incurred. The promoter refused, and Eddie continued to ignore my letters and emails for four years. Yet when our paths crossed at Snowbombing in 2022, the first thing he said was, 'I have some money for you for the theatre tour.' So I sent him my invoice, but once again received no reply.

I contacted Eddie again whilst writing this book to give him another chance to reimburse me and put it behind us, but once again he blamed the promoter – despite me sending him the emails from the promoter in which he makes it clear it was Eddie's decision. I remain out of pocket.

They say never meet your heroes. I'd say by all means meet them, just don't waste time trying to help them when they're down. If they rise again they have short memories.

The ginger troubadour's persistence paid off; he played a handful of songs shortly after one of our venues opened. His set was witnessed only by a handful of bar staff and crew – who were all blown away. The claim the unknown singer songwriter would be playing stadiums within three years of the phone conversation in March 2011 was, as I suspected, somewhat of an exaggeration. It took him four: Ed Sheeran sold out Wembley Stadium for three nights in 2015.

## When the Schnitzel Hits the Fan

In a crowded market it's important to have a USP. I once planned a party in London which was free to get in, but you had to pay to get out: the longer you stayed the cheaper it was. The night was going to be called 'Hostage!'.

We created a logo, sorted the line-up and even had a venue held, then the venue received legal advice that if someone refused to pay as they left, and we held them at the club, we'd get done for false imprisonment, so it never happened. Years later, I was asked to deliver a Backcountry Party at Snowbombing in the Austrian Alps for 'Taken!', an imaginative Shoreditch happening who ran one-off mystery destination club events. These required ticket holders to assemble at a designated meeting place and board buses, at which point they were blindfolded. They would then be taken to an undisclosed venue which had been prepared in advance with specifically themed décor.

For their alpine edition I'd suggested using a remote 200-year-old mountain hut and party barn.

We always consulted the Avalanche Commission when using the venue, as its location was in an avalanche gallery[9]. They gave us the green light, with the proviso that in the mountains the weather can always change, and we should be ready to react if it did.

The night was going really well until I took a call from my friend Zissi at the bus company, relaying her driver's concern that due to the heavy snow, the buses were unable to drive up the mountain track to the hit to collect us as planned as the snow was falling so ferociously that even though they had snow chains on, they could only wait at the bottom of the track for another thirty minutes before returning to the resort. As we had 200 people there, there were not enough toboggans for everyone, meaning a twenty-minute walk down the hill to the waiting buses. This meant I had to jump on the mic and end the party prematurely. You can imagine how that went down. People just didn't get how quickly the situation had changed.

---

9. A site susceptible to avalanches.

What I was also aware of was that the mountain track I had to walk the (by now 'loosened' group down was also avalanche prone, and in Spring in particular, a very real threat.

The thought did cross my mind to stay put and spend the night there. But the prospect of an all-night session in a small mountain hut with Hot Since 82, Dave Beer, Skream, a fully stocked bar, a sound system and 200 Snowbombers would've resulted in more casualties than terminating the party and heading back to civilisation, so, I pulled the plug, got out my head torch and led the group down the pitch black mountain track in the blizzard. Occasionally the mountains rumbled; a base, guttural expulsion which echoed in the darkness.

'Fighter jets, in this weather, well they're keen, I'll give them that,' Dave Beer expressed, surprised.

But it wasn't fighter jets. It was the most frightening sound I've ever heard; the rumble of snow. Until you've heard an avalanche you wouldn't believe how loud and violent snow can be. I swallowed hard and said nothing. No one suspected they weren't jets, but avalanches falling.[10] I could see the rolling script on SKY NEWS: '...British festivalgoers buried in avalanche...'

I was so relieved to finally arrive at the buses – just as they were getting ready to leave. The drivers, all very experienced, were on the verge of driving another mile down the road to the entrance of the tunnel, where they'd shelter and wait for us. This would've meant more walking in the driving snow on a frozen road when people were still in a party mood.

---

10. During the night, a thirty-foot-high avalanche came down on the road we'd walked a few hours earlier. We stopped using the venue after this as Spring is the most dangerous time for avalanches.

Carnage, in other words. In less than an hour, six inches of snow had fallen.

On getting back to Mayrhofen, I had supper with the promoter and told him all about my Hostage! concept, which he liked. As we spoke, he spoke about the bands his dad was in. After a while, I sussed out his dad was Bill Drummond from KLF, which made my night being a KLF fan (and contributor to their 'big burn', as I explain in my previous book!).

In Spring 2022. Russia was mercilessly shelling Ukrainian cities, and each night the BBC covered the carnage. International condemnation and pleas to cease the barrage fell on deaf ears. We had a dilemma. Snowbombing was an established brand but sat uncomfortably against a backdrop of indiscriminate air strikes. The resort was getting nervous. We weren't supporting the daily bombardment, yet they understandably felt it could appear in bad taste to dance, laugh and drink without a care in the world beneath a Snowbombing banner and sky exploding with fireworks while people cowered from *real* bombing 875 miles away.

There was talk about cancelling the festival, but after two years of postponement due to Covid, people were desperate for a release and had bought flights. We needed to show the resort we were aware of the situation and align with the calls for ceasefire, whilst delivering the event the sponsors, media partners and resort had invested in – but how?

Gareth gave me the weekend to come up with something. That night the Russians shelled a kid's hospital in Kiev. The footage was grim to the point I turned the television off.

I did what I always do in these situations. Asked for guidance. I recalled the time I 'became the universe' in Glastonbury festival in 1990 after eating two pieces of Space Cake which

I strongly suspect also contained LSD.

After my consciousness expanded to the degree I felt I was everything (in actual fact, I merely became aware of my connection to everything). In the presence of the divine all-knowing I became aware I could ask any question. So, I asked why there was a need. The answer I received didn't arrive in words so it's not easy to relay what I was told. The closest to it was 'the answer lies within: we have everything we need, basically'.

I looked again at the word which was causing such turbulence, SNOWBOMBING. 'The answer lay within...' I stared at the word without blinking until the letters became blurred and the answer to our problem revealed itself... we would rename the festival SNOWBOMBING.

I sent it to Gareth who loved it, as did the Mayrhofen Tourist Board. We printed special commemorative T-shirts and donated the proceeds and the pyrotechnic budget to War Child.

NO BOMBING 2022 was the first major music festival to take place after Covid – which was appropriate, as Snow-bombing 2020 was the first major music festival to be cancelled because of it.

### Loosely in the Sky with Jager

This was the year we filmed Suat and his walkabout mobile disco paragliding with former World Paragliding Champion Jurgen Stock – the clip is insane and was viewed over a million times in the first week.

The image was so defined and the alpine air so crystal clear that people said it was faked; that it was a green screen. But believe me, it happened, and wasn't the first time Jurgen

'David' Stock had done something of note.

I first met him at the turn of the century, when he would insist on taking me for a tandem paraglider flight at the end of the Kiss in the Snow week as a thank you for the business I'd brought him. Each year the flights seemed to get more interesting. We'd take off from further up the mountain or kiss (touch wings) with another pilot who would be carrying a mate, or he'd go into a longer and steeper corkscrew. After one particularly exhilarating descent which saw us almost loop the loop, I made the mistake of remarking that it felt like I'd done everything a tandem passenger can do in a paraglider. Big mistake.

'Next year we do a full moon flight!' Jurgen grinned.

The following year, a full moon fell on the last Thursday I was there with my wife and two-month-old baby. This changed everything. Someone now relied on me and needed me, and it was time to grow up and accept that I couldn't be reckless with my life any longer doing things like moonlit paragliding.

Consequently, I was hiding in the Scotland Yard pub, safely ensconced in a quiet corner drinking dunkel beer and chatting to CC who worked behind the bar.

The door then burst open and Jurgen's grinning manic face appeared.

'Tonight is the night. It is perfect!' His crystal-clear blue eyes were filled with mischief and excitement. This wasn't going to be easy. I walked outside and explained my dilemma to Jurgen, but he was having none of it, 'It's safe, the air is still and the light good. You made a promise!'

So, I agreed, but on the condition that I could write a note for my family to read in the event something went wrong. I crept into my apartment to find my wife and baby sleeping soundly and wrote a brief note which read:

*'If you are reading this, I won't see you again. I'm truly sorry but adventure is what makes life worth living. I love you both*

*xxx*

*Please forgive me.'*

We then set off for the Steinerkogl mountain hut which perches on a ridge 2,700 feet above the village, ascending and twisting ever higher around increasingly extreme hairpin bends through spectacular scenery which offered occasional glimpses of the Ziller valley below. At one point Jurgen turned the headlights off and drove the car using only the plentiful silver moonlight the mountainside reflected.

I was speechless with fear. If I could survive the drive up, the flight down should be no problem. Still, we climbed. Without warning, a large dark shape materialised on the road in front of us. Jurgen hit the brakes. I lurched forward and my hand hit the windscreen. Instinctively, I closed my eyes. From the footwell I heard the screech of brakes. I opened my eyes to see the most magnificent sight; a large stag deer bound out of sight up into the banking. Its silky hind legs momentarily shimmering in the moonlight.

'Maybe put the lights back on?' I suggested to Jurgen, which he did.

A few minutes later we finally reached the top and as I admired the view, Jurgen's girlfriend jumped in the driver's seat to drive the car back down, leaving only myself and Jurgen who was diligently preparing the glider. There was only one way down now. I strolled over and found Jurgen laying out the material on a small area of grass behind a line of pine trees which marked the edge of a steep rocky cliff. The cliff ended nearly 3,000 feet vertically below where it met the green valley floor. Get the take-off wrong and it was a long drop.

Now I was standing in front of Jurgen, being strapped in. Buckles clicked and nylon was pulled taut as he went through his pre-flight checks.

I knew the drill. On his signal, we would start running forward with all our strength as Jurgen pulled up the glider over his shoulders until it caught the wind and snaps tight. There then would follow what I called the stagger of uncertainty: a period where we'd run forward to get air moving over the wing, causing it to lift off the ground, which usually disappeared from beneath our feet as we'd run down a slope. Previously this had been down a gentle slope which inevitably got steeper until the lift kicked in, allowing us to take off. This time, however, I was running towards a bank of tall larch trees. With every step they appeared larger and more solid. I could now see the dark trunks. I drove forward like a prop forward, leaning into the night, the star-filled, beautiful night which all of a sudden possessed a lethal beauty. Onwards I drove, making scant progress as the wing of nylon ruffled and strained above my head.

Still no lift. The trees were closer now. I could see individual branches and started to aim for the gap between them which had presented itself. Now I was running but not getting anywhere at all. It's a recurring nightmare I have. Other people's nocturnes may be haunted by monsters, vampires or snakes, but mine is desperately trying to escape something but getting nowhere.

Then I realised why I'm not getting any traction. It's because we'd taken off!

Jurgen expertly steered his airborne cargo towards the gap in the bank of trees, where a younger tree was growing, which, although mature, was twenty feet lower than the rest of the trees. The fragrance of the pine, such a sweet aroma, filled my nostrils. I was staring at the top of the tree and we were going to crash into it. I closed my eyes and scrunched my face, readying for impact. But it wasn't the impact which scared me, it was what would happen next. With a bit of luck, the glider would get caught up in the tree and Jurgen's girlfriend would raise the alarm, prompting a mountain rescue as we dangled serenely three thousand feet above the ground.

Then, at the last moment, we ascended and only my boots brushed the very top of the tree, dusting off the snow from them.

'Fucking hell, Jurgen.'

'No problem,' he replied.

Once past the trees, the village glowed beneath us like a neon join-the-dots puzzle whose lights were gentle and static. I threw my head back and saw an array of rebel diamonds swirling at the edges of the wing.

This was the moment I'd been waiting for. I unzipped my jacket pocket and grasped the two small green bottles I'd bought before leaving Scotties. Jurgen's hands were full steering the 'glider, so I twisted off both metal tops and handed a bottle to Jurgen. We chinked them in mid-air and down them in one, the bitter twisted liquorice taste of cold Jagermeister cementing our derring do. I replaced the empty bottles and tops back in my pocket. It was then I noticed we were descending considerably swifter than during a daytime flight as the air is much colder and devoid of thermal currents which elevate the paraglider. As we banked to the left to make our final approach to the meadow in the middle of town we were now only fifty feet above the ground.

I felt a tap on my shoulder.

'When I shout 'now', make a war cry.'

'What?'

'Like they do in the movies.' Jurgen then placed his hand over his mouth and began a tapping gesture. 'Ow-ow-ow-ow-ow!'

I copied. I hadn't done this since I was a kid playing cowboys and Indians. In retrospect, it could be deemed cultural appropriation by reinforcing lazy stereotypes. At the time, it felt more like cultural appreciation; we were the noble savages in tune with nature defying the Sheriff.

I noticed we'd made the noise as we flew directly over a detached house at the perimeter of the meadow we were about to land in. Within seconds, we'd elicited the reaction Jurgen wanted. The balcony light went on and a figure emerged in a dressing gown shaking his fist. But we were now 300 metres away coming into land right next to a wooden fence. As ever the landing was just like stepping into the shower – a gentle step and we both remained upright. Jurgen unclipped me. 'Quickly, get in the car!'

Jurgens car approached on the other side of the fence. I hopped over and jumped in. A few seconds later, Jurgen threw a hastily bundled paraglider into the boot, jumped into the back seat and we sped off.

In the house a figure could be heard shouting in German.

Jurgen laughed. 'It's the chief of police. He knows it's me, but can't prove it as I use an unmarked wing.'

Five minutes later we were all sat back in the Scotland Yard Pub reliving one of the most memorable hours of my life. I felt elated. Adrenaline was coursing through my veins, mingling with the Jagermeister; a lunar-powered cocktail which kept me in there until 2 a.m., when I thanked Jurgen and walked back to the apartment where my wife and baby were asleep. Neither had stirred in the time I was away. I picked up the note I'd left, folded it neatly and slipped it into my rucksack. I planned not to tell Catherine what I'd done, but in Mayrhofen there's no such thing as a secret, and as we left breakfast the following morning, Harry the night porter heartily congratulated me on my full moon flight. News travels fast in Da Hoff – even when it isn't true!

Jurgen is a legend in paragliding circles. A double world champion, he once stayed in the air for eleven hours setting a new endurance record, or the 'pissing from a great height' record, as he refers to the necessity to take toilet breaks in the air and the distance record (200km), He once flew to Italy for a pizza, before flying back the next day when the wind changed – how cool is that?

Perhaps his biggest claim to fame was during the rainy summer of 2000 when he accepted a bar room bet to land on the roof of the German *Big Brother* compound. Making the front pages of every tabloid from Hamburg to Hoffenheim. As you can imagine, his reception from the security was less than cordial. He expected nothing less, which is why he made sure he was broadcasting live on a rival television station from his helmet cam. This saved him from a good hiding. The fine he received was more than covered by the live streamed footage and of course, he won the bar room bet!

**Top Tune: Yodel Song (Extended Mix) – Basement Jaxx (feat Sofia Shkidchenko) {Atlantic Jaxx}**

## BEHIND THE BROCHURE

There are certain sayings which apply to every area of life. One being 'it's nice to be important, but it's important to be nice'. In my experience, the important people, having gone through an asshole stage, show respect to 'lesser mortals' like road crew and especially lighting riggers, who risk their lives so that the star can bathe in the limelight.

One brass player for a band which played Snowbombing was evidently still in his asshole stage; lording it like he was Miles Davies, treating everyone like they were dirt, and generally giving it the big un. Making enemies and leaving your instrument unguarded at the side of the stage isn't clever – nor is a crew member using the mouthpiece to wipe his arse – an act which was deemed thoroughly deserved by all who heard about it, and explains the eager crowd waiting in the wings for the first trumpet solo…

# 27

# THE WUHAN CLAN

Friday January 3, 2019: The New Year's Eve hangover had dissolved into depression. The party was over, replaced by the calendar's cruellest comedown, the early January vacuum. The Christmas tree, having fulfilled its use, lay naked and dull on its side outside the front door like a teenage boy's Action Man; a mass of contorted limbs no longer appreciated. The Quality Street tin rattled with a few toffee pennies, the confectionary version of unsporty school kids who were always the last to be picked for football teams. Every other advert featured smiling nuclear families on a Tui, Jet 2 or First Choice summer holiday. They don't show the other side; the moody kids constantly on their phones as the parents argue about who stays sober to drive the hire car back to the apartment.

More holidays are sold during the two weeks either side of New Year than at any other time in the calendar. People need something to look forward to, and choose to illuminate the long dark nights with 'holiday porn'. Escaping the gloom and irritating in-laws for a blue sky and pool perv, working themselves into a 14 night, all-inclusive, transfers-included frenzy, before reaching the point of no return and clicking the 'BOOK NOW to receive a free room upgrade!' button, the image of the hot tub on the balcony burnt into their retina as spent and satisfied, they close their laptop the moment the Booking Confirmed email ejaculates into their inbox.

I'd just received my sales figures from my clearly very content booking agent Nick. We'd sold all of our beds and demand wasn't slowing. He urged me to buy more in. As he's on the front line, I always listen to him as he's rarely wrong. So, I actioned another fifty beds. This may not sound like a lot but it's an exposure of £25k.

Then my co-promoter Sam in Captured Festival called with similar news. We'd sold out of all Early Bird tickets for the festival the following September, and he was pushing to add another big name to the line-up which we were yet to announce. Ferry Corsten had played for us the previous year and was indicating he'd be available once again, but we both harboured a desire to book Paul Oakenfold who although available, involved a fee previously out of our reach. Eventually we agreed to go for it. It would be a big risk, but it felt right. Captured had grown in attendance and stature year on year, and booking Oaky would reinforce our position as one of the World's top trance festivals.

Together between Captured Festival, Ibiza Trance Event, and BTID in the Sun I was financially exposed like never before. My bank account was empty as ALL my money was with hoteliers and artist agents. The sales we already had on all three products were in an Escrow account, which we were unable to access until the events had been delivered.

But all three brands were established and growing. 'You got to speculate to accumulate', and all that. Trying not to think about the risk, I opened the bottle of Ribera del Duero I'd been saving for a rainy day or a celebration. This felt like the latter. The future was looking rosy. I thought back to all the bad luck I'd had to ride since setting up Radical Escapes twenty years earlier; the storms across the North Sea, the buses leaving me with 400 clubbers in Amsterdam, the backcountry party at Snowbombing we had to abandon because of an impending avalanche, my psychic medium being accused of being a fraud, 9/11, volcanic ash clouds, rail, baggage handler and air traffic control strikes, bankruptcies and insolvencies of debtors, fraudulent accountants and undercover customs operations, Remembrance and Royal parades – and far too many narrowly avoided death experiences to recount here.

Against all the odds, I'd survived and was finally about to reap the reward of all my hard work, long days and sleepless nights. I'd risked the roof over my head to be my own boss and provide for my young family, creating my own career path and doing travel *my way.*

The post-Christmas comedown hits hard. The magic is over for another year. As a boy, the next thing to look forward to was the FA Cup 3rd round which takes place on the first Saturday of the New Year. A day of non-league glory on sloping, muddy, pitches made for giant-killing and surprises. I checked the BBC website to look through the draw and see if Manchester United's tricky tie away to Wolves were going to be featured. On the homepage, the main story was about a new take on the iconic vampire Dracula which was written by The League of Gentlemens and Sherlock geniuses Mark Gatkiss and Steven Moffat. I made a mental note to watch it. Beneath this was a smaller headline:

*Mystery virus probed in Wuhan.*

Intrigued, I read on:

*Chinese authorities have launched an investigation into a mysterious viral pneumonia which has infected dozens of people in the central city of Wuhan.*

*A total of 44 cases have been confirmed so far, 11 of which are considered 'severe', officials said on Friday. The outbreak has prompted Singapore and Hong Kong to bring in screening processes for travellers from the city.*

*There has been speculation on social media about a possible connection to the highly contagious disease Sars (severe acute respiratory syndrome).*

*Wuhan police said eight people had been punished for 'publishing or forwarding false information on the internet without verification.'*

*The Wuhan health commission said on Friday it was investigating the cause of the outbreak.*

*In a statement on its website, it said it had already ruled out a number of infection sources – including influenza, avian flu and common respiratory diseases – but did not mention Sars.*

I twisted the chrome corkscrew clockwise, unaware that the world was about to start spinning backwards.

Here we go again, I thought, another health scare which won't amount to anything, recalling previous viral non-events like Swine and Bird Flu. As I didn't run trips to China, Singapore or Korea it wouldn't affect me, I mean, it's not like they were going to stop people from flying to Ibiza on holiday or anything stupid now, were they?

I heaved on the corkscrew like I was pulling back a longbow.

The cork made a 'plonk' as it was extricated. I noted it was a synthetic one – or genie cork as I call them, 'cos just like a genie, once they're released, try as you might, you can't get them back in the bottle. This proved prescient; in China the genie had indeed been let out of the bottle...

> **Top Tune: Gunman – 187 Lockdown (Original Mix)**
> **[Kinetic Records]**

## AfterLockdown
Excerpts from 'When the Dancing Stopped'

### #1
People have always convened and moved to music. Forging communities, challenging social divisions and taking pleasure in the beat of a drum (...bang!). Dancing has also been subject to regulation – rules about when, where and how they can move, rules about who is allowed to dance with who, rules about what dancers can wear and put inside their bodies...

I believe dance to be an affirmation of life, a celebration of the physical and acknowledgement of the spiritual – and a fundamental human right as important and precious as eating, drinking, sleeping and breathing...

### #2 Friday, 22 May, 2020
Ibiza's clubs' suggestion to run at thirty per cent capacity with seated VIP style tables for groups of friends, facemasks on entering and whilst walking around and using the toilet was blown into smithereens by Francina Armengol, President of the Balearic Government, who made the bombshell announcement that superclubs would also be closed for the

whole of the summer, *'and also 2021, or until a vaccine was found,'* as nightlife wasn't *'a priority'* (despite two thirds of the jobs in Ibiza reliant on tourism, and the clubs generating an estimated €20 billion).

This is the first recorded mention of closing for the summer of 2021 by any politician so far. So, either the tinpot Balearic Govt in Palma Mallorca has some info on the virus not even the WHO were aware of, or there's something else going down...

### #3 Thursday, 3 September, 2020
Opening day for my Ibiza Trance Event. On the event page I posted:

Today would've been 'wristband day' and the start of what would've been the greatest five days and nights of trance ever seen on the island.

But suitcases remain on the top of the wardrobe, passports gather dust in drawers and our hearts are tethered rather than getting set to soar.

We took the decision not to programme any virtual content, as there are lots of great streams out there already – and ITE is more – much more than the music, however immaculate it is.

Life's most treasured moments are when it's experienced with others. In unity there is beauty.

When we convene again it will be mighty: a laser-lit explosion of expression, joy and release.

Until then, remember a family is always a family, even when separated – bass is thicker than water!

### #4 Saturday, 24 September, 2022
WHOOOOOO! YESSSSSS!

The bump and screech of fuselage and rubber on tarmac

elicits an eruption the likes of which I've never heard in the eighty-plus times I'd previously landed in Ibiza.

It feels like my birthday, Christmas, NYE1999, VE Day and England winning the World Cup rolled into one. Ibiza is open for business – and its business is dancing! Everyone is smiling. The saying 'you don't realise what you have until it's gone' was never truer than in Covid. Everyone on today's flight realised alright – and everyone on today's flight has some serious catching up to do. Dancing is a release and this felt like the biggest release of my life so far.

'Please remain seated until the plane has come to a standstill and the captain has switched off the seatbelt signs, thank you.' The natives were restless and the cabin crew are struggling to contain them.

'We've been seated for two fucking years! It's time to dance!' some wag shouts. Another cheer. We're all wearing masks but are relieved to find Ibiza airport is longer carrying out health checks on arrival.

As we stand around the luggage hall waiting for the carousel to jerk into action, a few lads fool around, picking up their mate and clumsily depositing him on the empty conveyor belt. He crosses his legs, closes his eyes and adopts the Lotus position, evoking laughter. But not everyone is laughing. Across the hall green uniformed figures crane their necks for a better view and start to walk over, hands reaching their batons. The Guardia Civil welcome any excuse to correct an unruly Brit, and having been deprived of their food source for two summers are hungry for action.

I urgently approach the lad on the conveyor belt, getting his attention by shaking his shoulder. He opens his eyes to see the crowd part to reveal six shiny jackboots.

Leaning over, I cup his ear and whisper, 'The coppers in green are cunts. Don't mess with them 'cos they'll beat the fuck out of you... or even worse.'

My lockdown diary 'When The Dancing Stopped' can be found at kirkfield.substack.com

# EPILOGUE

# SUNSHINE IS MORE THAN DAYLIGHT

I've spent my adult life doing 'cool' things; singer in a band, a runner for a film company who made music videos, club culture journalist, rave MC, ski holiday host, clubbing travel pioneer, Ibiza festival promoter (and now author and rave raconteur). I always thought I was happy. But in my mid-fifties, I began to feel unfulfilled after meeting a surgeon who performs cataract operations. He told me that despite the long hours and working conditions, he went home feeling fantastic because he knew he'd 'made a difference'.

This got me thinking about how I'd spent my life; always focussing on myself, preoccupied with doing cool things. So, I decided it was time to put something back, and do something more useful for society than putting parties on and taking people on holiday so they could dance somewhere different,

I hoped my understanding of the relationship between young people and drugs may be useful in court, so I enrolled to become a magistrate. I volunteered for a charity which takes books to the housebound and terminally ill (the Home Library Service and Royal Voluntary Service). I found this rewarding and planned to do two more summers in Ibiza and then quit.

Then Covid happened, and it made us all reevaluate the everyday things we take for granted. Meeting a mate in a pub, dancing with others to the beat of a drum (Bang!) and going on holiday were but memories of how we used to live.

The longer lockdown went on, the more magical my memories became. I wondered if the thousands of people I'd taken on holidays across two decades were doing the same. What were previously throwaway moments were revealed as precious drops of glue which holds us together, and the 'selfish' job I did, now appeared valuable, and more importantly, valid.

I realised clubbing holidays are essentially a celebration of life; sharing music, sunshine and sensuality in like-minded company. Like youth, not having toothache and toilet roll, you only realise the true value of something when it's gone.

In late September 2022, after three years of inactivity, under an azure September sky, I was once again putting Radical Escapes wristbands back on excited wrists in Ibiza. The feeling of relief, joy and elation in everyone's eyes was unforgettable. People told me how they'd declined the refund we offered them in 2020, as they refused to believe they wouldn't be returning. Countless guests confided that their Ibiza holiday was the thing which kept them going through the dark times. One guest divulged he was going through deep depression, and the dream of playing a DJ set on the trip probably saved his life. Another girl wrote to me expressing her gratitude after finding a completely new circle of friends and way of life after we welcomed her into the group as a solo female traveller after she escaped a toxic relationship.

An often-forgotten aspect of holidays is they take place predominantly outdoors. Nature is a healer. While watching an alpine sunset from a mountaintop pyramid hotel where I'd organised an overnight stay, a gruff unit of a plumber from Catford started crying. 'It's just so beautiful,' he kept repeating as the mountains a razor-sharp kaleidoscope of orange and pink hues before our eyes.

He wrote to me a few months later to thank me for his holiday and to tell me he'd packed in the plumbing and was retraining as an outward-bound instructor for special needs kids.

Since then, many more have opened up telling me how their holidays sustain them through the year, often mending cracks in relationships and providing a shared experience which reaffirms their bond.

It reminds me why I started in the first place – to share the places I love and enable people to dance somewhere different.

Twenty-five years… over 100,000 guests… over one hundred events, including the UK's first international boat party, the World's first ski/snowboard clubbing holiday and an Ibiza holiday concept which has become the template. Along the way Radical Escapes has given hundreds of DJs the opportunity to play in the best clubs in the world. Some have gone onto make careers out of it (take a bow Jordan Suckley, D.O.D, Jon Kong, Leftwing & Kody), ALL have learned something about themselves and have memories which'll stay with them all their lives, which, I guess is the greatest gift.

We all share core human traits; a sense of belonging, family, community, love and purpose – they're what make us human (along with being able to select all images with a traffic light). All of these involve an element of supporting a fellow human being (except being able to select all images with a traffic light). Despite the all-pervading 'me' culture which worships individualism and independence, I believe we're happiest when we're helping others.

I may not be anything really useful to society like a surgeon, nurse or lollipop lady, so I've tried my hardest to ensure my holidays are the very best I can deliver, and hope that sometimes they've made a small positive difference to my guests – ninety-nine per cent of whom were an absolute pleasure to look after... the other one per cent have been immortalised in these pages!

All the stories I've written are true, but some names and identifiable traits have been changed to protect the privacy and anonymity of those involved.

Thank you for reading. Never forget that sunshine is more than daylight.

> **Top Tune: Summer Holiday (2003 Remaster) – Cliff Richard and the Shadows {Parlophone}**

# CREDITS

Thank you to: Dan Prince (quality control, structural integrity and confidence maintenance), Colin Steven @ Velocity for welcoming an unstable lad onto his stable, Paris Ferguson for her fresh pair of eyes and sprinkling some deftness on my daftness, Terry Neale, Sean Cummiskey, Kate Van Dyk, Don Eales, Dean Lightfoot, Leonie Barnard, Nick Halkes, Adam Lockhart, Danny Kirwan, Niall Rudd and anyone else who took time to read chapters and fed back with honesty.

A Hai Karate salute to my wingman, tour manager and audiobook producer Matt 'Mr Vinyl' Ward.

Big love to Red Jules @ Ibiza Clubbing for forty-plus, Samantha Bliss, Julia Antoni, and all the Solo Oldschool Ravers team for their sterling work; providing safety and security as well as smoke and lasers.

Radical Escapes would like to thank: Nick and Rachel Cade at Vacation Club, Damian Gelle, Erich Roscher, Lord Macey, JP Montgomery, Chris 'The Count' Good, Elliot Cox, Pabs and Shaggy, Stevie Sideburns, the late Mo Chaudry, Nick Ferguson, Andrew Duley and everyone who's ever worn a Radical Escapes CREW shirt, Nick Coles and every promoter who've been part of the journey.

Thanks to Pez for the artwork and Jules and Nick Dalton for their kind words.

My thanks to Paul Palmer-Edwards for designing the only jackets I wear except Belstaff. Neil O'Brien and David Shepherd for their belief. Norman Cook for being first off the mark to show love for Rave New World, and a generation of greyvers (copyright Nick Halkes!) for reading, listening, coming to my live shows and laughing in the right places.

This book is dedicated to those who have left the party far too soon, leaving those of us still here to appreciate it on their behalf. Until we join them at the afterparty, celebrate life, each other... and take that holiday.

A percentage of any profits from this book will be donated to The British Tinnitus Association, a registered charity (1011145) who provide free support to anyone with tinnitus or caring for someone with tinnitus and lead the charge for more investment in tinnitus research. More: www.tinnitus.org

**Big love to the rave new readers who preordered:**
Leyton Angell, Alan Appleton, Aleksi Arajärvi, Lisa Attfield, Darren Bailey, Heather Barker, Paul Barrett, Sharon Betts, Suzanne Blowers, Rebecca Booker, Scott Bonser, Alistair Brewin, DJ Lee Le Brie, Lou Brown, Lyndon Brill, Stephen Brown, Simon Burgess, Calum Butchart, Sean Butler, George Carrick, Alan Chicken, Jakub Cholewczynski, Luke Clarke, David "Clemo" Clement, Patricia Cobb, Simon Coleman, Nick Coles, Dave Cook, Marcus Cook, Lindon Cooper, Paul Courtney, Juliet Cromwell, Liam Cummiskey, Sean Cummiskey, Joseph Cusack, Rick B. Viss Davey, Nick Davidson, Stuart Dick, DJ Stocky, Bryan Donaldson, Sorrel Dryden, Natalie Ellengold, Ihab Elnaccash, Nova Ferguson, Eamonn Fevah, Richard Fish, Stefan Flannery, Teresa Fletcher, Andre Flitsch, Paul Franklin, Andrew Galliet, Dominic Garros, Tim Gibney, Scott Goldson, Jonathan Goring, Zachary Graham, Louise Hadlow, James Hamilton, Luke Harding, Daniel Hathaway, Kamilla Haufort, Tara Hawes, Glen Heslop, Steve Hill, Gary

Hiscock, Andrea, Richard Hollis, Joanna Honeywood, Richard Huish, Wayne Huntley, Dom Jay, Ben Jennings, William Keenan, Ross Kemp, Simon Kemp, Simon Kenway, Simon Kilmister, Steve King, Jan Korrubel, Konstantin Kukushkin, Jukka Kuronen, Dan Lane, Deborah Lannon, Brian Laurie, James Lawson, Adrian Lightly, Colleen Long, Krunoslav Lopandic, Kat Loughrey, Danny Manning, Sarah Mason, Alexander McFerren, Glenn McMaster, Wesley McRae, Rachel Micklewright, Goran Mikulic, William Millican, Kev Mooney, Neil Moore, Andrew Nelson, Hannah Nicholls, Kris Norrie, John Oddy, Gary Pagan, Leona Parsons, Karen Partridge, Craig Paxton, Lisa Penfold, Andreas Petrou, Chris Redmond, Olly Revest, Philip Reynolds, Tamarind Reynolds, Gareth Richards, Alex Robinson, Sandra Robinson, Justin Rosemeyer, Julio Santo Domingo, Fiona Schofield, Rob Seals, Mark Searby, Simon Searle, Colin Sengelow, Greg Sheppard, Leigh Sherlock, Matthew Shipp, George Simpson, Donald Sisson, Kevin Smith, Stepanie Snape, Helen Stainsby, Michael Tew, William Townsley, Gary Thomas, Liz Thomas, Nicole Thomas, Steve Turnbull, Justin Turner, Brett Vincent, Clare Wale, John Walls, Sebastian Weber, Glen White, Chris Willetts, Kirsty Willis, Marc Wilkie, Debbie Wogan, Thomas Wouters, Greg (Zogg)